Voices from the Middle

Volume 1 • Number 1 • September 1994

Responding to Literature

A Publication of the National Council of Teachers of English

Contents

Design: Doug Burnett

Cover photo: Jean Chen

Editing and Production:
Carol E. Schanche

 Printed on recycled paper

Message from the Editors

"So it has been for many of us," writes Robert Coles, "going back, way back to the earliest of times, when men and women and children looked at one another, at the land, at the sky, at rivers and oceans, at mountains and deserts, at animals and plants, and wondered, as it is in our nature to do: what is all this that I see and hear and find unfolding before me? How shall I comprehend the life that is in me and around me? To do so, stories were constructed—and told, and remembered, and handed down over time, over the generations." (p. 189)

Story. Humankind's way of figuring things out. Who am I? Why am I here? Who are all these others? What is going on, and what does it all mean? Has it always been this way? As we think about middle school classrooms, we think of diversity. We think of the range of students and teachers, all bringing dreams, hopes, fears, prejudices, opinions, and questions to school every day. At no other time in their lives will students' personal concerns be as relevant to the curriculum as they are now. Indeed, in many writing–reading workshops, students' lives *are* the curriculum. Story, in such classrooms, becomes the common language, the shared domain, the means through which we can look at our lives and at the world and ponder together the tough questions.

Voices from the Middle is an invitation to teachers to think with us about what matters most in our classrooms, and what matters most, of course, is our students. We struggle to help them find ways to make learning meaningful, purposeful, and enriching. We want them to know what school can do, that it can touch and change their lives, today, now. We want to share with them our passion for the poems and stories and books that have touched our own lives so profoundly,

the way *The Yearling* touched Katherine Paterson's life as a child and has continued to touch her as an adult writer, reader, and woman. *Voices from the Middle* begins with a celebration of literature because we believe that literature matters, that there is nothing as powerful as a poem, story, or book when the curriculum is, as it should be, the nurturance of good human beings.

As Bob Probst tells us, we "teach what we cannot know" when we bring literature into the classroom, as the words on any page are just part of the experience. We may know the specific literary elements of the text itself, and we may know the basis for our own reaction to it, but we cannot know what our students bring to the reading, for each is a separate human being, with values, experiences, and emotions unlike any others in the room. The knowledge that is woven when readers encounter text is a knowledge we cannot name. When we invite our students to enter into literature, we are offering them more than new information; we are offering them a way to look at their lives.

Students in classrooms from Edgecomb, Maine to Fairbanks, Alaska are using their writing to reflect on what they read, discovering and constructing new meaning in the process, as Marie Dionisio shows us in her students' journals. These sixth graders know the power of literature, just as they know the value of their own reaction to it. Through their writing, they ask questions of the text, speculate on authors' intentions, connect one text to another, make predictions and inferences. They feel empathy and, in examining characters' behavior, rehearse moral decisions they may face later in their own lives.

Louise Rosenblatt, in *Literature as Exploration*, says, "Though a free, uninhibited

Maureen Barbieri

Middle School Teacher, Greenville, South Carolina

Linda Rief

Middle School Teacher, Durham, New Hampshire

emotional reaction to a work of art or literature is an absolutely *necessary* condition of sound literary judgement, it is not...a sufficient condition.

"...he (the student) can begin to achieve a sound approach to literature only when he reflects upon his response to it, when he attempts to understand what in the work and in himself produced that reaction, and when he thoughtfully goes on to modify, reject, or accept it" (p. 75–76).

New Hampshire seventh graders go far beyond personal reaction to literature when they conduct research to understand more about what Lyddie, the character in a Katherine Paterson novel, endures. They discover a whole world of hardship, courage, and strength when they travel to the old Massachusetts mills, interview experts, and read related texts. They take what they have learned and create an extravagant, eloquent, dynamic musical production to share their new understanding and how they feel about it. They are, indeed, moving response beyond the personal. Through incredible collaboration, they invent characters, and write stories, scenes, and songs. Taking response further, they work with their music teacher to channel the feelings of their characters into melody, fitting the words to the notes, but careful that each bar of music conveys the intended meaning. Response goes beyond the expected. Learning becomes passion.

Mary Kitagawa's children spend extended time talking about their books. The act of talking becomes an act of generating meaning. Young speakers shape their ideas in words, but the words then shape new ideas, and the process becomes organic, recursive, just as writing does. Listening becomes an important element in response, as each reader brings new shades of meaning to the experience, and the literate community collaborates to develop a multi-textured understanding of a shared text. Reading is personal, but reading is also social, as Mary's children demonstrate.

When a group of teachers met last year to share our visions of what this new journal might be, Mary Krogness cautioned us to go beyond the tried and true, to dare to be innovative. As we present our first *Voices*, we are thinking of Mary and of all the other teachers like her who understand that middle school classrooms are in constant flux. Kids' lives are shifting, teachers' lives are more demanding than ever, and the whole nature of education itself is under scrutiny. But the more our worlds change, the more we will need literature, the more we will need creative, personal, and communal ways of responding to it.

Welcome to *Voices from the Middle*. Please respond.

References

Coles, R. (1989). *The call of stories: Teaching and the moral imagination.* Boston: Houghton Mifflin.

Rosenblatt, L. (1983). *Literature as exploration.* (4th ed). New York: MLA.

The Yearling *and* I

The green cloth binding is buckled and stained, showing the effects of a typhoon on the island of Shikoku in 1961, but the book itself is much older than that. On the flyleaf is a small sticker with my name, Katherine Womeldorf, and the Piedmont Avenue address where I lived from the time I was barely nine until I was just past twelve. I can't remember owning printed stickers with my name and address on them. They seem marvelously bourgeois. Yet there it is fifty years later, firmly proclaiming my ownership of this book, which was, as I recall it, the first book that ever exclusively belonged to me. Certainly it was the first book I remember my mother giving to me.

There were five of us children and I was the middle child. We had books because, poor as they were, my parents valued books and bought them for us when they could. But we shared them. The family name went on the flyleaf, not our personal names.

But somehow the year I was eleven going on twelve, my mother gave me this copy of *The Yearling*. The book had been published in 1938 and won the Pulitzer Prize the following year. No one in those days thought Marjorie Kinnan Rawlings had written a book for children.

I know that my conservative Presbyterian missionary mother had read it before she gave it to me. She would have remembered the jokes about the Almighty, the scenes where grown men and boys cavort about naked and are not ashamed. She would know that death hovered over its pages like a vulture over the Florida swamp lands, and that when the characters invoked the Lord's name, it was often not in prayer. She might well have known that Mrs. Rawlings herself was something of a scandalous woman who had left behind comfortable, civilized society

and gone to live an unconventional life in the Florida wilds. She must have known all these things, yet sometime that year when I was just the age of Jody Baxter, my mother, returning from a trip where she had gone to speak to Presbyterian ladies about foreign missions, brought me the gift of this book that she knew I would love.

My mother was right. I did love *The Yearling*. It was so live with atmosphere, so rich in emotion, that all the other books I had loved until that time seemed to blanch in comparison. It never occurred to me to wonder about the author. If I'd even known, which I didn't, that she was a wealthy, educated journalist from up north, I wouldn't have thought to question how she could know so much about the hummock country of Florida or, indeed, so much about the heart of a rough and lonely child. I had no curiosity at all about the author. *The Yearling* didn't belong to Marjorie Kinnan Rawlings, it belonged to me. It was a world I had discovered. And I was Jody Baxter.

A year or so later, we moved to a house that backed on woods, and for the first time in my life I had a puppy of my own that followed me everywhere. At thirteen, when other girls were beginning to experiment with lipstick and making eyes at boys, I was romping in the woods with my mongrel at my heels, feeling that we had become Jody and Flag in *fact* and not just in imagination.

I never discussed the book with other people. I feel sure that my seventh-grade teacher would have been shocked if she had known not only that I had read it, but that my mother had given it to me. In reading class in those days, we had basal texts. The library at Calvin H. Wiley School was a good one, and the librarian one of my life's heroes, but reading books from the library

Katherine Paterson

Author

Katherine Paterson at thirteen

was something teachers tolerated rather than encouraged. It was all right to read library books in one's spare time, and the occasional required book report took as much joy as possible from that enterprise, but reading books for pleasure mustn't be allowed to interfere with one's education.

I do remember Mother once pointing out the white tail in a picture of a deer. "I never see the white tail of a deer without thinking of Fodderwing," she said. And I remember being proud that she and I had a secret. We both knew strange, crooked Fodderwing who saw visions of the departed Spaniards and who could converse with wild critters. But I don't remember ever really talking about the book even with my mother.

I'm not sure I'd have known how to talk about it. The connection I felt with the story was so intense. How could I have expressed it in ordinary language? Although, if I had met someone my own age who felt as passionately about the book as I did, wouldn't that have given us a special bond? But I didn't know a teacher like Mary Kitagawa in those days. None of my teachers would have given over precious school time for students to explore meaning in a story, much less dared to explore emotion or belief.

When I was sixteen, I met a girl who had grown up in Africa. The summer we became friends, Mary read aloud to me Alan Paton's *Cry the Beloved Country*, rolling the beautiful Zulu words off her tongue like exotic music. In Paton's tragic story of his beloved South Africa, I saw for the first time what was happening all around me in the American Southland of the late 1940s. Reading a great novel is a conversion experience; we are never quite the same afterwards.

Mary and I are still the closest of friends and still introducing each other to books we love. She taught me that books can provide a common language and enrich the best of friendships. So in a way, I'm sorry that I didn't have a friend to discuss *The Yearling* with—to watch with me, hushed, at the dance of the whooping cranes—to recoil in horror when Penny was struck by the rattler—to track old Slewfoot across the frozen

> *Reading a great novel is a conversion experience; we are never quite the same afterwards.*

swampland—to stand close to me when Jody put the muzzle against Flag's soft neck—and to weep with me for a friend and a childhood that were gone forever. But I didn't have anyone at twelve who I thought would understand those feelings, so I kept them to myself.

When the movie of *The Yearling* came along, I was in high school and more sophisticated than when I'd first read the book. I cried in the movie. I always cried in sad movies. Still, I couldn't help noticing that Gregory Peck was far too tall and handsome to play the wiry little Penny Baxter. I could talk about the movie and did, but it didn't occupy the same wild acreage in my heart that the book had claimed three years before.

Not until I reread the book fifty years later did I realize just how profound an effect it had on me. Echoes from *The Yearling* reverberate through my own books. In *Come Sing, Jimmy Jo*, as if in answer to Hollywood casting, I have given James Johnson a father very much like Penny Baxter in size and wisdom. Jerry Lee loves his son just as Penny does, and he, as well as Penny, will, out of love, make the hard decisions that will appear harsh and unloving to his son.

I've had other surprises as I've reread *The Yearling*. If anyone had asked me where the theme for *Gilly Hopkins* had come from, I would have told her the story of my friendship with Barbara Thompson. Barbara and I were in high school together in a small West Virginia town. I moved to Charles Town in October of my junior year from a fine city high school in Richmond, Virginia. It was Barbara, cheerleader, homecoming queen, president of the junior class, who mysteriously reached out to me and liked me as I was—shy to the point of arrogance, intellectually starving, desperately lonely, with all my friends hundreds of miles away.

Barbara, like Mary whom I met the following summer, has remained a friend through the years. Our lives have gone in quite different directions. I married late and happily. She married her troubled high school sweetheart and is now divorced. In one of our all too infrequent visits since we were young, Barbara said something that haunted me until I was able to incorporate it into a book. "Kathy," (Barbara is one of a handful of people who can call me Kathy without making me cringe) "why don't we ever tell children that life is tough? We feed them all these fairy tales about happily-ever-after and then they feel cheated. We need to tell them early on that life is really hard."

When I began writing *The Great Gilly Hopkins*, I named the town where Gilly finds unconditional love "Thompson Park" in Barbara's honor, and I put into the mouth of the most loving of all my characters words that echo Barbara's concern.

> Gilly was crying now. She couldn't help herself. "Trotter, it's all wrong. Nothing turned out the way it's supposed to."
>
> "How you mean supposed to? Life ain't supposed to be nothing, 'cept maybe tough. . . . Sometimes in this world things come easy, and you tend to lean back and say, 'Well, finally, happy ending. This is the way things is supposed to be.' Like life owed you good things. . . . And there is lots of good things, baby. . . . But you just fool yourself if you expect good things all the time. They ain't what's regular—don't nobody owe 'em to you."
>
> "If life is so bad, how come you're so happy?"
>
> "Did I say bad? I said it was tough. Nothing to make you happy like doing good on a tough job, now is there?" [*The Great Gilly Hopkins*, pp. 147–48]

There are few among my friends who have done better on a tough job than Barbara or have been happier in the doing. You can understand, I think, why I thought *Gilly* was Barbara's gift to me. But when I reread *The Yearling*, I was startled to find another seed for Trotter's philosophy in Penny Baxter's speech to Jody after Fawn's tragic death, Jody's flight, and his son's return. Perhaps I was able to hear Barbara's words as an adult because I had read Penny's words first when I was a child.

> You figgered I went back on you. Now there's a thing ever'man has got to know. Mebbe you know it a'ready. 'Twa'n't only me. 'Twa'n't only your yearlin' deer havin' to be destroyed. Boy, life goes back on you. . . . Ever' man wants life to be a fine thing, and a easy. 'Tis fine, boy, powerful fine, but 'tain't easy. Life knocks a man down and he gits up and it knocks him down agin. . . I wanted to spare you, long as I could. I wanted you to frolic with your yearlin'. I knowed the lonesomeness he eased for you. But ever' man's lonesome. What's he to do

then? What's he to do when he gits knocked down? Why, take it for his share and go on. (*The Yearling*, p. 426)

I'm sure those words were an enormous comfort to me at twelve, just as Barbara's words were a prod years later to share this comfort with other lonely and hard-pressed children.

In *Shadowlands*, C.S. Lewis's most troublesome student says to him, "We read to know that we are not alone." *The Yearling* let me know that I was not alone, and I am grateful that children have written me to say that reading *Gilly Hopkins* has tempered their loneliness.

Although the relationships among *Come Sing, Jimmy Jo* and *The Great Gilly Hopkins* and *The Yearling* were somewhat oblique, even hidden to me, I think I knew almost from the beginning that Jesse Aarons was a cousin to Jody Baxter. Their homes are hundreds of miles apart, but they are both lonely country boys. Jesse Aarons, Sr. is not Penny Baxter, but after Leslie's death when he comes to find Jess at the creek bank, his compassion for his grieving son stretches toward the love Penny daily displays towards his. Jess's father does not teach his son to hunt and farm, but he would envy Penny's opportunities to do so. Life has been hard for both men, but it has driven Jesse Aarons off the land, and his loss is immeasurable.

At the core of both books is friendship. It would be unjust to Leslie to compare her to Flag. Her friendship is one that opens up the world for Jesse, while there is always a hint of danger in Jody's love for a wild creature that cannot understand the constant struggle with starvation on Baxter's Island. But Leslie herself is a beautiful, untamed creature. She has the imagination to destroy monsters and to create new worlds. I think one reason many adults are uneasy with *Bridge to Terabithia* is just this untamed element, for imagination will not bend to neat rules and so threatens complacency and conformity.

Years ago when I was trying to learn how to write fiction, I made up a motto for myself that would run through my head like a mantra: *Something's got to happen. Someone's*

> *I think one reason many adults are uneasy with **Bridge to Terabithia** is just this untamed element, for imagination will not bend to neat rules and so threatens complacency and conformity.*

got to change. In books for children, the someone who must change is, of course, the young protagonist. And the last lines of *The Yearling* still make me weep, even as I know, and knew when I was twelve, that the yearling Jody must grow to be a man.

> He did not believe he should ever again love anything, man or woman or his own child, as he had loved the yearling. He would be lonely all his life. But a man took it for his share and went on.
> In the beginning of his sleep, he cried out, "Flag!"
> It was not his own voice that called. It was a boy's voice. Somewhere beyond the sink-hole, past the magnolia, under the live oaks, a boy and a yearling ran side by side, and were gone forever. (*The Yearling,* p. 428)

In *Bridge to Terabithia,* I see I could not quite dare that bleak a conclusion. Jess would have to take Leslie's death for his share and move on, but as he went, May Belle would tag along—May Belle the pest, the peek, the exasperating voice of all his own inner doubts and fears. And though many readers, young and old, have argued the worthiness of May Belle, it is a measure of Jess's change that he at the end takes her into Terabithia. For if we were rewarded according to our worth in this life, where would most of us be?

> "Whatcha doing, Jess?" May Belle had followed him again as he had guessed she might.
> "It's a secret, May Belle."
> "Tell me."
> "When I finish, OK?"
> "I swear on the Bible I won't tell nobody. Not Billy Jean, not Joyce Ann, not Momma—" she was jerking her head back and forth in solemn emphasis.
> "Oh, I don't know about Joyce Ann. You might want to tell Joyce Ann sometime."
> "Tell Joyce Ann something that's a secret between you and me?" The idea seemed to horrify her.
> "Yeah, I was just thinking about it."
> Her face sagged. "Joyce Ann ain't nothing but a baby."

> "Well, she wouldn't likely be a queen first off. You'd have to train her and stuff."
> "Queen? Who gets to be queen?"
> "I'll explain it when I finish, OK?"
> And when he finished, he put flowers in her hair and led her across the bridge—the great bridge into Terabithia—which might look to someone with no magic in him like a few planks across a nearly dry gully.
> "Shhh," he said. "Look."
> "Where?"
> "Can't you see 'um?" he whispered. "All the Terabithians standing on tiptoe to see you."
> "Me?"
> "Shhh, yes. There's a rumor going around that the beautiful girl arriving today might be the queen they've been waiting for." (*Bridge to Terabithia,* pp. 127–28)

My mother never knew what she gave when she gave her child a book. Neither will you as you give many books to all sorts and conditions of children. But I hope in this reflective history of one child and one book, you'll realize something of the riches you have at your disposal and will give them away, as my mother did, with perception and delight.

Editors' Note: Below is bibliographic information on books mentioned in Katherine Paterson's article.

Lewis, C. S. (1991). *Shadowlands.* New York: NAL-Dutton.

Paterson, K. (1977). *Bridge to Terabithia.* New York: Crowell Junior Books.

Paterson, K. (1978). *The great Gilly Hopkins.* New York: Crowell Junior Books.

Paterson, K. (1986). *Come sing, Jimmy Jo.* New York: Avon.

Paton, A. (1977). *Cry the beloved country.* New York: Macmillan.

Rawlings, M. K. (1938, out of print). *The yearling.* New York: Grosset & Dunlap. [Now available 1988, New York: Macmillan.]

> *And the last lines of* The Yearling *still make me weep, even as I know, and knew when I was twelve, that the yearling Jody must grow to be a man.*

Teaching What We Cannot Know

My students have taught me many things, but perhaps most important of all is that I can't know what I'm teaching. Not, at any rate, when I'm teaching literature.

I should have learned that long ago, but I caught on slowly, despite dramatic lessons my students, or circumstances, arranged for me. Once, for example, sometime during my second year of teaching, I decided to pull together a collection of poems that dealt with war. Vietnam was cranking up at the time, and the students were interested in what was happening over there, although for most of us it seemed a long way off. We knew war through John Wayne movies and the evening news and so it was a confusing mix of glory, noise, heroism, savagery, excitement, dirt, and pain. We did, however, know people who were there, or would be going there soon, and so it seemed appropriate that we reflect, somehow, on the experience they were entering. I thought that the poetry of Wilfred Owen, Sigfried Sassoon, and others like them would be as good a way as any of encouraging reflection on the war, of giving the students, I optimistically believed, some knowledge of the experience.

So I spent several weeks compiling a small collection of the poetry that had come out of World Wars I and II, figured out how to justify it in the curriculum, and began one Monday morning with "The Death of the Ball Turret Gunner" by Randall Jarrell. It seemed a good opening, because it was short, powerful, unromantic, and understated. I thought that its provocative contrast with the glorification of war in the movies my students had seen would yield some interesting discussion and at least get us started.

The Death of the Ball Turret Gunner [1]

From my mother's sleep I fell into the State,
And I hunched in its belly till my wet fur froze.
Six miles from earth, loosed from its dream of life,
I woke to black flak and the nightmare fighters.
When I died they washed me out of the turret with
    a hose.

Randall Jarrell

My first period class, however, went miserably. By the time it was over, it had been a long, grueling week. When I read the poem aloud, they seemed not to hear it. When they looked at the text, they seemed not to see it. When I commented or questioned, they seemed not to hear me. No one looked at me. They looked at the empty board behind me, at the backs of the students seated in front of them, down at their desks, up at the flickering fluorescent tubes hanging from the ceiling—anywhere but at me. The hour ground by tediously, the clock ticking more and more slowly, as if conspiring to extend my torment as long as it possibly could. I had no idea what I was doing wrong or how I could escape from the situation I had somehow created for myself.

Ultimately, mercifully, the bell rang and the students, all but one, packed up their books and slipped silently away. That one student came up to me apologetically and explained that they were all sorry class had gone so poorly, but they had just found out that a friend of theirs, a quiet young woman in my second period class, had learned over the weekend that her brother, who had left for the war only a few months ago, had on Friday been cut in half by a machine gun in

Robert Probst

Professor of
English Education,
Georgia State
University

---

[1] "The Death of the Ball Turret Gunner" from THE COMPLETE POEMS by Randall Jarrell. Copyright ©1945, 1969 by Mrs. Randall Jarrell. Reprinted by permission of Farrar, Straus & Giroux, Inc.

some nameless swamp in Vietnam. She was in school, nonetheless; she would be coming into my room within the next few minutes, and they had sat through "The Death of the Ball Turret Gunner" anticipating its effect on her, worried for me, and imagining—or trying not to imagine—the dying of a young soldier, someone they had known, who had, in essence, just been washed out of the turret with a hose.

Thinking back over the class, I realized how little I knew or could know about what I was teaching. I began the day not knowing, at least, the simple facts of the student's life; how those facts might shape her response; why she was there, and what that might mean about her state-of-mind, her circumstances at home, her relationship with her family, her relationship with her friends; how her friends and others in the class might react to a traumatic scene in the classroom; how I would be able to help, or how I might hurt her further, by my own choices in the class.

I knew the text well enough, I suppose—I could have explained flak and described the ball turret on a bomber, and I could have helped them through the subtleties and ambiguities of the first several lines—but the experience they were likely to have with these five lines obviously was going to involve a great deal more than defining a few terms, sketching a B-29 on the board, and wrestling with a metaphor or two. I knew very little about what poem that short text would become when my students read it.

At the time, abandoning the unit seemed the wisest course; I had no confidence in my ability to handle the situation, though I've occasionally wondered since then if she came to school that day searching for something that a better teacher, with that same poem, might have given her. Not given her, perhaps, but helped her to find, because just as I didn't know what she brought to the class that day, I didn't know, couldn't know except in the most general terms, what she might need to, or be able to, take away. Because I couldn't know her well enough, I couldn't know what she would do with the poem, what it would be for her. Nonetheless, though I didn't have the courage to attempt it, I believed that the poem had something

significant to give her, that it somehow carried knowledge in its lines and that if I could have handled the delicate situation within the classroom, we'd have been able to extract it. Knowledge, after all, was what we were pursuing when we read. We have always thought of the libraries, the great books, as the repository of knowledge. We go to those shelves hoping that the writers will share insight, wisdom, understanding, knowledge. Why else spend the time with difficult texts?

I saw knowledge, I think, as something knowable. Literature somehow contained it, or embodied it, and my students and I, if we worked diligently at the task, could dig it out, polish it up, and take it home to show our parents. That knowledge was complex. Nothing so simple as facts, lists of dates and names and places, but still it was there to be known, a collection of observations, insights, inferences, and principles—something that could be articulated and grasped, some object for my verb, "know."

It seemed reasonable enough: if you *knew*, then you knew *something*. There was an object, an element or unit of something out there in the world to be grasped intellectually in some way, articulated, classified, and filed away satisfactorily in the mind, leaving you with the sense of peace and harmony that wraps itself warmly around you at moments such as those when your checkbook finally balances, if it ever does, or with that sense of conquest and accomplishment that gratifies you when you finally arrive, after struggling with obscure and incomplete directions, at the right address. It's that sense of emotional and physical calm, that feeling of well-being that tells you that you know. At such moments, you can state, plainly and simply, what it is that you know, even—if pressed—how you know it, and it's a pleasant feeling. But I've begun to doubt that literature offers knowledge, not knowledge of that sort, at any rate. I've even begun to wonder if "to know," when we refer to literary experience, is a transitive verb at all.

Knowing, literary knowing, at any rate, seems to be an elusive concept. The poets themselves seem to dance around it cautiously. Levertov, for example, writes of two girls who come to know the secret of life.

> I've even begun to wonder if "to know," when we refer to literary experience, is a transitive verb at all.

The Secret [2]

Two girls discover
the secret of life
in a sudden line of
poetry.

I who don't know the
secret wrote
the line. They
told me

(through a third person)
they had found it
but not what it was,
not even

what line it was. No doubt
by now, more than a week
later, they have forgotten
the secret,

the line, the name of
the poem. I love them
for finding what
I can't find,

and for loving me
for the line I wrote,
and for forgetting it
so that

a thousand times, till death
finds them, they may
discover it again, in other
lines

In other
happenings. And for
wanting to know it,
for

assuming there is
such a secret, yes,
for that
most of all.

                    Denise Levertov

There's knowledge here, and not just knowledge, but the ultimate knowledge, the "secret of life." Perhaps the knowledge isn't here, exactly, not in this poem, but it's available in those other lines Levertov alludes to. It's unfortunate that they've all forgotten the name of the poem, and that they've misplaced the secret of life. You'd think, having found something so significant as the secret of life, they'd try to hang onto it, put it in a safe place and remember where that place is. Levertov reassures us, however, that they'll find it again, and will do so over and over in other lines of poetry, other happenings. She

doesn't, however, give us much hope that when they do, they'll hang onto it. On the contrary, she knows that they'll forget it, and they'll do so a thousand times, so that they may rediscover it a thousand times.

This isn't the sort of knowledge, apparently, that finds its way into the encyclopedias, the sort that is carefully recorded and organized and passed on, like a secret family recipe. Rather, it is ephemeral, elusive, slippery. It's a leprechaun, darting from bush to stone to rabbit hole, laughing out loud at our clumsy attempts to capture it. By the end of the poem, Levertov seems almost to doubt that the secret is there at all. She loves the two girls, she says, for assuming that there is such a secret, and in that word, "assuming," questions the existence of the secret in the first place.

And yet she never seems to question the value of the search. In fact, it is the search, rather than the secret itself, that seems to matter. Levertov's cheerful acceptance of her young readers' carelessness with the secret of life, and of her own inability to know the secret they had found and lost, led me to realize that in all the literature I'd ever read, with all of its references to secrets and to knowledge, no one had *ever* told me what the secret is. The poets allude to it, talk about it, dance around it, but they never share it with us. After years of reading poetry, short stories, and novels, I have yet to find one that reveals the secret. Granted, little secrets are revealed. Mysteries, for instance, are built around hidden information—secrets—and of course they are revealed by the conclusion of the stories. These are secrets of another sort, however, secrets of the kind we had as children, little bits and pieces of information that we could conceal or share, trade like little trinkets, use to bribe or blackmail or otherwise annoy our friends. They were knowable secrets, knowable but insignificant. Perhaps that's why so few mysteries are considered great literature—they are about the little mysteries that can be dis-

> *In fact, it is the search, rather than the secret itself, that seems to matter.*

_____

[2] From Denise Levertov, *Poems 1960–1968.* ©1968 by Denise Levertov. Reprinted by permission of New Directions Publishing Corporation.

pelled, while we value more highly the mysteries that remain eternally mysterious, the secrets that remain hidden, the knowledge that eludes our knowing. The secrets of Levertov are dramatically different from the secrets of Agatha Christie.

Dunn deals with this epistemological problem in writing, as Levertov did, of someone who has found the secret, seen the light, arrived at knowledge, pure and clean and perfect, but he broadens the issue by addressing our problem, the problem of the teacher, one who hopes to somehow bring the knowledge to his students:

Allegory of the Cave (1990)[3]

He climbed toward the blinding light
and when his eyes adjusted
he looked down and could see

his fellow prisoners captivated
by shadows; everything he had believed
was false. And he was suddenly

in the 20th century, in the sunlight
and violence of history, encumbered
by knowledge. Only a hero

would dare return with the truth.
So from the cave's upper reaches,
removed from harm, he called out

the disturbing news.
What lovely echoes, the prisoners said,
what a fine musical place to live.

He spelled it out then, in clear prose
on paper scraps, which he floated down.
But in the semi-dark they read his words

with the indulgence of those who seldom read:
It's about my father's death, one of them said.
No, said the others, it's a joke.

By this time he no longer was sure
of what he'd seen. Wasn't sunlight a shadow too:
Wasn't there always a source

behind a source? He just stood there,
confused, a man who had moved
to larger errors, without a prayer.

Stephen Dunn

Like Levertov's two girls, he has figured it out. He has the secret, he possesses knowledge. Unlike them, he doesn't misplace it, but hangs it carefully, with his car keys, on the hook assigned to them, so that he'll know where it is when the others, who haven't climbed out of the cave, are ready to share it. Thoughtful of his less fortunate friends, he tries to teach them, tries to share

with them the knowledge he has acquired, as best he can. They, however, remain blissfully in the shadows, and after awhile, he begins to think he may be in the shadow, too—a different shadow, but a shadow nonetheless.

Wasn't sunlight a shadow too:
Wasn't there always a source
behind a source?

That knowledge that he'd painfully acquired and now floats down on scraps of paper to the benighted friends he left behind, is gradually coming to seem much like their ignorance. He is still confused; he has moved to larger errors; he is not freed but encumbered by his knowledge; he is no better off than before. Perhaps he's worse off, because he's out here in the bright but unenlightening sunlight, without a prayer. And once again, like Levertov, he's been evasive about the nature of the knowledge he has acquired. He doesn't tell us what it is, though I suppose it hardly matters if knowledge is just another form of ignorance.

If literature offers us only such insubstantial knowledge as this, knowledge that slips away to hide in corners like that in "The Secret," or knowledge that suddenly transforms itself into another form of ignorance, like that in "Allegory of the Cave (1990)," then what are we doing when we read literature? Why bother with it if its secrets present themselves one moment and then vanish the next into thin air, if its knowledge is consigned to paper scraps that vanish down the mouth of a cave to be half-read and wholly misunderstood?

The term "knowledge" may, however, be robust enough, and encompassing enough, to include other ways of apprehending or comprehending than those that result in some consensus about the way the world works. In addition to references to information grasped—"I know what it costs," or "I know the address"—we speak of know-

---

[3] "Allegory of the Cave (1990)" is reprinted from *Landscape at the End of the Century* by Stephen Dunn, with permission of the publisher, W. W. Norton & Company, Inc. ©1991 by Stephen Dunn.

> "I know what you're going through," for instance, speak not so much of your grasp of facts and figures as of your compassion and your shared human experience.

ing to refer to sympathizing or perceiving. "I know how she felt," or "I know what you're going through," for instance, speak not so much of your grasp of facts and figures as of your compassion and your shared human experience. Not reducible to numbers, it is still a form of knowledge.

We may also use the term "knowing" to mean reconciling or determining or accepting. Some time ago a friend, struggling with frightening choices, said, at the end of a long and sad conversation, "I know what I have to do." Naively, but logically, I suppose, I interrupted the silence that followed that short, resigned statement with the question, "Well, what *are* you going to do?" and he replied, with no sense of self-contradiction, "I don't know." He didn't yet know the steps he'd take, he didn't have a map, a chart, or a diagram, and in that sense, he didn't know. But he was resigned to his situation, he had mustered his resolve to deal with it, he was reconciled with the pains he would suffer and inflict, he had accepted a reality that he would have preferred to banish, and in that sense, he *knew*. Knowledge takes various forms.

And what does that mean for the literature program? It means, in part, that we don't know who and what we're teaching. We try, and that's probably appropriate, but we will always find the secret dancing away from us or peeking shyly from around a corner. It means that knowledge, like Ithaca for Ulysses, serves us—serves literature teachers—best as a goal rather than as an acquisition. More important, it means the knowledge we're pursuing is knowledge that can be found—or, more accurately, can be made—only by the students themselves. Like the secret in Levertov's poem, it's not available

to the author of the text, or to the teacher, but only to the reader, the student, the individual into whose life the literary work must be assimilated. Such knowledge, unique and personal, is acquired in the journals Dionisio writes about, in the exploratory talk Kitagawa describes, and in the creative expression Rief discusses. It is the sort of knowledge that is inscribed not in the pages of encyclopedias, but rather in the minds and hearts of individuals slowly and perhaps painfully coming to grips with their place in the world.

Not knowing who and what we're teaching doesn't necessarily imply that we can't teach, or that our teaching is insignificant. On the contrary, it suggests a reconceiving of our instruction as the sustained engagement in an aesthetic and intellectual life that will yield not discrete bits and pieces and chunks of knowable data, but rather will yield sympathy and perception and reconciliation with the world. There was no way for me to give my young student information—knowledge—that could reconcile her with her brother's death in some distant jungle. Ultimately, however, reading and writing and talking, when the time and the text and the people are right, could yield for her some articulation, some reconciliation or acceptance, some knowledge of that loss and her pain. It isn't a knowledge that we can spell out, chart, diagram, and measure. It is nonetheless very significant knowledge, and we have to try to defend it and hold a place for it in our schools. We may not know what it is we teach when we bring a literary text into the classroom, but it is vitally important for us all that we keep teaching it.

It means that knowledge, like Ithaca for Ulysses, serves us—serves literature teachers—best as a goal rather than as an acquisition.

Responding to Literary Elements through Dialogue Journals and Minilessons

Marie Dionisio

Louis M. Klein Middle School, Harrison, New York

The author has adapted this article from one that appeared as: "Responding to Literary Elements through Mini-lessons and Dialogue Journals," *English Journal, 80* (1), January 1991.

When the kids in my sixth-grade class are reading, so am I. That book often becomes the subject of a book talk. It doesn't take long for kids to start asking "How's your book?" in their letters to me. I always respond honestly, as in the following letter:

Dear Emily,

Right now I'm reading *The Facts and Fictions of Minna Pratt* by Patricia MacLachlan (1988). The techniques of characterization in this novel are superb. It has just the right balance of telling and revealing character traits. Minna is a very unique and yet very ordinary teenager. Her mother is a writer and never asks her any ordinary mother questions. Minna hates this. Also she is experiencing love for the first time. It happens while she's playing Mozart on the cello. His name is Lucas and his family is normal. At least that's the way Minna sees it at present. I have a feeling things may change. MacLachlan has written this in the present tense so it reads as if it is happening at the very moment that I'm reading it! Thanks for asking.

Ms. D

We read for sustained chunks of time in class and choose our own books from a variety of sources: classroom, school, public, and personal libraries. Students are required to write at least one letter per week in a reading dialogue journal. Every class begins with a five-minute minilesson, during which I focus on the strategies mature readers use, present book and author talks, and model my own responses to the adolescent novels I read (Atwell, 1987). My classroom library contains more than 600 paperbacks chosen especially for adolescent readers and includes novels, poetry, short story collections, and nonfiction material.

Early in the year, I give a series of book talks about adolescent novels I have read and loved. I read a carefully chosen excerpt that is sure to grab readers' interest, and I model

my own responses to the book. In book talks, I've mentioned my understanding of Jody's anger, confusion and unending pain in *The Year without Michael* by Susan Beth Pfeffer (1988), my empathy for Louise in Katherine Paterson's *Jacob Have I Loved* (1988), and my awe at the beauty of Natalie Babbitt's language in *Tuck Everlasting* (1985).

The realization that I find value in adolescent novels gives kids the validation they need for their own feelings about these books. Being a member of the community of readers in my classroom stemmed from my increasing familiarity with, and respect for, adolescent literature. I began reading adolescent novels in order to be able to recommend books to kids, but my response to these novels took me by surprise. The more I read, the more I wanted to read. As a result, I've discovered a plethora of quality literature written expressly for teenagers, and I have been compelled to share my enthusiasm for these books with my kids. As Nancie Atwell (1987) says, "Living the literature becomes possible for students when teachers live the literature, too" (p. 200).

When kids begin to choose books that I've mentioned in book talks, I focus minilessons on the things I notice in the literature: author's use of setting, characterization, theme, conflict, use of language, and the relationship of the author's ideas to my world. I use adolescent literature I have read to illustrate these points.

Setting

Julie of the Wolves by Jean Craighead George (1972) exemplifies the different ways in which an author might use setting in a novel. George's vivid description of the Alaskan tundra pulls readers into the story, making them feel as if they are there. She also uses setting to signal changes in action, to manipulate the reader's feelings, and to express ideas. Since *Julie of the Wolves* is a survival story, the setting also affects the actions and reactions of the character. I discuss these uses of setting in separate minilessons and always illustrate by reading a passage.

The connection between the character and the setting is evident in many passages from this novel. George uses the setting to emphasize the character's feelings in the following passage:

> The wind, the empty sky, the deserted earth—Miyax had felt the bleakness of being left behind once before.
>
> She could not remember her mother very well, for Miyax was scarcely four when she died, but she did remember the day of her death. The wind was screaming wild high notes and hurling ice-filled waves against the beach, Kapugen was holding her hand and they were walking. When she stumbled, he put her on his shoulders, and high above the beach she saw thousands of birds diving toward the sea. The jaegers screamed and the sandpipers cried. The feathered horns of the comical puffins dropped low, and Kapugen told her they seemed to be grieving with him. (p. 75)

I ask students how this scene looks in their minds' eye, how it makes them feel, and how they think Miyax and Kapugen are feeling. I allow them to respond, to agree, and to disagree with one another. In this exchange, all ideas are respected and none are deemed wrong. The suggestion of a parallel between the barrenness of the scene and the sorrow and loneliness of the characters emerges from this sharing. I conclude the discussion by suggesting that they try to notice the ways authors use setting in the novels they are reading.

Near the end of class, I bring the kids together and invite them to share anything they have noticed about the minilesson topic in their books. During one week-long discussion of setting, students shared what they noticed about the settings in the books they were reading. Bobby commented, "In *Hatchet,* the way the author describes the place makes me feel as scared and cold as Brian." Janet, who was reading *Julie of the Wolves,* remarked, "I found another place where Jean George makes me feel warm inside just like Miyax feels. It says about Kapugen's little house: 'It was rosy-gray on the outside. Inside, it was gold-brown.' That feels warm and safe." The wonder in their voices impressed me more than their words. They seemed surprised to have made such discoveries in their reading. What's more, others chose to read those books the very next day.

A few weeks later I received the following journal letter:

Dear Ms. D,

I'm reading *Snow Bound* by Harry Mazer. I remembered what we said in the mini-lessons a few weeks ago, the setting ones. I think Harry Mazer did some of those things too. In one part Tony is walking away from the car. He is just like a speck in the white snow walking and walking. The way Mazer wrote it I can see Tony in my mind. It makes me feel like he's so alone and will probably die. I think Tony feels like that too. And Cindy too because she sees him from the car window.

Ken

I doubt that Ken will ever forget that authors can use settings to manipulate readers' feelings and responses.

Allowing kids to select their own books, and to respond to them personally, provides them with a safe way to explore literary elements without fear of being wrong. In my response, I reinforced the kind of exploration Ken was doing:

The wonder in their voices impressed me more than their words.

Dear Ken,

Mazer sure does use setting in *Snow Bound* in many of the ways that we saw Jean George use setting in *Julie of the Wolves*. The example you used in your letter is great. It illustrates an author using setting to make the reader feel a certain way. The picture of Tony getting smaller and smaller as he walked up the snow-covered hill made me feel hopeless too. It made me think that the chances of their surviving were next to impossible. You made a good point. Thanks for sharing it with me.

Ms. D

Theme

As a junior high student, theme was difficult for me to identify in literature. As a result, I was utterly amazed at the ease with which my students began to note the universal ideas and feelings behind the stories they were reading and to connect those stories with their own lives. The following journal letters illustrate how the students talked about theme.

Dear Ms. D,

I just finished *The Friendship and The Gold Cadillac* but in this letter I will be zeroing on *The Friendship*. I've seen something in *The Friendship* that I think has something to do with peer pressure. When Tom Bee saved the white shopkeeper's life, he said he can call him by his first name, but now he changed his mind because the other white men said that it was bad that he was letting a black man call him by his first name so he backed out of the deal. He didn't do what was right and he listened to others even though he promised. What do you think?

Amy

Dear Ms. D,

In *Midnight Hour Encores* she was a very feeling person. Her love for her father was hidden in other things she did, like fighting and music.

He [Bruce Brooks] was saying love comes in many different ways, not just hugging and kissing.

I finished *The Shadow Club*. It was so full of hate for certain people, it burned.

Kay

My response to letters such as these is crucial, for it is in my letters to students that I am able to prod each one a little further. Many times that prodding is affirmation for their ideas and explorations. It is human nature to continue taking a risk when you receive positive feedback for the ones you have already taken.

Dear Kay,

I must read *Midnight Hour Encores* now because of the theme, "love comes in many different ways." Most of us think hugging and kissing are the only expressions of love. The fact that this book points out other ways love can be expressed makes it an important novel.

Oh no! You always say things that make me have to read the book. *The Shadow Club* is a must now too. The ad in the Trumpet Club brochure is what made me buy the book for our library. Your remark, "It is so full of hate...it burns," should replace their ad! Would you do a book talk?

Ms. D

When I return to theme in later mini-lessons, I use books that students have suggested in journal letters and share times. This year's suggestions included *A Wrinkle in Time* by Madeleine L'Engle (1976), *Roll of Thunder, Hear My Cry* by Mildred D. Taylor (1981), and *The Outsiders* by S. E. Hinton (1982, 1967). These suggestions change from class to class and from year to year. That fact alone suggests the richness of allowing students to freely explore the literary value of the books they choose to read.

Conflict

In discussing conflict, I always choose a novel that has a combination of internal and external conflicts. This year I used *The Island Keeper* by Harry Mazer (1981) because a student had recently done a book talk about it. Conflict always creates lively share time discussions and detailed journal letters. Perhaps the turmoil of adolescence makes it easy for these readers to identify with both external and internal conflict, especially in novels that have teenage characters. These letters, written by students of varying abilities, each exhibit a very real understanding of conflict.

Dear Ms. D,

I am still reading *Let the Circle Be Unbroken*. In it I like the way Mildred Taylor shows the inner conflict of Stacey, like when he walks off into the woods or when Cassie asks him questions. I think one of Mildred Taylor's inspiring authors was Mark Twain because it's kind of about the same topic and the style of writing are similar. I can understand how Stacey feels with a girl he likes getting

I was utterly amazed at the ease with which my students began to note the universal ideas and feelings behind the stories they were reading and to connect those stories with their own lives.

pregnant with a white man, and learning about being a man and all the troubles you have to face, and doing it without Papa there. It would be hard.

Dennis

Dennis focuses on more than one conflict in Taylor's novel, but he doesn't stop there. He goes on to compare Taylor and Twain! Is this simply reading or is it literature study? I say it's both. Dennis's sophisticated response to this book indicates real involvement as a reader. He is doing much more than a surface reading.

In the next letter, Anne's response goes beyond a single book. She has begun to group books by theme and conflict.

Dear Ms. D,

At the beginning of the year I read *The Twin Connection*. It wasn't a great book but it relates to *Pen Pals, Rumble Fish, The Makeover Summer,* and *Just As Long As We're Together*. All these books are by different authors but the type of conflict is the same. JELOUSEY is the most popular area of conflict in my book because people of different ages can take part in feeling the same way. Jelousey can be an interesting area of conflict if you look at it with the right conclusion. Sometimes the jelousey is open and jumps from the page to your mind like in *The Twin Connection, Pen Pals, The Makeover Summer,* and *Just As Long As We're Together,* and sometimes it's hidden in the character's heart like *Rumble Fish* where you have to read between the lines to find it. I like these types of books.

Anne

Again, my response reinforces the risk Anne took with her thinking about books and conflicts:

Dear Anne,

You're really thinking. Noticing how conflicts are repeated in a number of books and seeing how the same conflict is treated differently in those books is exactly the kind of thinking I'd hoped you would do this year. Keep it up.

Ms. D

The more literary elements I highlight in minilessons and the more I share my responses to adolescent novels, the more kids talk about their books in those terms. The mutual honesty that grows from shared interests, shared respect, and a common ground of literature is at the heart of my students' willingness to take risks in their

responses to books. Before I had even addressed the idea of symbolism in a mini-lesson, Eric brought it up in his letter.

Dear Ms. D,

I just finished *The Dollar Man*. I loved it. I really liked the ending when he left the money and the watch behind on the bus seat. I guess that was to show he was leaving his father behind him.

Eric

I asked Eric to read this letter during the next day's share session. One student added, "I didn't think of that, but now I see what you mean. Keeping the watch and the dollar was a way of keeping his father in his life but it didn't help him at all." A debate about this symbolism resulted in kids bringing up other books. John said,

In *Rumble Fish*, when Motorcycle Boy broke into the pet store, took the fighting fish, and brought them to the water to be set free, it signified the rage inside of him being let out. He didn't express himself violently like I expected. Instead, his actions alone were symbols of his feelings.

The learning that grew out of this sharing of ideas among students can't be equalled in any other atmosphere. It is a forceful reminder that student sharing is a powerful instructional tool. With Eric's permission, I used his letter to introduce symbolism to my other classes.

In the final journal letter of the year, I ask students to write to me about how they had changed as readers and about their feelings about books and reading workshop. Their letters are always revealing:

When I came here I thought of reading as a bunch of words on paper that you just read. Now after minilessons and share times, I see that reading is an experience. I am now able to find the true meaning of a book. Minilessons taught me about books and their meanings. The one that influenced me most was the one where you talked about the universal message of a book. This taught me to look beyond the words on the page and see what they really meant.

Share times helped me to see the changes that were happening to me by sharing the things I had noticed in my reading that day.

The reason I have changed from a plain old reader to a reader that looks farther than the cover of the book is the journal.

The mutual honesty that grows from shared interests, shared respect, and a common ground of literature is at the heart of my students' willingness to take risks in their responses to books.

I used to think good literature was a book with a good plot, but now I judge a good book by its characters.

At first I was embarrassed to share my ideas or to give my opinion on a certain book. But now I've learned that your opinion on a book can't be wrong.

There is magic in our classrooms when kids discover their own ideas. It happens because of the atmosphere we create, because of our enthusiasm for literature, and because kids have the freedom to choose their own books and to have their own ideas without fear of being wrong. But most of all it happens because we respect kids and their ideas and insist on the same from them. We are equals in the world of literature. A mutual honesty permeates our written and oral talk about books and the ideas they spark in us. This atmosphere is safe. It supports taking risks as readers and as thinkers. It validates each individual's ideas and promotes the exploration of new ones. This atmosphere allows for the transaction between the text and the reader that creates what Rosenblatt (1978) calls the poem, the meaning, and the merit of the literary experience. It creates a place where books become literature in the minds and hearts of adolescents.

> *There is magic in our classrooms when kids discover their own ideas.*

References

Atwell, N. (1987). *In the middle: Reading, writing, and learning with adolescents.* Portsmouth, NH: Boynton/Cook.

Rosenblatt, L. (1978). *The reader, the text, the poem: The transactional theory of the literary work.* Carbondale: Southern Illinois University Press.

Adolescent Literature Cited

Babbitt, N. (1985). *Tuck everlasting.* New York: Farrar, Straus, & Giroux.

Blume, J. (1988). *Just as long as we're together.* New York: Dell.

Brooks, B. (1988). *Midnight hour encores.* New York: Harper Junior Books.

George, J. C. (1972). *Julie of the wolves.* New York: Harper Junior Books.

Hinton, S. E. (1982, 1967). *The outsiders.* New York: Dell.

———. (1983, 1975). *Rumble fish.* New York: Dell.

L'Engle, M. (1976). *A wrinkle in time.* New York: Dell.

MacLachlan, P. (1988). *The facts and fictions of Minna Pratt.* New York: Harper Junior Books.

Mazer, H. (1974). *The dollar man.* New York: Dell.

———. (1975). *Snow bound.* New York: Dell.

———. (1981). *The island keeper.* New York: Dell.

Pascal, F. (Creator). (1990). *Sweet valley twins: The twin connection.* New York: Bantam.

Paterson, K. (1990). *Jacob have I loved.* New York: Harper Trophy.

Paulsen, G. (1988). *Hatchet.* New York: Penguin USA.

Pfeffer, S. B. (1988). *The year without Michael.* New York: Bantam.

Shusterman, N. (1990). *The shadow club.* New York: Dell.

Taylor, M. D. (1987). *The friendship and the gold cadillac.* New York: Dell.

———. (1983). *Let the circle be unbroken.* New York: Bantam.

———. (1981). *Roll of thunder, hear my cry.* New York: Bantam.

Weyn, S. (1988). *The makeover summer.* New York: Avon.

Wyeth, S. D. (1989). *Pen pals.* New York: Dell.

Suggestions for Introducing and Exploring Literary Elements

Familiarity with literature, freedom to explore and apply new knowledge without risk of evaluation, and multiple opportunities to share new discoveries or try out new thoughts are at the heart of my reading workshop. Whenever I introduce a literary element, I provide the technical term and a definition in "middle school" language, but the heart of each minilesson consists of actual examples that illustrate the element and the way in which authors use that element. The examples always come from books my students and I have read, books that are readily available in our classroom library. I end each minilesson with an invitation to "find other examples in your own reading and contribute them to a future class discussion."

Connecting the literary elements to passages from familiar books puts them within the grasp of middle schoolers and gives them meaning within specific reading experiences. Definitions alone seem to create little thinking or learning. Only when a definition is within the context of examples the students can touch through their own reading do the definition and the term make sense.

A large percentage of the students seek out the very books I have used in my minilessons. During share time and in journal letters, they mention finding the very examples I cited in the minilessons. Using those examples and others, they explain, in their own words, the literary element and its power in the story. Students tell me that reading the book from which I have taken an example of the literary element helps them to see the element in a larger and more personal context. It also helps them to easily locate additional passages that illustrate the element we have discussed.

A workshop classroom is an exciting place to be. For me, the excitement comes as much from what I learn each day as it does from what my students learn. It seems that the more I plant seeds of learning by using examples of the books I've read, the responses I've had, and the thinking I've done, the more they push their own thinking and, in turn, mine. *This* is where I truly see their growth.

Lingering Questions

- How can I involve more students in preparing and presenting minilessons that reflect the discoveries students have made and pose questions for their classmates to explore?

- How can I enable students who are satisfied with plot summary to ask big questions of themselves and of the literature they read?

- How much should I push readers to think and rethink the questions and ideas they have in response to their reading?

- How much can I use an individual reader's journal reflections or responses as a jumping off point for class sharing?

Threads of Life: Reading, Writing, and Music

Linda Rief

Language Arts
Teacher,
Oyster River
Middle School,
Durham,
New Hampshire

with **David Ervin**,
Music Teacher,
Oyster River
Middle School

It is June, and the night before the last day of school. There are 150 seventh graders performing their original musical for more than 300 parents, teachers, and other students. We are packed elbow to elbow. We have created a makeshift theater-in-the-round from the gymnasium in our middle school. I am behind the audience attempting to keep 149 members of the cast relatively quiet, despite the stifling heat. Sweat runs down my arms, drips off my elbows, my eyebrows, my nose. The lingering odors from years of basketball and volleyball games hang heavy. Hundreds of play programs fan the still air. Dave, the music teacher, strikes a chord on the piano, as Josh joins in on guitar. Scene 3. A dim spotlight finds Matt, a seventh grader who often can't answer his biggest question about school, "What's this for?" Tonight he is playing the role of Rico. It is the 1990s. Rico, a high school student and the head of a gang known as the Pounders, is alone in an abandoned textile mill. Alone and hiding. Blamed for a crime he didn't commit. He opens his mouth and sings:

> I sometimes wonder what happened to me.*
> I was left alone, dropped on the street.
> Just eight years old; left to fend for myself.
> Nothing really matters, not even life itself.
>
> This is my life. This is how it goes.
> When you live the way that I do
> You get used to the blows.
> But somethin's goin' down,
> Someone's got to fall.
> This is my life, up against the wall....

For several seconds after Matt stops singing, I notice that the whole room is holding its breath. Then it exhales into thunderous applause. Matt, too, exhales. It is no easy task singing a solo in front of one's peers, especially when you have never sung, or

acted, or wanted to. And this is no easy song. It is laden with emotion, laden with high notes. But Matt hits them all. It doesn't matter that it's June, or that it's the night before the last day of school. For the first time in seventh grade, Matt has his answer to "What's it for?" And not just Matt. As the lights come up, I notice Alyssa and Julie. They are rows apart but find each other's eyes. They, too, know the answer. They wrote the lyrics to this song.

For years, Dave Ervin, the music teacher, and I talked about planning a project together, believing that what the seventh graders could do in one class would be doubly enhanced if they were guided through it in two classes. But we never found the time to design a plan. We admitted finally that we would never find the time. "Let's just do it," we said. We believed, but never said out loud, that our similar philosophical beliefs would guide us through this project.

Music, like writing, is a mode of expression that attempts to describe those things that we do not yet understand. In both the music and language arts classes, we are asking students to raise the questions that a text brings to mind. What surprises you? Perplexes you? What do you want to know more about? The text may be a novel, a poem, a song, an essay, a picture, one's own writing, or an observation of the world around you. In this case, their answers to these questions took the shape of narrative scripts, lyrics, and music.

In order for any form of expression to have value, it must be meaningful, purposeful, and enriching.

---

* Copyright pending by Linda Rief and David Ervin for scripts, lyrics, and musical arrangements. Reprinted by permission.

■ Meaning is that which makes an intellectual and emotional connection with the learner.

■ Purpose is that which leads the learner from one meaning to another.

■ Enrichment is that which gives the learner a deeper understanding of herself or himself, others, and the world.

Both of us strive to make those experiences we offer our students meaningful, purposeful, and enriching. We know that about each other.

I wanted to teach the seventh graders how to conduct research. Dave wanted them to write and perform an original musical. Both of us wanted as many students as possible to find success in many different ways. Both of us wanted them to have fun.

In language arts classes, students concentrated on the drafting and refining of a story, the turning of a narrative into a script, the language of the characters, and the drafting of poetry for lyrics. In music classes, Dave also guided them through the development and refinement of the story, the refining of the scripts, the refinement of the lyrics, and setting the lyrics to music. Could we work collaboratively with little planning and a lot of intuition and trust to guide us? We had six weeks to find out.

In Language Arts

I have two basic purposes for teaching research skills. I want the students to really learn about something in depth—something that is meaningful, purposeful, and enriching—and I want them to leave my classroom knowing how to learn. I learn best when I have some input into what I will learn. Our students need to be given that same option.

There are times, however, when I like to be pushed in directions I might not choose for myself. I think there are times when we need to set some of those same parameters for our students. It pushes their thinking.

For most of the year, students had read books of their own choosing. Although we had read numerous short stories, poetry, journalism articles, and picture books together, we had not read a novel as a whole class. Since individuals read in a variety of ways, I offer students all those possibilities.

This time, I wanted all of us to read and respond to a novel together. Too often we choose books to read together with a male protagonist, so I wanted the main character to be a girl, one who is feisty despite the odds. I wanted the book to be fresh, new to me also. And I wanted the book to be historical fiction, because I've noticed few students choose it for themselves.

Most importantly, we had to consider our constraints of time and numbers. We had 150 students brainstorming ideas for a musical. We had six weeks in which to make it happen. All 150 students had to be part of the performance on stage. We needed to confine the topic for our sake as teachers, as well as for the students. We decided that the research would focus on the mills during the Industrial Revolution. We would have the students read *Lyddie* by Katherine Paterson, we would take them to the Boott Mill in Lowell, Massachusetts, and we would ask them to write a musical based on their wonderings and findings. I wanted the students to respond to this reading in more than a personal way. I wanted them to take apart the layers of this novel, and construct their own meaning through a new medium, one that was unfamiliar to them and me—in this case, a musical.

I wanted them to take apart the layers of this novel, and construct their own meaning through a new medium, one that was unfamiliar to them and me—in this case, a musical.

Reading Lyddie

Before reading *Lyddie,* I asked the students to take three minutes to jot down in their journals everything they knew about mills in New England or the Industrial Revolution. After just thirty seconds they were looking around the room staring at each other. They knew little. My list wasn't much longer. I would be learning right along with them.

After reading the first chapter, I was hooked. I read a few passages to the students. They wanted to hear more. Students bought their own copies. (I provided books to those students who couldn't afford it.) I wanted them to write in the margins, underline, question, react . . . .

I gave the students eight days to read *Lyddie*—about three chapters, or twenty-five pages a night. I asked them to make notations in their books by underlining, starring, or bracketing key phrases or paragraphs that would be helpful to them in developing characters, writing dialogue and scenes, and understanding relationships during this time period. I asked them specifically to note (in their books or in their journals):

■ personal reaction to each night's reading

■ examples of language and/or expressions that you would most likely not use or hear today

"Oh Lord, deliver us!" (p. 2)

"You want I should go with you as far as the village?" (p. 6)

. . .she minded mightily being beholden. (p. 7)

■ metaphors and similes that described situations, places, or people

Lyddie could feel the rage oozing up like sap on a March morning. (p. 20)

Mistress Cutler watched Lyddie like a barn cat on a sparrow . . . . (p. 24)

Missing Charlie was like wearing a stone around her neck. (p. 24)

Fatigue was like a toothache in her bones. (p. 138)

> All of this reading and writing was meant to connect them with the time period— immerse them in the language, sensitize them to the issues, feel the emotions of real people.

■ descriptions that stick with you/bring things to mind for you

A factory was a hundred stagecoaches all inside one's skull, banging their wheels against the bone. (p.63)

■ examples of ways young women were treated, and expected to behave

■ conditions on the farms, in the mills, in the boardinghouses

■ things you notice about Lyddie

issues/problems/people Lyddie must contend with

ways she handles herself

characteristics you admire in Lyddie

the significant messages you take away from Lyddie's story

■ questions that come to mind as you read

I read with the students, often starting each day with a passage I loved (or hated), talking about what they and I had discovered, giving them time to read, and sometimes asking them to try a quick-write. Over the course of two weeks, I asked the students to write for three to five minutes in their journals in each of these ways:

■ Draft a letter as a mill girl to four different audiences: a family member, a best friend, the overseer, the newspaper, about what it's like in the mills.

■ Pour out a journal entry as if you are loving or hating your new found "freedom" as a factory worker (conditions, expectations, treatment, hopes, dreams).

■ Draft a petition to the overseer about the conditions you can no longer tolerate (make suggestions about what might be done better).

■ Read pages 74–80 again. What does reading mean to you?

All of this reading and writing was meant to connect them with the time period—immerse them in the language, sensitize them to the issues, feel the emotions of real people. They were sketching out ideas every time they read and wrote, not knowing

Clip and File

Reviews of Books for Middle Level Readers

Reviews for Kids by Kids

The Master Puppeteer
Katherine Paterson

Harper Trophy, 1989, 192 pp., $3.95
ISBN 0-06-440281-9

Jiro, a thirteen-year-old boy, wants to work at a puppet theater to earn money. Jiro leaves his mother and very ill father who have neither money nor food. At the puppet theater, Jiro meets Kinshi, the son of the puppeteer, Yoshida. Kinshi will let Jiro live at the Hanza Theater to learn to control the large puppets. It takes about four months just to learn how to operate one part of a puppet. Jiro tries to get reward money by finding Saburo, a bandit who robs the rich and gives to the poor. Saburo is a character similar to Robin Hood, but mysterious.

Katherine Paterson researched puppet theaters and historic things about Japan. The book is set in the time of a terrible rice famine in the late 1700s in Japan. About 200,000 people died of starvation at that time. People who want to know a little about puppetry and about old Japan would like this book.

Saray Nop, Grade 6
Amherst, Massachusetts

The Flip Flop Girl
Katherine Paterson

Lodestar, 1994, 120 pp., $13.99
ISBN 0-525-67480-2

The Flip Flop Girl is a wonderful fiction story about an eleven-year-old girl named Vinnie whose dad has just died. Her mom can't support the family, so they move to Brownsville, Virginia with Vinnie's annoying grandmother. There, her problems begin. Ever since her father's death, her brother Mason has not said one word. Vinnie doesn't get to sing songs with her mom or play dolls with her grandma anymore because they're always trying to get help for Mason. Vinnie hates Brownsville. Not only does she lack for attention at home, but none of the kids at school seem to like her, except for her handsome teacher, Mr. Clayton. Then one day she sees a tall, lanky girl playing hopscotch. Lupe has a weird family, but Vinnie finds out that they are best friends when Lupe sticks up for her. She appreciates Lupe more and more, as she realizes she can't be totally independent from others. I think the author did a great job expressing the feelings of Vinnie in this book.

Jennifer Betras, Grade 8
Spartanburg Day School, Spartanburg, SC

Come Sing, Jimmy Jo
Katherine Paterson

Avon Books, 1986, 192 pp., $2.95
ISBN 0-380-70052-2

This book tells the story of James who cherishes the happy evenings on the patio with his grandmother. It doesn't matter to him that she sings the wrong notes, because he cares more about being with her, laughing, singing, and playing his guitar. James's father, mother, and uncle Earl have a country band and travel to different cities singing for people all year. James almost never gets to see his parents, to get to know them from the inside.

On one of the family visits, the band's new manager, Eddie, hears James sing and decides that James should join the band because he sings better than anyone else. James doesn't feel happy about leaving his grandmother behind and knows that he will have to face new problems in the city. This is the saddest part of the book because Grandma's and James's bond is now broken a little, and both feel very sad.

I think that Katherine Paterson did a good job forming and developing these characters, especially James and the grandmother.

Vanessa Kuhn, Grade 8
Spartanburg Day School, Spartanburg, SC

Park's Quest
Katherine Paterson

E.P. Dutton (Lodestar Books), 1988, 160 pp., $12.95
ISBN 0-525-67258-3

Park's Quest is about a boy whose father, a Vietnam War veteran, died before he was born. Park wants to find out who he was and why his mother acts strangely when he mentions him. Though different in appearance, father and son both have the same name, Parkington Waddell Broughton. Park the Fifth asks his mother questions, reads and studies the books his father used to read, and even goes to the Vietnam Memorial. Later he gets an invitation to visit his grandfather. There he feels confused and in the way, and a pesky Vietnamese girl named Thanh follows him around. At first they dislike each other, but later realize they share something important.

This book contains excerpts from stories of the times of King Arthur, which makes the story more enjoyable: "Who is yonder knight on that great white horse?" I also liked the effective repetition: "Geek, geeeeek. Geek, geeeeek." The story seems to be a mystery and a fiction story in one. Readers who enjoyed *Bridge to Terabithia* will enjoy this one, too.

Andy Tam, Grade 8
Spartanburg Day School, Spartanburg, SC

Bridge to Terabithia
Katherine Paterson

Harper Trophy, 1987, 144 pp., $3.95
ISBN 0-06-440184-7

In *Bridge to Terabithia,* Jess meets his new neighbor, a tomboy named Leslie. Paterson presents Leslie as a person who doesn't care how she looks or what other people think of her. This strange couple develops a friendship that will change them forever. Jess loves drawing and running, and practices hard to be the best. The friendship grows after the day Leslie gets to run, and soon they invent Terabithia. I like their secret place, because I always wanted a secret place where I could get away from people. Paterson gives the impression that anything can happen at Terabithia.

I know how it feels when everything is going perfectly, and then you get some bad news, and it hits you like a mack truck. The feeling remains with you and won't go away. The only way to escape feelings like this is to run, just as Jess does. I like this book a lot. It shows you that you don't know how valuable your friends are until you lose them.

Jennifer Sams, Grade 8
Spartanburg Day School, Spartanburg, SC

Lyddie
Katherine Paterson

Puffin Books, 1992, 192 pp., $3.99
ISBN 0-14-034981-2

I love the book *Lyddie.* Katherine Paterson is a great author who paints a detailed picture of the 1840s and helps me understand this time in our history more clearly. I grew to love Lyddie and wanted everything to turn out for the best. I liked the whole theme of the story—a young girl's having to be mother to her brothers and sisters and having to go out in the work force at such a young age. This book teaches responsibility and is inspirational. I especially like the parts of the book where Lyddie is all on her own. Paterson really makes me feel for her. I can just imagine the boarding house and the factory. It is funny, but serious at the same time, when the boss tries "to take advantage" of the girls.

The book is a perfect mixture of seriousness and humor. It also teaches how you should stand up for what you believe in. I commend Katherine Paterson on such a great job. *Lyddie* is one of my favorite books.

Kristin Lemaster, Grade 8
Spartanburg Day School, Spartanburg, SC

Jacob Have I Loved
Katherine Paterson

Harper Trophy, 1990, 256 pp., $3.95
ISBN 0-06-440368-8

In the book *Jacob Have I Loved,* Katherine Paterson tells the story of two sisters who, like Jacob and Esau, fight for attention and a birthright. In the process, we get a sense of what life might be like on Rass Island. With Caroline playing the part of Jacob, the younger and more perfect twin, Louise fades into the background and longs for the attention and love of her parents. She fights a battle within herself, looking for someone to blame for all this heartache. She states that "the only time I've ever been happy was the first two minutes of my life," before her sister Caroline was born.

As a result of her feeling out of place at home in the presence of a hateful grandmother and an indifferent family, Louise turns to the ocean and her friend Call for comfort. On the water, Louise finds a reassurance that makes her feel that she is worth something, and in Call she finds a friend with whom she can laugh and cry.

Jenny Neely, Grade 8
Spartanburg Day School, Spartanburg, SC

The Great Gilly Hopkins
Katherine Paterson

Harper Trophy, 1987, 192 pp., $3.95
ISBN 0-06-440201-0

Galadriel Hopkins is left by her mother when she is three years old. From that time on, she is sent from one foster home to another and soon becomes "the problem child." Gilly dreams of finding her birth mother, Courtney Rutherford Hopkins. But then she is sent to Mrs. Trotter, who receives Gilly with a different kind of caring and love. She and her son treat her as if she has always been there. Although Gilly is still looking for her birth mother, and still telling herself how ugly and fat Mrs. Trotter is, she has never felt this safe before. One day the search for Gilly's birth mother almost reaches completion; Gilly buys a ticket to California but is later sent to her real grandmother where all she does is write letters to Trotter.

I really liked this book because it is a combination of a funny story and a girl's family crisis. The mystery in Trotter and William Ernest is humanity, which allows Gilly and all kids like her to feel understood.

Marie-Theres Franke, Grade 8
Spartanburg Day School, Spartanburg, SC

Mill
David Macaulay

Houghton Mifflin/Sandpiper, 1989, 128 pp., $7.70
ISBN 0-395-52019-3

Mill, a combination of historical fiction and fact, captures the rise and fall of the mill age. It outlines the construction and operation of 19th-century mills in the imaginary town of Wicksbridge. Macaulay's precise, intricate black-and-white drawings (from intriguing perspectives) show how the mills were constructed and how the actual machinery worked. In the course of the book, several mills are erected and destroyed. With each new mill, more advanced technology is used.

Using bits of journal entries to highlight the real-life happenings in the mills, we learn of the hardships and risks for the mill workers. *Mill* shows how easy it was for someone to be seriously hurt or killed by the fast-moving teeth, looms, and shuttles operated mostly by young girls. Despite the attraction to leave farms to earn money in the mills, the conditions during the boom in the textile industry were horrid because of economic hardships and competition with automation. Throughout *Mill*, you not only learn how mills were built, but you get a real sense of what life was like then.

Marc Swanson with Patrick Aber, Grade 8
Oyster River Middle School, Durham, NH

The Clock
James Lincoln Collier and Christopher Collier

Delacorte, 1992, 161 pp., $15.00
ISBN 0-385-30037-9

Although this story is fiction, it is based on real conditions and events. Annie Steele wants to become a teacher. But her father is deeply in debt and sends Annie, only 15 years old, to work in the new wool mill. Annie not only works long and grueling hours in the dangerous mill conditions, but she must contend with the mill's cruel and offensive overseer, Mr. Hoggart. The intrigue deepens when Annie realizes that he is also a thief. Throughout the story, the *clock*, which Annie must now answer to daily at the mill, remains a metaphor for progress—and all that progress means. The authors make us wonder if giving up control of one's time and life for material possessions is worth the price of progress.

This work of historical fiction gives us a new perspective on our own technological advances in view of the drastic changes our ancestors experienced as a result of the mills. Is all the progress for the better? There are no answers in this book, but it certainly leads to some valuable class discussion.

Linda Rief, teacher
Oyster River Middle School, Durham, NH

The Lorax
Dr. Seuss

Random Books for Young Readers, 1971, 70 pp., $12.00
ISBN 0-394-82337-0

"Protect it from the axes that hack. Then the Lorax and all of his friends may come back." When you first hear the words "picture book," you relate them to children, but the reality is that they often address serious topics that even older students can enjoy.

The Lorax is a delightful story that makes a serious point: by being too greedy we can lose everything. The rhythm, combined with colorful pictures, tells us that if you really love something, save it! Dr. Seuss lets us step into his world of Truffula trees and the Brown Bar-ba-loots, led by the wise old Lorax. Their enemy, the Once-ler, narrates the message about planet earth. Once there were crystal waters and clear skies, now tarnished with pollutants. Now certain animals and plants can only be read about—or seen in science books. Like the Truffula Trees, the Brown Bar-ba-loots, the Humming-Fish, and the Swomee-Swans, we have our own animals and plants in jeopardy. Dr. Seuss wants us to care for and respect the world around us.

Casey Hopkins, Anne Duperault, and Michele Labreque, Grade 8
Oyster River Middle School, Durham, NH

A River Ran Wild
Lynne Cherry

Harcourt Brace Juvenile Books, 1992, 26 pp., $14.95
ISBN 0-15-200542-0

"They came down from the mountain, and at the river's edge they knelt to quench their thirst with its clear water. Pebbles shone up from the bottom. 'Let us settle by this river,' said the chief of the native people. He named the river Nash-a-way— River with the Pebbled Bottom." Centuries later the Nash-a-way River was declared ecologically dead, the shiny pebbles and clear water smothered by years of waste dumped into the river by textile mills.

Through beautiful illustrations and descriptive words, Lynne Cherry tells us the history of the Nashua River, an Algonquin tribe's home. It is the story of industry and progress begun by the colonists, of terrible pollution and disrespect for the environment, and of the inspiring salvation of this beautiful resource by ordinary people. The clever, beautiful illustrations bordering the pages give the reader a better idea of the times and place in which this story takes place. The book inspires us to respect the environment and to save our lakes and rivers while we still can.

Kristen Cosby, Grade 8
Oyster River Middle School, Durham, NH

Clip and File

Reviews of Books for Middle Level Teachers

Reviews: Lanny van Allen, Texas Education Agency, Austin, Texas; Robert Probst, Georgia State University

---

The Spying Heart:
More Thoughts on Reading and Writing
Books for Children
Katherine Paterson

Dutton (Lodestar), 1990, 208 pp. $8.95

ISBN 0-525-67269-9

Through this compilation of articles, speeches, and book reviews (even a Miss Manners book), Paterson shares a variety of comments and insights about herself, her associates, her ideas and philosophy, and books, ones that she's read and ones that she's written. She shares ideas about writing—hers and others'—and why Story is so important to all of life, why imagination is vital if we are to make "connections" (like Einstein and E=mc^2). She talks about a writer's point of view and a writer's responsibilities. More specifically, she talks about her characters, her word choices, her books' endings, and how her favorite, Gilly Hopkins, came to have that name. Paterson wishes kids were all "flashlight readers," wanting to continue reading past bedtime so badly, they read in the closet or under the covers using a flashlight—just as she did!

I would get new batteries for my flashlight to read this lovely book, especially the very rich chapters "The Spying Heart" and "Do I Dare Disturb the Universe?"

Radical Reflections:
Passionate Opinions on Teaching, Learning,
and Living
Mem Fox

HBJ, 1993, 192 pp., $12.95

ISBN 015-607-947X

If teachers want to read only one book this year that will give them renewed energy and make next year different and more rewarding, then this book is The One. This book validates the changes you want to make to have a live, student-centered classroom.

Mem's title warns the audience that she is "radical" and passionate in her opinions. Fox, a teacher for twenty years, knows Real Language works because she has used it (and lived it). She points to classroom writing and reading experiences, notes and poems of her own and of her students, and reflects on her childhood reading experiences as well as her experience teaching her baby Chloe to read. She says, "Fine writing teaches reading whether we intend it to or not." And she firmly believes basals do not have fine writing. Students may learn to read with basals but will not learn to become readers! The literary desert, Fox calls them. It's far, far better to work with real writing rather than "messing about with unattached parts of language." Mem Fox is a spark, a sparkler, and this book is dynamite!

Response and Analysis:
Teaching Literature in Junior and
Senior High School
Robert E. Probst

Boynton Cook, 1987, 279 pp. $17.50

ISBN 0-86709-203-3

Most of us had teachers who told us what the writer meant by each word and line of a piece of literature. (Perhaps at least a few of us have even done that ourselves!) How exciting and liberating, then, is this book! Probst, drawing on Louise Rosenblatt's work, tells us, "The task in teaching literature is to help students think, not to tell them what to think." Probst, like Rosenblatt, argues that literature is experience, not information, and that the student must be invited to participate in it, not simply observe it from outside.

Probst's book is replete with thoughtful strategies for teaching literature—such as pairing of texts, reading in groups, and writing in response to reading. After a good review of genres, Probst provides excellent thematic lists of YA books, sections on visual literacy (and how to address it in classroom work), and testing/evaluation. His final chapter is devoted to others who have made significant contributions to reader-response theory. Probst offers us a thorough, highly readable text, one that we'll use often and hurry to buy for our teacher friends.

The Reader, the Text, the Poem:
The Transactional Theory of the
Literary Work
Louise M. Rosenblatt

SIU Press, 1978, 214 pp., $22.50

ISBN 0-8093-0883-5

In *The Reader, the Text, the Poem*, Rosenblatt elaborates the theory of literature developed earlier in *Literature as Exploration* (1938). Rosenblatt herself expresses the focus of the work most succinctly in the first sentence of her preface: "The premise of this book is that a text, once it leaves its author's hands, is simply paper and ink until a reader evokes from it a literary work—sometimes, even, a literary work of art." *The Reader, the Text, the Poem* is about that process of evoking meaning from texts. Rosenblatt draws a lucid picture of the acts of reading, rejecting a monolithic view of reading for a more complex vision that differentiates between reading for information—efferent—and reading for fuller immersion in the imaginative worlds of poetic and fictional texts—aesthetic. The vision she presents of autonomous readers fully involved, intellectually, emotionally, and aesthetically, in literary texts is wonderfully democratic in its respect for the integrity of the reader and the vitality of the literary work of art.

where or when those ideas would find their way into song lyrics, a setting, a script.

Krista drafted a diary entry for one quick-write. Part of it said: "I shar a room with six other girls. We are so cramped its like putting all six of us into one set of clothing. Wone girl has a cof and won't see a docter. I heer her nite after nite hacking like a sik cow...."

After finishing the book, she wrote in her journal, "*Lyddie* was one of the best books I've ever read,...I'm not sure if you noticed, but I wrote all of my favorite quotes in my log instead of the book because I treasure the book and I would like to pass it on to my children....This book really gave me a 'flavor' of the 1800s and helped a lot in writing the play. I felt like I really learned something. History is not one of my favorite things to study, but I'm really into what we are doing in L.A. and music....My absolute favorite quote in the whole book was [after Lyddie crammed the fire bucket over Mr. Marsden's head for what he was doing to Brigid], 'Behind in the darkness, she thought she heard the noise of an angry bear crashing an oatmeal pot against the furniture' (p. 161). It seems that that was what the whole book *Lyddie* was about."

Once students finished reading *Lyddie* as a whole class, I expected them to continue reading and responding in their journals to additional recommended titles. (See References.) This worked especially well for those students who read *Lyddie* in a day or two and wanted more to read. I also read several books aloud: *The Lorax* by Dr. Seuss, *Mill* by David Macauley, and *A River Ran Wild* by Lynne Cherry.

As they read, the students wanted to know more.

"How come the girls left their farms to work in such awful places?"

"Were the mills really that bad?"

"How come they worked under such horrible conditions?"

"Why were they treated so terribly? How could the overseers get away with that?"

"Why were there only girls working in the mills?"

To help students in their search for answers, we took them to the reconstructed textile mills in Lowell, Massachusetts. After working on hand looms, listening first hand to the deafening clatter of actual machines, and learning about the working conditions, we returned to our classrooms. In language arts classes, I asked the students, "What surprised you? What do you want to know more about?" Their answers, in the form of questions, surprised me. "Do you think the ghost of Lizzie Ryan still haunts the mill?" "How did they stand the noise of those machines?" "How did they breathe with all that dust around?" "Why didn't they protest?" "How come they didn't just go back to the farm?"

The park ranger who had acted as our guide had told the story of a girl named Lizzie Ryan. The students remembered every detail. She was a real mill girl in the 1800s. She died when she fell five stories while trying to slide down the bannister for a quick retreat to supper. Supposedly "her ghost still haunts the Boott Mill," the ranger said.

During their tour through Lowell on the old trolley car, students noticed groups of students hanging out behind the present-day high school near the mill. High schoolers seemed to congregate in definite ethnic groups. To our seventh graders, these groups of older students were intimidating. For days, their talk always circled back to Lizzie's ghost and the gangs of high schoolers. As we formulated questions for our research, "What we want to know more about," ideas seemed to head in those two distinct directions.

What if Lizzie really did haunt the mills? What if she could come back to life? What would she be like? Would she fit in? Why would she haunt the mills? How could she come back to life? What would she be like if she did? What would she find today?

Were those real gangs hanging out behind the high school? How were they divided up? What are their lives like? Is each gang different? What would have happened if someone had taunted them? Would they have tried to hurt us? Are these the great-grandchildren of the men and women who were immigrants in the 1800s? Are these the

> *They were sketching out ideas every time they read and wrote, not knowing where or when those ideas would find their way into song lyrics, a setting, a script.*

descendants of the boys and girls who came off the farms to work in the mills? Were these kids new immigrants?

In their research, reading, and writing, the students continued to return again and again to their own questions about Lizzie Ryan and about gangs. The students' questions about conditions in the mills, their continued interest as we read *Lyddie*, and their curiosity about gangs indicated there was enough interest to sustain their research. In both language arts and music classes we asked the students to focus their ideas for a story around the Industrial Revolution, concentrating particularly on its effect on women in the mill towns. We had no idea how their interest in gangs might connect, or even if it would connect at all.

In Music Class

The drafting of story ideas began in Dave's music class with "What ifs?" The students' "What ifs?" ran the gamut from aliens having root canals in a dentist's outer space office to a former mill worker being born again as a cowboy. Although no "What if?" was wrong, only the ones that could be built upon from student to student ever survived the process. The students kept going back to the ghost of Lizzie Ryan and today's gangs in cities. The focus began to become clearer as one class went around the room:

What if a Hispanic gang in 1993 is accused of killing another gang's leader? What if they run to the abandoned mill and hide? What if they hear police sirens and quickly get into an old elevator? What if the elevator suddenly jerks to a start and they're carried into the past when the mills were working? What if a member of the gang doesn't want to leave the past? What if the gang members are expected to work? What if they form a strike? What if one of them is killed by a machine? What if they try to take the mill workers with them back to the present? What if one of the mill workers looks, talks, and acts like one of the gang members?

The "What ifs?" continued in music classes for several days until the students had the beginning of a story that had to do with the ghost of Lizzie Ryan from the mills and something to do with gangs of today.

Those ideas came back to the language arts classes where I had students break into two groups, those who wanted to focus on ideas that had to do with Lizzie Ryan, and those who wanted to discuss possibilities associated with the gangs. We then brainstormed ways of connecting the two. Once we had the connection, students broke into groups of three to five to come up with an outline for a whole story. Ideas were shared with the whole class; the best-liked ideas went down to music classes where they were further refined.

Once we had an outline, we broke it into six scenes (some clearer than others), giving the responsibility for developing each scene to an entire class of seventh graders (we had six sections of seventh graders).

Producing the Musical

Refining the script in language arts

Once we had a scene for each class, I broke the students into groups of three to five, gave them a brief summary of the scene, and asked them to write a one-to-three page narration which they then turned into a three-to-five page script. Each group read their parts as they acted out their scenes. We voted on the most effective ones, attempting to combine the best from each. Minilessons included: setting the scene; turning narration into dialogue; refining dialogue based on language of the time, character, and need; writing narration; writing description; finding appropriate places for songs; writing poetry/lyrics; rhyming; writing effective titles; and use of literary devices (such as metaphor and simile).

Of the six seventh-grade language arts classes, I had only two of them. The four I did not have worked on this musical with David only. My entire 50-minute period with my two classes was devoted to researching and writing their scripts and songs. At night, I often took the rough draft scripts from the other four classes home to give them my written response, questions, and suggestions. I listened to their songs after school, and offered my response in a similar fashion.

> *The drafting of story ideas began in Dave's music class with "What ifs?"*

One of my classes was responsible for the opening mill scene; the other was responsible for a contemporary classroom scene. Unfortunately, we had little time to read about inner city gangs. In the class responsible for the gang scene, I did read several passages from *The Outsiders* by S. E. Hinton, and asked the students to listen to the news and clip articles from newspapers for any information about gang-related incidents. I asked them to pay specific attention to the attitudes of the gang members, if they were able to glean that kind of information. I also had these students do several quickwrites in their journals, using the prompt, "As a gang member, draft a letter to your best friend, your worst enemy, a teacher, a family member, and a potential employer about what life is like for you in the inner city."

I cut out every article I could find and posted significant stories. I related a story to the students about why collecting research was so important to understanding a character, especially one that might be difficult to relate to. In 1988, while on a fellowship at the Kennedy Center in Washington, D.C., I met Victoria Clark after her performance as Madame Thenardier, the tavern owner's wife, in *Les Misérables*. In order to understand her role as a "child abuser," she kept an artistic journal in which she collected every article or passage she could find (from life and literature) that related to abusive treatment of children, so that she could understand the emotional, psychological, and physical aspects of such a character. If there had been more time, we should have spent it on reading so much more about gangs—who the kids are, what their lives are like, why they need the gangs, how they talk, what they do and do not value, how violence is a part of their lives, etc. But we had less than a week to finish the scripts. We worked with what the students knew.

As we worked on the scripts, I found the most difficult part was trying to keep all twenty-five students in each class completely occupied with the scripts or songwriting. It did not always work. Some students were completely committed to the tasks. Others lost interest once the initial script was written. Because

there were no props or sets for the production, there was little else for these students to do.

Casting parts in music

Once we had the six scenes, we figured out who the main characters were. In music classes, David used two rough draft songs (one about the mills, the other about gangs) for auditions. Anyone could audition for any part. Every student in the class then voted on which two or three students should get a callback. At callbacks, the three students from every class who received the most votes tried out using the same two rough draft songs. Two students from each section, who didn't want to try out, ranked the students. After the session, David and I held a closed-door discussion with the selection committee. We went around the room. We each voted on one person who we thought absolutely had to have a major role. We could name someone who had been named or someone different. Then we listed the best student from each section, based on strength and quality of voice, ability to portray a particular character, ability to connect with the audience, etc. The only requirements that had to be met were: there must be one major role in each seventh-grade section, and there must be a balance of girls and boys in major roles. Being fair is more important in seventh grade than always giving the lead to the very best because the best is often the same person year after year. We have to be more trusting that kids will rise to the occasion when given an opportunity that really challenges them. So often they do.

Scripts and songs were refined and polished like any piece of writing: readers (students and teachers) continually pointed out the places that worked or stuck with them; asked questions to refine the pace, the accuracy of the language, or the story; and made suggestions.

Setting text to music

Dave Ervin *is* what he teaches: a musician, a composer, and a singer. He holds high standards for kids, and they know it. He puts great trust in them. But he also teaches

> *We have to be more trusting that kids will rise to the occasion when given an opportunity that really challenges them. So often they do.*

them. He believes that singing is natural in all of us: that we start life singing before we even begin to talk. We almost have to *learn* to talk, to speak *without* pitch. Therefore, his job is to encourage students not to fear uttering pitched sounds again. He also believes that music is a language of emotion; the music behind words is there to make the emotion of those words more understandable. Setting words to music means convincing kids of those two premises.

Dave has found a process that helps kids take their words, find the emotion in them, and discover the music that is already there. He:

■ has the students break the text into word groups, phrases, and/or sentences.

■ has the students explore the meaning and emotion of the phrase or word group through speech, saying it over and over dozens of times until they feel ready to perform the line in a play.

■ has the students add more and more pitch to their speech, as if they were giving an impassioned soap box sermon. He continually reminds them, however, not to change the meaning. They must only add pitch to their speech.

■ has the students discover the notes and rhythms of the line.

■ and finally, helps them to set an accompaniment to their melody.

Once kids speak their lines in an emotionally clear way, the music is lying there. The trick is to get kids to say the words until they get the exact emotion, which takes a lot of trust in a safe environment. David creates this environment by accepting all that kids say and do with ideas. He helps them see how they could be better. Once the kids' words connect with their emotion, they can begin to hear the notes. As David explains, "If students see the text without doing this, it rarely makes the meaning and emotion of the words more understandable. At best, they create beautiful words attached to beautiful but unrelated music. At worst, it is beautiful words that are caged within a nursery school

melody, canceling out all real emotion."

In music classes and after school, David worked with the students who had major roles. He also helped the students who wrote the songs through this process by orchestrating and arranging the music so that it fit the mood, the character, the story, and the lyrics. All of the lyrics, musical scores, and scripts were written by students with our guidance and suggestions.

Because every seventh grader was in the production, older students accompanied on piano, guitar, and other musical instruments. There were no props. With twenty-five students frequently on stage, props got in the way. Students used hand motions, facial expressions, and body language to indicate various props. Costumes were simplified also: homespun for the mill girls, different colored T-shirts for the gang members. At various points during the production, slides of the mills were flashed on all four walls of the gymnasium.

Reflection

This kind of project was not an easy task. There were many times during the six weeks that I asked myself, "What am I doing this for?" But the production itself, still a rough draft, was testament to the entire process. When that whole room exhaled into thunderous applause for Matt, I knew exactly what David and I were doing this for. It's always for Matt, and Rachel, and Casey, and Jeanne, and Jeremy, and Alyssa, and.... It's for all those reasons. And they all have names.

In *Lyddie*, Katherine Paterson says, "The next day in the mill, the noise was just as jarring and her feet in Triphena's old boots swelled just as large, but now and again she caught herself humming....Tonight after supper, Betsy would read to her again....there was a delicious anticipation, like molded sugar on her tongue....it wasn't so much that she had gotten used to the mill, but she had found a way to escape its grasp. The pasted sheets of poetry or Scripture in the window frames, the geraniums on the sill, those must be some other girl's way, she decided. But hers was a story." (p.79)

For many students, school tends to be as jarring as those mills. We have to find ways of helping them put "geraniums on the sills." We have to recognize that it is our job to find meaningful, purposeful, enriching ways of learning with which kids can connect. We have to offer students all of these same opportunities for responding to "story." Some write, some sing, some listen. They all need to read. And pushing their thinking beyond just personal, immediate response, helps them understand not only themselves, but others. Through reading, writing, and music, students were truly reflecting on their responses to literature and all that it encompasses. Like Matt, they found themselves humming. What better response can we get from readers?

References

Cherry, L. (1992). *A river ran wild.* Orlando, FL: Harcourt Brace.

Hinton, S. E. (1967). *The outsiders.* New York: Dell.

Hugo, V. [1887] (1961). *Les miserables.* New York: Fawcett.

Macaulay, D. (1989). *Mill.* Boston, MA: Houghton Mifflin.

Paterson, K. (1991). *Lyddie.* New York: Dutton Child Books.

Rosenblatt, L. M. (1983). *Literature as exploration* (4th ed.). New York: MLA.

Seuss, Dr. (1971). *The lorax.* New York: Random Books for Young Readers.

Recommended Reading

Collier, J. L., & Collier, C. (1992). *The clock.* New York: Delacorte.

Dublin, T. (1981). *Farm to factory: Women's letters 1830–1860.* New York: Columbia University Press.

Larcom, L. (1961). *A New England girlhood.* Gloucester, MA: Peter Smith.

Lord, A. (1981). *A spirit to ride the whirlwind.* New York: Macmillan.

Robinson, H. H. (1976). *Loom and spindle.* Kailua, HI: Press Pacifica.

Weisman, J. B. (Ed.). (1991). *The Lowell mill girls: Life in the factories.* Lowell, MA: Discovery Enterprises.

Lingering Questions

- How can I keep all the students working on a project as big as this so that they are interested through final drafting?

- What are some other ways to get students to respond to literature that push them beyond just an emotional/personal re-sponse?

- In what ways might the social studies teacher get involved in a project like this also?

- Is there a way of making this a true interdisciplinary project with all teachers involved?

- What are some other books/issues that could be studied in the same way?

- How could we find mentors to work with the students as they write, arrange, and orchestrate the music for such a production?

Things I wish we had done, but had no time to do

- Interview people who worked in the mills in New Hampshire and New England in the 1900s.

- Visit mills closer to home, in addition to the ones throughout New England.

- Read more books about the mills, the Industrial Revolution.

- Read more books and articles about gangs.

When Research and Response Intertwine

Purpose of Research

- to really learn about something in depth

- to learn how to learn

Considerations for Research

- When is the last time you really learned about something in depth?

- How did you go about learning it? (I've learned that if I do, or learn about, what I love to do, or love to learn, I do it well. Our students need to be given those same options. However, I think there are times when I like to be pushed in directions I might not choose for myself. I think there are times when we need to set some of those same parameters for our students. It pushes their thinking.)

Contributing Factors to the Research/Learning Environment

- Choice of topics/issues, ways of researching, ways of presenting:

  at times, free choice

  at times, within parameters (of themes, topics, issues)

- Time: minimum six weeks

- Positive, constructive response to progress and to final products

- Organization: available resources, written guidelines, schedules, deadlines

- Demonstrations:

  examples from previous students/present students

  from the teacher (I try what I ask the students to do. If it isn't good enough for me to do, then it isn't good enough for them to do.)

Structure of Research Studies

- brainstorm topics/issues/questions

- gather information (from primary sources: people, literature)

- organize information

- present information

Requirements of Research Project

- research through 3 different genre/media (e.g., novels, picture books, field trips/interviews)

- present findings through 3 different genre/media

- include process paper

- self-evaluate: What did you do well (process, content, mechanics)? What could you have done better?

- "Test": If you had to research another topic/issue, how would you do it?

Sample Script

Scene 1: Mill, City in New England in the 1800s [1]

Songs:

Mill Girls (Lizzie, all mill girls)
Well, That's Lizzie (all mill girls)
Weave a Fortune (Lizzie, Ruth)

We hear the sound of the looms while it is still dark. The lights come on and the mill girls begin to sing **Mill Girls.** The sound of the looms goes off during the song. When the song is done the sound of the looms comes back on.

Mill Girls

Mill girls run as fast as fire
The bell tolls loud, hard work its desire.

Chorus

The shuttle flies from end to end
Weave and spin, weave and spin
Break and mend, break and mend
I'd give my soul for silence
The giant beast roars like thunder on the plain
The cotton dust flies like furious rain.

Chorus

Their fingers twirl, their feet are sore
The looms don't rest, just cry for more.

Chorus

Day after day the bell is rung
Their only wish that day is done.

Chorus

The machines demand total compliance
I'd give my soul for silence!

Overseer: Get back to work! (The sound of the looms continues softly in the background. The spotlight goes on Lizzie and Ruth.)

Lizzie: Back to work, ey? That's all we do is work. Me be gettin' so angry at Mr. Hamilton. Nothin' we do seems good enough for him.

Ruth: I know what you mean. But don't you be thinkin' of doin' anything you'll regret later, ey?

Lizzie: What do you think I'd do? (sarcastically)

Ruth: I know you, Lizzie. Know you be goin' to play some kinda trick... (pause)...oh damn!

Lizzie: Hard day, ey?

Overseer: Hard day? Lord, none of you girls knows what a hard day is. Ruth! What are you trying to hide? You're doing that all wrong! Can't you get anything straight? If you don't straighten that cloth and get those warp threads tight... Look at this.... your weaver's knot ain't holdin'...If you continue to do this incorrectly I'm going to have to dismiss you, hear?

Ruth: I-I-I'm sorry Mr. Hamilton. Puttin' me on 6 looms is harder than tryin' ta git milk from a dried up cow. I'll try to keep it all straight. (Overseer mumbles under his breath and walks away.) He's right. Ain't nothin' I do is right. These threads are so confusin' ...(Ruth starts to cry. Lizzie, who has heard the entire conversation, walks over to Ruth.)

Lizzie: (comforting) It's all right, Ruth! Now, you better stop that blubberin' or your bolt will be ruined for good, ey. (Pause.) The only thing confusin' is Mr. Hamilton's expectations. I expect I kin unconfuse him. Here, let me help get these threads straightened for you. (Lizzie helps Ruth fix her material. The overseer walks over again to check Ruth's loom.)

Overseer: (to Ruth) Sorry, dear, it's just that your work isn't as good as your looks. (He pats Ruth's butt. As the overseer walks away, Lizzie pushes a bucket out into the aisle that trips him.) Damn you girl! You're the blister on my heel...

Ruth: That weren't Lizzie's fault, sir! That was a mistake.

Lizzie: (to the overseer) The only mistake was him talkin' to you like that. Creation! If the Lord don't git even. (sarcastically) Lord knows you ain't got no right to talk to her like that. An' you sure ain't got no right to touch...

Overseer: (Quickly jumps in.) Touch? What I can touch is your weekly pay. You watch it missy, or you'll be losin' more than a few warp threads.

Lizzie: You bein' the only thing that's warped around here... (said under her breath at the overseer)

ALL: Lizzie!

Ruth: Whatta ya think you be doin', Lizzie? You nearly lost your pay too.

(Overseer walks away.) I can't believe he don't blacklist you...

Lizzie: Ruth, you be seein' anyone who works eight looms alone blacklisted? I ain't afraid of no overseer. You gotta be tough here...

Song: **Well, That's Lizzie**

Lizzie, that girl
She's our friend, she's our pal
Makin' life tolerable
in the mill on the canal.

Chorus

Well, that's Lizzie
She's crazy as can be
Always livin' life
As if she were free
Lizzie always talks back
Not afraid to fight
While we weave meekly
Spin and weave in fright.

Chorus

On the boardinghouse roof
Is where she often hides
Talkin' with the stars
Takin' life in strides.

Chorus

Slidin' down the bannister
To get to supper first
Never thinkin' of the danger
Never fearin' for the worst.

Chorus

The supper bell rings.

Ruth: Creation! These warp threads keep snappin'... An' if only I could block out this wretched noise...

Lizzie: (Yelling over the looms. She finishes hers, then says) You want I should help you, Ruth? We'll have to work fast, eh?

Ruth: It ain't your fault my threads keep snappin'.

Lizzie: Well it ain't your fault neither.

Song: Weave a Fortune (Ruth and Lizzie)

I wanted to weave a fortune...
To turn riches out of rags...
But you'll never be rich
If there's a hitch in your stitch
And your money bag's strikin' snags.

Ruth: Lizzie, you be so good to all us newer girls, 'specially me. You be the only friend I got. Don't trouble yourself more now. (The supper bell rings.) I have to go. I'm obliged to set the table for supper.

Lizzie: Go. I'll finish it off for ye. I'll be there in the flash of a lightnin' bolt.

Ruth: Lizzie, you promise me, you ain't gonna be slidin' down no bannister agin, ey? You be the only real friend I got here. Cross your heart?

Lizzie: Cross my heart and hope to die on the Sabbath if I do. Now don't you fright yourself. (Lizzie has her fingers crossed behind her back.)

Ruth: I don't want to see you hurt, ey.

Lizzie: (Continues to work until she finishes Ruth's bolt. In her rush, though, she catches her hair in the loom. Must cut off a huge hank of hair to release the hold—or be scalped. When she falls, she lands in a bucket of red dye, which splatters all over the other side of her head. All this trouble hardly fazes her.) Damnation! I be really late. (Lizzie runs to the stairway and leaps onto the bannister. She misses, plunging 5 flights to her death.)

Mill Girls

Up Against the Wall

It's About Time to Talk

"So, what was this book all about?" I asked the six students who were discussing *Bridge to Terabithia* (Paterson, 1977). After two sessions in which these fifth and sixth graders had raised issue after issue about Leslie's drowning and Jesse's conflicted feelings of grief, I expected them to say "death and courage" or "grief and healing." But I was wrong. "Friendship, a powerful friendship," they agreed without hesitation. Yet, their talk had involved almost role-playing Jesse's suffering. They requested an extra session before moving on to a second novel, apparently trying to achieve a sense of closure on this one.

An essential ingredient in literature study is time: time over several sessions for a group to coalesce, time for each session to take shape, time for returning to topics that do not feel settled, and time for each speaker to explore thoughts at the point of utterance without interruption.

I give the groups time to coalesce by having them work as a unit for three weeks. Each group has two fifty-minute discussion periods a week, long sessions so that everyone can be heard. We meet Tuesdays and Fridays so there is time between sessions to read whatever amount the group assigns itself. By enlisting interns, counselors, and resource teachers (special education and ESL), many groups can meet at the same time, most with an adult participant. (In years when other adults were not available, I rotated sessions, and allowed other students to read in class instead of expecting them to do it all as homework. I also had more student-only groups, after they got used to the format.) We open the door between two classes so that students may form groups from among about forty-four peers. Groups are determined by which of six or seven books offered in each round of study have been selected by individual students. I feel satisfied with the time these arrangements provide.

An unhurried pace in a long session allows students to reopen previously abandoned topics. Students who know they will always be heard can be patient while thoughts percolate to the surface through many exchanges, some of which may seem random. There is time for silence and time to look at notes or double check something in the text. The pace allows for turns lengthy enough that speakers can vacillate along the way about the position they are taking.

I often either step up the pace or slow it so that each group can find and refine its optimal pattern of turn-taking. Over six sessions together, the exchanges naturally become more spontaneous. Turn allocation that is too formal deadens the pace, but too lax a system allows so much overlapping that students finish nearly all of each other's sentences. An ideal balance rests between an exchange rapid enough to hold the attention of impatient contributors and slow enough for each speaker to develop ideas that emerge at the point of utterance.

As the transcript of a taping of the *Bridge to Terabithia* group's fourth session indicates, interpretations emerged both within speakers' turns and over the course of several exchanges.

Sarah: (leading off by bringing up Jesse's belief that Leslie's death had only been a dream) Um, on page 107, when he's trying to get rid of Leslie being dead. He's afraid and everything. He's like, (She reads aloud, ending with the words "his unremembered nightmare.") So its like, it wasn't a nightmare, but he thought it was and he couldn't remember it, and he was scared to go to Terabithia.

Mary M. Kitagawa

Marks Meadow School, Amherst, Massachusetts

Teacher: (reading) "He could explain it better in the daytime when he had shaken off the effects of...." So, particularly, you are focusing on "his unremembered nightmare."

John: (almost taking on Jesse's state of denial) I don't think he'd go and explain it to her anyway.

Sarah: (following John's lead) Yeah, he's thinking of what he could say.

Teacher: I'm still puzzled. I'm still trying to process what you said, because, to tell you the truth, I didn't notice all this.

After the students clarified that it was around midnight that Jess awakened, they began to imagine what the "dream" must have been, almost role-playing the emotional blur that Jess was experiencing. John and Clayton began speculating about when the "dream" started, reciting as evidence anything that differed from the family's normal lifestyle.

John: He thought it was like a dream. But, wouldn't it seem a little long? 'Cause, if that happened to me, uh, I'd think,—It had some association with "The Perfect Day" (a chapter title). That wasn't a dream. It was sort of weird. That has to have a clue.

Clayton: Well, the dream probably started when he came home. The dream probably started the minute he walked in the door and the TV was off and Brenda was sitting there. Brenda said, "Your girlfriend is dead." Yeah, that's probably when the dream started. And he's thinking about what he'll say to her, about what he'll do tomorrow, and apologizing for not asking so she could go to the art gallery. It was just, all a dream.

John: Yeah, you know how the TV is off in his house. Wow, that's weird. He probably thought that was a little like a dream. You know, everyone's sitting on the couch together and the TV is off. There's no food, uh, sort of seems weird, so that's probably why he could sort of think it was a dream.

After reinforcement of their ideas about when the supposed dream began, they discussed how long it served to buffer him from reality.

Clayton: Well, that dream helped him until the morning, when he was eating his pancakes and his dad said, "We have to go and pay respects." It worked all the way until when his dad said that, and he said, "I know it's hard for you that Leslie's dead." That's when his comfort stopped.

Sarah: Well, actually I think it didn't stop there. I think he kept on not believing it until he got to the reunion—thing with the—not the reunion but the, uh, where he was going to pay respects.

My main role in these groups is to support reflection while the agenda takes shape from within. I have read and discussed this novel at least seven times with students, but no group ever played out the dream the way this group did. No one would create a lesson plan expecting this of students. My primary role was to show my genuine interest as they got rolling and to remain silent while they refined their image of the dream. I can contribute speculatively myself, but I try to hold off raising any new topics that might usurp the agenda. I also do not want to beat someone else to a topic. The words I dread hearing after I have brought up a new idea are, "Oh, that was the issue I was about to raise."

The group proceeded from the dream segment to consider Jesse's dismay at not being consulted before deciding to have the body cremated. It was Zack who launched that issue.

Zack: Uh, page 114. They're uh—It says: (He reads a long section in which Jess begins to awaken to the truth about Leslie's death upon hearing that she would be cremated.) Hummm. Anger. I brought that up 'cause he was hoping that he could see Leslie just one more time before she was buried, but she was cremated, so he would never get to see her again. That also brought him a lot of pain.

As if actual peers of Jess, the students were fairly critical of Leslie's parents.

John: You know how it always seems she's trying to be with her parents more and help them out and stuff? It doesn't really seem like they know what she wants, 'cause they're always saying, "Oh, she would have wanted you to have her paints." "No, she wouldn't want you to have her dog." And how they thought she'd like it here, but she didn't really like it a whole lot, you know, and I think that's why Jess said she belonged to him, or something. And, he should have a little bit of say in it because she—if they know so much and they keep getting it wrong, how do they know that she would want to be cremated and Jess'd never see her again? And, so that's sort of why I think Jess was really mad and stuff.

John had destroyed the parents' credibility quite eloquently, "they keep getting it wrong." I thought the parents were getting a bum rap, but I did not point that out. It was Tory who prevented closure, a reflective role she favors so much that "cept" is often the first word of her utterances.

Tory: Um, 'cept, I wonder why he thought that she was mostly his and that they didn't really care about her.

Sarah: (after reading aloud how Leslie's father explains why he isn't giving Jess the dog) You know, it's Jess who's saying he [Leslie's father] should have P.T. [the dog]. And I don't think he meant "She [Leslie] belongs to me." He was just going through something, you know, like, "She was mine," like, "Why did she have to go?"

John: (bridging from his earlier thoughts to incorporate what Sarah had just said) Just because she was closer to him doesn't mean that he can say if she should be cremated.

Clayton: He's going through one of the stages when someone dies. There's anger, there's sadness, sometimes there's "I could have prevented it." So that's one of the stages, the anger: Why did they have to move here? Why did they have to be here in the first place, and why didn't they just stay away and, he would rather not have been friends with Leslie than have her die.

Since they related to Jess as a peer, it took time for them to consider the perspectives of the adults in the story. Just as they often do about their real life issues, they readily complained about the adults in Jess' life before tempering that with other possibilities.

Literature study conducted by students with restrained adult support is a powerful experience of introspection as well as social discourse. Adults who have sat with groups usually come away saying, "If only I had had such opportunities when I was their age."

But literature study is not merely a personally meaningful experience. The rationale for spending almost two hours a week in speculation, hypothesis building, group reflection, and elaboration of emerging thinking about literature is that students read better and develop new perspectives. They read carefully in anticipation of the discussions, and they read analytically in preparation for defending their interpretations.

It is such experiences with discourse about a text, based upon the reader's individuality and the unique dynamics of the group, that tap what Douglas Barnes (1992) calls "action knowledge," or everyday knowledge as distinguished from what he calls "school knowledge." And action knowledge is the basis for finding relevance in a text.

When the boundary between "school knowledge" and "action knowledge" is low and easy to cross... we can expect pupils to be able to take an active part in the formulation of knowledge. But it will only happen if the teacher allows for it and sets up a communication system in which pupils have a considerable *influence over moment-by-moment strategies* [emphasis mine]. (p. 30)

Within a loose structure that sets norms of focus and turn-taking, students learn how discourse works. Their control over the moment-by-moment direction of the talk gives them control of the agenda. It is critical for the adult to be someone who can yield that internal control of discourse strategies to students but still be enough a part of the group to influence the pacing and encourage reflection.

Focus is promoted by having everyone bring notes and by setting the norm that speakers should usually build upon what a previous speaker has said. Topic shifting is somewhat formalized by a rule that to change the subject we have to ask permission of the one who raised the current issue. At the beginning of each session we look over our notes and see who wants to raise the first issue. Then, when the first exchange loses steam, someone suggests a new issue. (We don't call them questions, because what we want is speculation about some aspect of the novel, not answers. Of course, some issues are first raised as questions.)

> *Literature study conducted by students with restrained adult support is a powerful experience of introspection as well as social discourse.*

Besides formally asking to shift topics, students frequently alter the focus by prefacing their remarks with a comment like, "This is sort of related to what Seija said..." or, "I don't think this is exactly a new topic...."

One of the advantages of tying leadership to issue raising is that relatively uninvolved discussants can launch a topic and then participate as leaders by simply introducing the subject. This has often been the start of participation by shy students, less able readers, and students not yet fluent in English.

Turn-taking is the trickiest aspect of structure for me, because each group has its own dynamics, requiring its own blend of freedom to interrupt and restraint of eagerness to speak. Our norm is to start the three weeks together by requiring hand raising and to let whoever launched the current issue call on speakers, but groups are encouraged to abandon hand raising as soon as they find they can take turns spontaneously. Once a group has achieved a comfortable balance, my participation is guided by the group norm.

Beyond these loose rituals and preparation requirements, it is the strategies of "real world," natural discourse that facilitate the group's interactions. Since a school context and about six years of conditioning usually mean that students all too readily yield control to a teacher, it is necessary for adults to actively signal reluctance to assume leadership, or to find a way to "lead from behind" by subtle means.

When listeners have eye contact only with me no matter who is speaking, or when the speaker maintains eye contact only with me, I agonize over how to break that recitation mold. Sometimes when I find that only the speaker and I have our eyes locked, I pour over my notes and the text to see if my looking occupied will cause students to begin to direct attention to each other. It rarely works! Usually my only recourse is to spell out my concern and remind them to address each other directly. Sometimes I use a circular hand motion invented by our Chapter I teacher for the same purpose.

Literature circle conversations differ from other collaborative groups in that there is no product or expected outcome except to know that we have heard each other thoroughly. Because of the transiency of talk, it is extremely process-centered. Each of us carries away an independent version of the commonly created text that emerges as we talk. Unlike authors' circles, no written draft has been presented by its creator or will be carried away for revision toward a final product. By learning to negotiate meaning on a text for which none of us has the emotional fragility of authorship, students get valuable practice for the more delicate task of critiquing in authors' circles.

It is important that students who discuss literature also have authoring experiences themselves. A student who is writing every day brings to literature study an insider's view of what makes a text effective. The following discussion by sixth graders I taught several years ago occurred in response to my question, "How does writing make you a better reader and reading make you a better writer?" It was never clear which part of the question each student was answering, which illustrates how intertwined reading and writing are.

Rolando: You notice things the writer does, like at the end of the chapter, instead of stopping, he makes you say, "Oh, I know what will happen," so you read on to see if you're right. The author puts in some foreshadowing like, "I thought that was the end of it, but I didn't know how wrong I was."

Gonzalo: Details. You notice how the writer puts in lots of details. You stretch out the action, too. You stretch it out with more details when the action gets more important.

Adrian: In Eucario's story he used description of the clothes his character wore to show what kind of person he was, not just what he looked like.

Rafael: But, you let the reader do some of the thinking. The Lloyd Alexander books help me think of stories but mine are different. If you pay attention you see how the plot builds up.

Viet: Like if you want to make the details important you don't just say "blue eyes" but you say "eyes blue like the sky." And you don't say it right out, all the details. You let the reader guess a little and you show what you mean little by little.

> *Each of us carries away an independent version of the commonly created text that emerges as we talk.*

Rafael: I know a technique. Someone's talking for a long time, but you have to put breaks where the other person talks to show that the listener is still there, or the reader will forget.

Viet: Also, you understand a writer's techniques like flashbacks because you've used them in a story too. So you notice how the writer gets back to real time, like his mother calls him and he stops thinking back.

I cannot say for sure which of these strategies the students learned from being avid readers, from engagement in many literature study discussions, or from being writers accustomed to peer conferences. They had all explored literature through collaborative discussions that were paced so that there was time in which to create tentative observations that could be validated or disputed. According to Walter Loban:

> Those subjects who proved to have the greatest power over language...were the subjects who most frequently used language to express tentativeness...supposition, hypotheses and conditional statements (1963, cited in Barnes, 1992, p. 69).

Carol Gilles refers to literature study by a wonderful phrase, "cycles of meaning" (1993, p. 206). The recursive quality stems from the fact that students engage in what Barnes (1992, p. 28) calls "exploratory talk" as opposed to "presentation." Rather than predetermining what they will say, they plunge in and discover their meaning as they speak. By mutually creating a flow of talk, the group as a whole and the individuals who agree, or agree to disagree, explore the dimensions of their novel in ways that could never be anticipated, indeed should never be anticipated, in a lesson plan.

It seems that the reason for both ample time and the presence of a reflective adult is that tentativeness requires a framework in which trial balloons stay aloft long enough to be tested and modified. If a group needs to have its pace adjusted, the adult participant can overtly or subtly influence the flow. Contributions such as "I want to be sure I got that. Can you explain more?" if sincere, not only help keep the floor for the speaker who is struggling, but also slow the pace so that others can reflect before their turn to speak.

(If not sincere, however, students will spot the difference and show that they feel manipulated by a quick switch to recitation mode.)

The goals of slowing the pace and delaying premature closure are quite contractive to the typical hurried curriculum in which teachers are trying to cover ground by moving students along rapidly. Rather than looking for the most efficient, effective prompts for eliciting a desired reader response, according to precepts of literary criticism, this sort of study builds upon students' emerging discovery of relevance, a process that takes time and often requires doubling back over ideas that are transformed within a speaker's turn or over the course of many exchanges between speakers.

This type of study works well with students of any reading level. One of the most exciting aspects of this curriculum is that it not only works with all students, but it enables heterogeneous groups of students to work with the same text. Even nonreading special education students participate in some of our literature circles, basing their contributions on novels they have heard through a tape recorder or had read to them by a parent. This year I have an Ecuadorian student who reads the novels in Spanish. At first he used bilingual classmates to translate his contributions, but by second semester he was communicating through broken English and some pantomiming.

Anyone composing thoughts at the point of utterance is liable to be ungrammatical, even in their native language. In the case of young adolescents, utterances are also sprinkled with "like," "you know," and "stuff like that." These are not simply teenage slang but serve to hold the floor while the speaker changes gears or repairs the grammar of a sentence that is taking a new direction. Examples of this strategy occurred in the following exchange in which some of the students hypothesized a happier ending, the rescue of Leslie.

Clayton: Well, uh, see, Jesse was a chicken, very big chicken, when—before Leslie came. He still was a little one after—he still was a little one when she was alive. And, I bet you, if she fell in when he was there, I bet

> *In the case of young adolescents, utterances are also sprinkled with "like," "you know," and "stuff like that."*

you his fear would just overcome him and he would be stiff. And I don't think he'd be able to do anything. Especially 'cause she hit her head on the rock, he doesn't know how to swim, the water is going fast, she'd be carried downstream, and I think she'd still die.

Tory: I don't really think that she would've died because like sometimes when you're really afraid then you—it goes really fast and you don't really just stand there, like, sometimes you don't really think about what you're doing, you just sort of...so you just sort of like go for whatever you're afraid of. So, it's—I think that he would've jumped in and tried to save her, but it might not've done much good, but it might've.

John: I was going to say, about what Clayton was saying—You know how fiction stories are, you know, there's a kid who, even though he's a chicken, heroically he climbs down. Duh de duh de duh de duh (theme music) and then he goes and saves her somehow, you know. He just happens to make it, you know. And so it's happily ever after. But I guess he did-n't because he wasn't there. So it's less of fic-tion.

Seija: I was thinking to myself. That can't be true. Main characters never die.

Not every speaker gets acknowledged. At one point in the earlier discussion about Jesse's anger over Leslie's being cremated, Seija brought up a topic that was not well-timed.

Seija: (without any preface) I was thinking about his drawings and about the museums where the buffalo were being, were falling off the cliff and dying, and Leslie fell off the rope and died. I was thinking about that.

Sarah, ignoring what Seija said, con-trolled the direction by saying, "I want to go back to what Zack said" and proceeded to speculate on whether or not Leslie's parents should have moved there in the first place.

My teacher-self wanted to protect Seija from rejection, but several things prevented me. Her topic had been discussed in a previ-ous session and, furthermore, was not relat-ed to the current issue. Although students often violate the routine for changing topics,

with or without acknowledgement that they realize what they are doing, Seija was shift-ing the focus when the dream topic was still hot. She misjudged the group's willingness to let go of their immediate interest. I try not to bail out students like Seija unless it seems to be personal discrimination. The discus-sion was providing her with gentle, but valu-able, feedback on group dynamics in dis-course.

With tentative ideas supported by time and a focusing framework, student-led liter-ary discussions, ideally with an adult partici-pant, are a way to explore belief systems. The exchange of ideas seems to fill a niche for preadolescents because talk is a double-edged sword for them. On the one hand, it matters greatly what their peers think, so they are intensely curious about the attitudes of classmates; on the other hand, their con-cern about appearing different in public makes self-revealing conversation risky. Perhaps that explains the popularity of liter-ature circles: the opportunity to hear and test opinions in the context of vicarious experiences, to be able to formulate ideas collaboratively, and most of all, to be fully heard by peers who have time to listen deeply. These are heady experiences.

Discipline problems are nearly absent in groups sitting "knee to knee and eyeball to eyeball," hearing each other and being heard. Sometimes, though, a discussion turns into a debate and students have to be reminded that we are not engaged in a "win–lose" contest. Usually that only hap-pens when personal conflicts intrude from beyond the study of literature.

Preparation for class, by both students and teachers, means just reading many nov-els and taking notes. Grading can be as sim-ple as keeping track of who comes prepared and participates actively. Reading prowess and enjoyment grow dramatically. It is the one part of the academic schedule that most draws complaints from my students whenev-er we have to postpone it.

> The exchange of ideas seems to fill a niche for preadolescents because talk is a double-edged sword for them.

References

Barnes, D. (1992). *From communication to curriculum.* 2nd ed. Portsmouth, NH: Boynton/Cook.

Gilles, C. (1993). "'We make an idea': Cycles of meaning in literature discussion groups." In K.M. Pierce & C. Gilles (Eds.) *Cycles of meaning: Exploring the potential of talk in learning communities* (pp. 199–217). Portsmouth, NH: Heinemann.

Loban, W.D. (1963). *The language of elementary school children.* Research Report No. 1. Urbana, IL: National Council of Teachers of English.

Paterson, K. (1977). *Bridge to Terabithia.* New York: Crowell Junior Books.

Lingering Questions

■ Although I like the "three weeks—six sessions" time frame for groups to coalesce and have time to develop their ideas collaboratively, that provides only about ten groupings a year. Groups often finish a novel in less than three weeks. What would be the advantages and disadvantages of shortening the three weeks to two, with perhaps four sessions instead? Should the norm be "two weeks—four sessions" with the possibility of some groups staying together for four weeks (eight sessions) if the book is unusually long or if the students want to read a series together? (The rationale for a common time frame is so that groupings include the widest possible ranges of classmates and book choices. That would not be the case if there were staggered time frames.)

■ The gain in opening the door between two classes and mingling students is that students have more books to choose from and more potential discussants. Is the loss of community involved in going beyond a single classroom worth the gain?

■ Should we be concerned that, no matter how we try to avoid it, each adult with a group will naturally differ in amount and style of involvement?

■ Since the main advantage I see in adult participation is pacing, how can students be encouraged to pace their student-only discussions so that each speaker has the opportunity to explore an idea in-depth and turn-taking flows smoothly?

Novels that are popular with my students include the following by Katherine Paterson (see Clip and File section): *Bridge to Terabithia, The Great Gilly Hopkins, The Master Puppeteer, Jacob Have I Loved,* and *Lyddie.* (There may be others they would particularly enjoy, but I do not yet have access to multiple copy sets of them.) Novels by other authors that seem particularly productive for literature study discussions include the following, ranked approximately by my appraisal of them as literature study novels (chosen from among those I have available for my students.)

Babbitt, N. (1975). *Tuck everlasting.* New York: Farrar, Straus & Giroux.

Hamilton, V. (1974). *M. C. Higgins, the great.* New York: Collier Books.

Taylor, M. (1976). *Roll of thunder, hear my cry.* New York: Bantam Books.

Taylor, M. (1981). *Let the circle be unbroken.* New York: Bantam Books.

Lunn, J. (1981). *The root cellar.* New York: Puffin Books.

Alexander, L. (1964). *The book of three.* New York: Dell Publishing Co., Inc.

Alexander, L. (1965). *The black cauldron.* New York: Dell Publishing Co., Inc.

Alexander, L. (1966). *The castle of Llyr.* New York: Dell Publishing Co., Inc. (Some groups read also the other two in the Prydain series:

Alexander, L. (1967). *Taran wanderer* and (1986) *The high king,* both also from Dell Publishing Co., Inc.)

Collier, J. L., & Collier, C. (1974). *My brother Sam is dead.* New York: Scholastic, Inc.

Collier, J. L., & Collier, C. (1978). *The winter hero.* New York: Scholastic, Inc.

Yep, L. (1975). *Dragonwings.* New York: Scholastic, Inc.

Myers, W. D. (1982). *Won't know 'till I get there.* New York: Viking Penguin.

Soto, G. (1990). *Baseball in April and other stories.* New York: Trumpet Club.

Avi. (1984). *The fighting ground.* New York: Harper and Row.

Pitts, P. (1988). *Racing the sun.* New York: Avon Books.

Yolen, J. (1988). *The devil's arithmetic.* New York: Viking Penguin.

MacLachlan, P. (1991). *Journey.* New York: Dell Publishing Co., Inc.

Rylant, C. (1992). *Missing May.* New York: Dell Publishing Co., Inc.

Voight, C. (1982). *Dicey's song.* New York: Fawcett Juniper.

Babbitt, N. (1970). *Kneeknock Rise.* New York: Farrar, Straus & Giroux.

Bibliography

Andrasick, Kathleen Dudden (1990). *Opening texts: Writing into literature.* Portsmouth, NH: Heinemann.

Atwell, N. (1987). *In the middle: Writing, reading and learning with adolescents.* Portsmouth, NH: Boynton/Cook-Heinemann.

Atwell, N. (Ed). (1980). *Workshop 1: Writing and literature.* Portsmouth, NH: Heinemann.

Atwell, N. (Ed). (1990). *Workshop 2: Beyond the basal.* Portsmouth, NH: Heinemann.

Barbieri, M. (in press). *Sounds from the heart: Early adolescent girls' literacy.* Portsmouth, NH: Heinemann.

Benedict, S. & Carlisle L. (1992). *Beyond words: Picture books for older readers and writers.* Portsmouth, NH: Heinemann.

Eagleton, T. (1983). *Literary theory: An introduction.* Minneapolis, MN: University of Minnesota Press.

Fox, Mem (1993). *Radical reflections.* New York: Harcourt Brace & Company.

Johnston, P. (1993). Assessment and literate "development." *The Reading Teacher, 46* (5), 428–429.

Kaywell, Joan F. (Ed). (1993). *Adolescent literature as a complement to the classics.* Norwood, MA: Christopher-Gordon.

Kitagawa, M. (1994). Revisiting Britton, as in James. *Language Arts, 71* (2), 116–120.

Krogness, M. (1994). *Just teach me, Mrs. K.: Talking , reading, and writing with resistant adolescent learners.* Portsmouth, NH: Heinemann.

Langer, Judith A. (Ed). (1992). *Literature instruction—a focus on student response.* Urbana, IL: National Council of Teachers of English.

Murray, Donald M. (1993). *Read to write.* (3rd edition). Fort Worth, TX: Harcourt Brace Jovanovich.

Paterson, K. (1990). *The spying heart.* New York: E.P. Dutton.

Peterson, R., & Eeds, M. (1990). *Grand conversations: Literature groups in action.* Richmond Hill, Ontario, Canada: Scholastic-TAB Publications.

Probst, R. (1991). Response to literature. In J. Flood, J. Jenson, D. Lapp, & J. Squire (Eds). *Handbook of research on teaching the English language arts.* New York: Macmillan.

Rief, L. (1992). *Seeking diversity: Language arts with adolescents.* Portsmouth, NH: Heinemann.

Rosenblatt, L. M. (1978). *The reader, the text, the poem: The transactional theory of the literary work.* Carbondale, IL: Southern Illinois University Press.

Rosenblatt, L. M. (1983). *Literature as exploration.* (4th edition). New York: Modern Language Association.

Sloan, G. (1991). *The child as critic: Teaching literature in elementary and middle schools.* New York: Teachers College Press.

Whaley, Liz & Dodge, Liz (1993). *Wearing in the women.* Portsmouth, NH: Boynton-Cook.

Voices from the Middle

Volume 1 • Number 2 • November 1994

From At-Risk to Promise: Pathways to Literacy

A Publication of the National Council of Teachers of English

Contents

It is the policy of NCTE in its journals and other publications to provide a forum for the open discussion of ideas concerning the content and the teaching of English and language arts. Publicity accorded to any particular point of view does not imply endorsement by the Executive Committee, the Board of Directors, or the membership at large, except in announcements of policy, where such endorsement is clearly specified.

Copyright 1994 by the National Council of Teachers of English. Printed in the United States of America. ISSN 1074-4762.

 Printed on recycled paper

Message from the Editors

*V*oices from the Middle was born of many teachers' caring. The need for greater care in our profession and in our classrooms seems to us acute right now, and we hope this journal will be a means of forging compassionate connections among teachers and students alike. From all accounts, the launching of *Voices from the Middle* has been most felicitous, and we are gratified by the response we have received so far. Readers tell of sharing the journal with colleagues, administrators, and even students. Since it is students' voices as well as teachers' that this journal seeks to heed, we are touched by fourteen-year-old Jennifer's recent letter:

Thanks for the magazine. I love it! The article by Robert Probst, "Teaching What We Cannot Know," was wonderful, especially the poems "The Secret" by Denise Levertov and "The Allegory of the Cave" by Stephen Dunn. The article that you got Katherine Paterson to write was wonderful also. I like how she goes into her past and tells about how she wished she could have talked about *The Yearling*. I also liked how she gave a quote from her friend which later helped her write *The Great Gilly Hopkins*. In the article Marie Dionisio wrote— it was good too—the first journal letter written by Ken was exactly how I felt. The idea that Linda Rief had reminded me of our poem performance. That sounded so cool. . . .

Jennifer reminds us never to underestimate our students. She is a reader, writer, and thinker who knows no bounds. She will be happy to find other student voices in this issue, young people who, like her, are wildly excited by the books they are reading and the kinds of classroom talk their reading ignites. These are students of amazing teachers who see themselves as writers, researchers, and most of all, learners. They are not teachers who allow themselves to be content when seventy-five percent of their students are thriving. Instead, they are teachers who care

about every last kid, determined to find a whole panoply of ways to reach the most resistant in the room. They are teachers who come together in a true literacy community to pool their knowledge, collaborating to discover new possibilities for learning.

It is Carol Pope who inspires them. Dr. Pope is a person of strong convictions who believes that when teachers are eager to learn, there is no limit to what they can accomplish. Under her leadership, such a group began to read professional literature—beginning with Nancie Atwell's *In the Middle: Writing, Reading, and Learning with Adolescents*—and to explore concerns about their students who, for various reasons, seemed at risk of failure in school. Beginning with a discussion of students' strengths, the teachers formulated a plan to implement reading and writing workshops for all students in their rooms. They decided to conduct case studies on students who represented their biggest challenges, documenting their practice as well as the children's responses to it. Dr. Pope trusts that when teachers link what they know and believe to what they want to happen with students, miracles are possible.

Just as she trusts teachers, the teachers in her research group trust their children. Virginia Smith trusts Mike to get his writing done. She talks to him writer to writer, values his idiosyncracies, and expects great things of him. She struggles with ways to sustain the excitement of writing workshop in the face of her district's incessant preoccupation with mandated assessment of expository writing, but is fierce in her commitment that her students' own stories come first.

Sue Coty is interested in the role effective communication plays in her classroom,

Maureen Barbieri

Middle School Teacher, Greenville, South Carolina

Linda Rief

Middle School Teacher, Durham, New Hampshire

sharing compelling accounts of the changes she observed when she and her students took the time to focus on ways of talking to one another. Sue is another teacher eager to learn from her students, and her classroom research has profound effects on her plans for future practice.

Carole Jacobs, a member of the original research group, now lives and teaches in Oregon. She brings to her new school the same trust and commitment Sue and Virginia share. She has tremendous faith in students. "Even though some students may not be producing according to my expectations," she writes, "they may have abilities they keep to themselves." Carole wants to discover and nurture this incredible range of abilities, and it is her classroom research that gives her the means to do so.

These are three of dozens of teachers in Carol Pope's teacher research group, three who challenge us with their philosophy and their tenacity. Their classrooms are not panaceas, they tell us; things do not always work well, some kids still slip away. But these teachers will not give up. They see every student as unique, every day as a challenge, and every classroom as a place to learn more.

Nel Noddings, Professor of Education at Stanford University, urges an ethic of care in classrooms: "We need the special attitude of caring . . . if we are to survive and be whole. At every stage we need to be cared for in the sense that we need to be understood, received, respected, recognized. . . . Caring cannot be achieved by formula. It requires address and response; it requires different behaviors from situation to situation and person to person. It sometimes calls for toughness, sometimes tenderness . . ." (Noddings, 1992).

Carol Pope and her colleagues know all about caring. We are grateful to them for sharing what they know with us.

References

Atwell, N. (1987). *In the middle: Writing, reading, and learning with adolescents.* Portsmouth, NH: Heinemann.

Noddings, N. (1992). *The challenge to care in schools: An alternative approach to education.* New York: Teachers College Press.

> Sue is another teacher eager to learn from her students, and her classroom research has profound effects on her plans for future practice.

Building Pathways for At-Risk Students and Their Teachers

We need to provide not only a promise, but also a pathway by which to reach the promise.

—Joel A. Barker (1990)

Do you have them too? Those haunting faces—the faces of students you feel you somehow failed? I have many such faces in my collective classroom conscience. Dexter, "Red," Lawrence, Dianne, Stephanie are just a few of the students I was never able to touch, ones I failed by my own limitations, by the nonproductive ways I used their time in my classroom. As a teacher, I found myself at a loss as to how to guide the learning of those who were unmotivated, less able, and often disruptive—how to provide a structure in which they could thrive.

For years I carried these faces with me as I searched for ways I could have done better. Along my journey, I have met other teachers who suffer similar frustrations, feelings of guilt and angst, who carry their own covey of haunting faces. As a result of many interactions with middle school teachers and their "at-risk" students, I constructed a theory: If I could 1) bring together a group of highly competent middle school English language arts teachers; 2) expose them to what we know from research about teaching English language arts, about middle school adolescents, and about academically disadvantaged students; 3) support them in the development of a sound individualized approach that built on students' promise; and 4) provide continuous follow-up through regular meetings and an interactive support system, they would become teacher-researchers intrigued by documenting the growth of their less advantaged students. I had confidence they would choose to institute a pedagogical approach stimulated by and adapted from their reading of Nancie

Atwell's *In the Middle: Writing, Reading, and Learning with Adolescents* (1987). My plan was that while they would be guiding and documenting the progress of their challenging students, I would be researching *their* development as professionals.

The Teachers

The voices you hear in this issue represent our PAL (Power and Literacy for Disadvantaged Youth) group, a contingency of middle school teachers who made a commitment to work with at-risk students in their English language arts classrooms. The PAL project, funded by the Z. Smith Reynolds Foundation (Winston-Salem, N.C.), originated with fifteen teachers who applied for fellowships to attend the PAL Summer Institute in 1990. As Director of PAL, I used the grant money to award each participant a stipend and to purchase for them texts, materials, and a classroom set of young adult literature titles. Based on the success of the first PAL group, Z. Smith Reynolds also funded an expansion of the project in 1991. Four years later, the group includes more than forty-five teachers from seven different school systems and twenty different middle schools. Our common belief is that *all* students have a better chance to succeed and belong in an environment that honors them as individuals and builds on their strengths, rather than focuses on their deficits.

We began our Summer Institute by reading Nancie Atwell's text, as well as a host of literature about "at-risk" students and middle school adolescents. At this stage in our work, as the "grant-getter and leader," I was more than a little apprehensive. I was taking a constructivist approach to reaching the goal of having teachers *choose* to implement a

Carol Pope

Associate Professor of English, North Carolina State University

with **Candy Beal**, Doctoral student in Curriculum and Instruction, North Carolina State University

variation of workshop in their classes. Throughout our two weeks, I kept wondering in my journal, "Will they want to try some variation of a reading/writing workshop approach? Will they want to make a shift in their already successful classroom instruction? Will they proclaim, 'This is too idealistic!'? Or will they bond and become an ever-evolving group of teacher-researchers as I hope?" While I was pondering their possible responses to my agenda and the parameters of the grant, the teachers were thinking more practically. "Will this really work for all students? Can I do it? Will I have the administrative support to try?" There was one question, however, that we all shared: "Will we really be able to see our at-risk students grow and improve in a more independent, self-directed classroom format?"

Defining "At-Risk"

The first challenge we undertook in our two-week institute was to identify and describe our at-risk students. In pairs, we shared stories and observations about the students we considered at-risk of academic failure. We generated a list of characteristics that included such descriptors as: Undisciplined, Impatient, Brash/Hostile, Inattentive, Unmotivated. We also described them as students who often have low self-esteem, defy authority, seek attention, and set unrealistic goals for themselves.

Further discussion revealed that these students often have no adult role models and little parental care. They move frequently, live in dysfunctional circumstances perpetuated by poverty, drug abuse, and violence. Story after story emerged, and we got quieter and sadder. The sheer magnitude of our task was looming. Sue Coty, a seventh-grade teacher who writes later in this issue, broke off the discussion by blurting out, "All these descriptions are *so* negative!"

Taking her observation as a cue, I asked, "Are there qualities of these students that we find admirable or positive?" Voices began to rise, and we perked up as we formulated another list: They get themselves and their siblings up in the morning; they

make sure everyone catches the right bus; they prepare meals; they have strong socialization skills outside of school; they know how to protect themselves and their younger siblings in the neighborhood; they question/challenge openly; they are good nonsense detectors.

In short, the at-risk students we referenced in this discussion are, despite the odds against them, survivors. And even though their experiences in *our* worlds are limited, they are, by no means, limited in the life and language experiences of their *own* worlds.

From this more balanced perspective on our at-risk students, we reviewed what we know from research and experience about English language arts instruction for middle grades students and about successful programs for students who are at risk of failure. We thought we had a pathway with reading/writing workshop, but we were looking for the promise of success.

Research on Middle Grades Students

A look at the literature regarding adolescent development and the research concerning middle school students holds few surprises. The middle-school age is a unique time for those experiencing it and for whose with whom they share their lives. It is a transition from childhood to adolescence marked by a need for exploration, security, and acceptance. It is a time when students need sensitivity and consistency from their adult community (Erikson, 1968: Feldman & Elliot, 1990; Muuss, 1988).

Physical changes for young people are greater during this period than at any other time in their lives. While they want to be seen as unique, they also do not want to be seen as "different." Sexual changes and social considerations are these students' utmost concern. Emotional development, often characterized by uneven mood swings, challenges the best of parents and teachers. *Steady* and *predictable,* words often associated with elementary-age children, are left in the past. The new watchwords for adolescents are *changeable* and *challenging* (Van Hoose & Strahan, 1989).

Opportunities for cognitive development are great, but must be addressed in the context of these myriad factors. Students at this age respond positively to collaboration, independent decision-making, and individual attention. They want a high degree of participation at school, and they want a curriculum as well as activities that are meaningful. They are truly self-involved, but they are also beginning to see themselves in the context of the world outside themselves (Alexander & George, 1981; Garbarino, 1985).

Research on At-Risk Students

Much of the research on at-risk students refers to programs that involve the whole school, focus on community activities, or employ "pull-out" approaches. Our goal was to find a way to work with these students *within* English language arts classrooms. In our shared readings on this topic, we were encouraged again by Nancie Atwell, as well as by such authors as Mike Rose (1990), Kenneth Weber (1974), and later in our development by Linda Rief (1992) and Susan Stires (1991).

An analysis of successful programs for at-risk students have the following characteristics in common. They provide supportive, caring environments where students participate in meaningful activities to achieve realistic, useful, self-selected goals. The leaders in these situations, who are themselves organized and straightforward, set high expectations for the students, respect them, and provide support as they try, fail, and try again. The means by which the students achieve their goals are flexible and involve collaborative experiences with peers or the leader of the program. Cultural sensitivity and language acceptance are crucial (Lehr & Harris, 1988; Presseisen, 1988; Wells, 1990).

Clearly, the needs of at-risk students are not entirely different from those of any other middle grades students. Their wish is to draw little attention to their own differences. They may already be larger, smaller, taller, shorter, overdeveloped, underdeveloped, having a good or bad hair day, strug-gling with complexion problems. Couple these characteristics with the knowledge that they are not measuring up academically, and at-risk students erupt. Not only do they already feel that the whole world is watching them, but now, as a result of being unsuccessful in school, the fragile self-concept takes another hit. Stick out? They may feel as if they have a bull's eye on their shirt and are just waiting for the next target practice.

A Pause for Reflection

Given what we had reviewed and learned about middle school students and those who are at risk of failure, we paused to think about the implications for us as teachers. We began constructing guidelines for ourselves:

■ Recognize the negatives as positives. We can put these qualities to productive use in class.

■ Be accepting. At-risk characteristics overlap with regular middle school students' characteristics.

■ Be clear to ourselves. Establish a vision for a way we want to be with *all* our students, not just those who walk in straight lines.

■ Learn by making mistakes and encourage students to do the same.

■ Change the definition of authority. Look at choice rather than rules.

■ Recognize the importance and impact of the home and the community on literacy as well as the school and my classroom.

■ Remember that the real influences on our students' choices may not be immediately visible to us as teachers.

Research on English Language Arts

The research on English language arts is well known to most of us. In teaching writing, for example, a process approach coupled with guiding and scaffolding students' writing experiences more likely produce positive results in writing achievement (Hillocks,

> *Students at this age respond positively to collaboration, independent decision-making, and individual attention.*

1986). In order to discuss the importance of helping students explore their own methods of composing, we deconstructed a process approach by reviewing the value of invention strategies, the importance of context (audience, purpose, and form), and the usefulness of separating revision from editing.

Contributing to the discussion and summary of writing research, we added the information about writing-to-learn, peer conferences, writing response groups, and student-teacher conferences. As a refresher, we reviewed some of my favorite English educators (Britton, 1970; Graves, 1983; Kirby, Liner, and Vinz, 1988; Moffett, 1992; Murray, 1987) and saw in these sources the touchstones for the writing workshop procedures Nancie Atwell describes in what came to be our most valued text, *In the Middle*.

To support our growing intention to implement a reading as well as writing workshop, we also examined the research and theories regarding young adult literature and reading. The concept of saturation and diffusion described by Daniel Fader in *The New Hooked on Books* (1976), and supported historically by other research (Coryell, 1927; LaBrant, 1937; Atwell, 1987), convinced us of the value of sustained reading. Our own love of reading, Atwell's argument about using class time for what we most value, and the urging of Frank Smith (1988) easily convinced us on this score. The value and importance of using young adult literature as the "curriculum" were reinforced by professional voices (Donelson & Nilsen, 1989) and our emerging state curriculum guidelines, which support young adult literature in middle school.

The roles of listening, speaking, and viewing are intertwined in writing and reading instruction. The necessity of working with students to become effective listeners is obvious, given the value of conferring about writing and responding to others' writing. Our group also discussed the advantages of such approaches as reading aloud, listening to recordings of literature, creating videos of responses to one's own reading and others' writing, and talking as a means by which we learn (Golub, 1989). Sue Coty's article in this issue reveals how she helped students build their speaking and listening skills so as to be effective communicators during their peer conferences.

Throughout all of our reading, analyzing, discussing middle grades students and at-risk students, and revisiting English language arts instruction, four important concepts kept reappearing: 1) Relationships, 2) Individualization, 3) Modeling, and 4) Success and Self-Esteem. The theoretical framework in Figure 1 became the rationale for our pedagogical decision to implement adaptations of a reading/writing workshop approach.

The teachers were convinced! Clearly, reading/writing workshop was the way to go. With this rationale and the helping hands of Sue Coty and Carole Jacobs, who were already experienced at using a reading/writing workshop, each PAL teacher developed an implementation plan for working with at-risk students in a workshop atmosphere. The belief that students and teachers are learners together propelled the teachers to consider a plan for becoming teacher-researchers in their classes and engaging students in that same enterprise. The path for my research and for theirs was mapped.

Some Rocky Spots

For the past four years, the PAL teachers and I have worked together to discover what works with at-risk students in reading/writing workshop. As you might imagine, the stories told in our meetings have not always been happy ones. One such story was of Lakesia, an economically and academically disadvan-

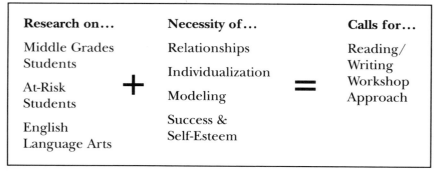

Research on...		Necessity of...		Calls for...
Middle Grades Students		Relationships		Reading/ Writing Workshop Approach
At-Risk Students	**+**	Individualization	**=**	
		Modeling		
English Language Arts		Success & Self-Esteem		

FIGURE 1. PAL's pedagogical rationale

taged young girl who showed great promise as a writer in Virginia Smith's sixth-grade class. One sad day the school discovered that, based on the school system's districting plan, Lakesia was attending the "wrong" school. She was immediately transferred to her "right" middle school, where she fell in with a group of students who were dubbed "troublemakers." In her desperate attempt to find a way to belong, she lost her interest in writing, began misbehaving, and ended up in a tracked "lower-level ability" language arts class. Virginia was crestfallen by this turn of events and tried to contact Lakesia as well as her teachers. All to no avail.

Then there's Robert, with whom Jakie Glick, his seventh-grade teacher, had finally built some trust after several months of painstaking encouragement. Robert had begun to write some heartrending personal narratives, when practically overnight he was moved to Florida to live with his grandmother. His North Carolina family's situation was unstable, and they were unable to continue caring for Robert.

At one winter meeting, Joyce Walker told the story of her eighth-grade student, Bernice, who had a reputation for being continuously disruptive. Most of the time Bernice did not cause any trouble in Joyce's reading/writing workshop class, but she was not productive either. One day during status-of-the-class (Atwell, 1987), as Joyce was urging the students to make progress in their writing because the end of the quarter was approaching, Bernice looked at her with dismay and complained, "Miz Walker, you always be wantin' us to *do* somethin'!" In her gracious way, Joyce responded, "Yes, Bernice, you're right. I *do* want you to be doing something." As we discussed this incident in our PAL meeting, Joyce still seemed stunned and worried about what to do next. The PALs pointed out to her that probably Bernice had been through a number of public school years without being asked to do much. Now she was being urged daily to produce; no more hiding until test time. However, no hiding for Bernice also meant no avoiding this resistant behavior for Joyce. She had to negotiate with Bernice every day.

Exploding the Myths

In the face of such personal trials, what have we learned about working with at-risk students? Some of the early lessons we learned were "myth-busters." The often-repeated statements about these resistant students have proved not to be true.

They need skill drills: Contrary to what we often hear and see recommended in traditional settings, we have found that a "drill and kill" approach is not necessary for at-risk students to grow as writers and readers. Mike, whose story Virginia Smith tells later in this issue, benefited from the opportunity to write about what he knew and cared about. He, like many other students the PAL teachers have followed, grew more rapidly from writing about things that mattered to him. We find, too, that students read more when the topics interest them and the characters, settings, or conflicts are ones with which they identify.

You can't let them move around; they are too disruptive: We have also found that making middle school at-risk students sit in straight chairs in straight rows with their feet on the floor does *not* make them more effective learners. They can, indeed, function effectively in a classroom that allows some freedom; they will no more take advantage of an environment that permits movement and alternative seating than they will of a classroom that requires absolute silence and passivity.

Their presence in heterogeneous classes will pull down the quality of other students' learning: What have we found about our at-risk students' abilities to respond to their peers' writing and to their reading? As Carole Jacobs's article in this issue reveals through her story of Sheronda and Vonnie, the heterogeneous grouping (on which we insist in our classes) does not precipitate a social class or ability separation; rather, our students who are at-risk can and do give helpful responses to other students' content, and they like being heard. They gradually develop the confidence to respond to literature, and they expand their vocabulary, fluency, and insights simultaneously.

> *Now she was being urged daily to produce; no more hiding until test time.*

The heartwarming story Sue Coty renders in her article about Belinda and Gina's interaction is a perfect example of what we have learned about students working together. We have seen social barriers broken among students in reading/writing workshop. Students broaden their group of peers to include others who may not be in their established cliques. None of these results come, of course, without the guidance, modeling, and mentoring of an exemplary teacher like Sue.

They cannot handle freedom: What about structure? Can at-risk students handle the freedom that comes with reading and writing choice? We have found that all our middle school students like some kind of predictability in their classrooms. That does not mean that every assignment has to be rigid; rather, a firm classroom organizational structure provides stability and comfort. Once the students grasp the daily pattern of reading/writing workshop, they adjust and thrive—usually much better than they did in a more teacher-centered lecture/independent practice format. And yes, we have found that it is okay to "smile before Christmas" and to let them smile, too; they return to the tasks at hand readily and do not take advantage of the flexibility.

What More Have We Learned?

Besides exploding the often-held myths about at-risk students, we have also discovered that there is no panacea for working with these challenging students. They have lots of external baggage that we cannot carry for them, and they often cover their lack of confidence and expertise with bravado and disruption. However, we now know that these students are academically capable, that given a supportive, individualized, caring pathway, they can and will succeed. They will join their teachers as researchers, set realistic goals for themselves as readers and writers, and will revel in the power of what it means finally to be heard. They can respond to individual attention positively, and they appreciate the respect they garner from both the teacher and their peers.

It is important to note here that these results have been gleaned from a study of individual students, each with a unique story. We would never be able to document the growth and change of our students if we considered them only as a group; each of them, after all, is different and brings a different set of personal and academic circumstances to the classroom. Therefore, most of our PAL teachers have chosen to develop case studies about their at-risk students. Only by following the students individually over time are they able to discern the degree of their growth. The articles in this journal represent just some of the stories they have uncovered, some of the lives they have touched, some of their joys and sorrows.

Risk-Taking Teachers

The PAL teachers are risk-taking teachers. Why else would these highly skilled, respected educators even consider trading their successful whole-class units for an individualized reading/writing workshop approach? A possible answer to that question lies in Erik Erikson's "Theory of Epigenesis."

Erikson suggests that in our lifelong effort to become identity achieved, we go through a series of defining conflicts. With each satisfactory conflict resolution, we become stronger, know our developing selves more completely, and are better able to arrive at our own identity. Once we are identity achieved, we go through even higher levels of development that allow us to trust ourselves and others, to find success through those that we guide, and to give back to those who will carry on to the future.

The PAL teachers have moved through identity achievement as excellent teachers to a new role as facilitators of a reading/writing workshop. This way of working with students has given them the ultimate gift—the satisfaction of mentoring those they value and cherish in a way that enables their students to own their processes and achieve their own independence.

Along the way, the PAL teachers also have fun. They like and respect each other, their students, and teaching. They enjoy the

> *We now know that these students are academically capable, that given a supportive, individualized, caring pathway, they can and will succeed.*

challenge of implementing a promising way of guiding adolescents, and they are natural researchers in their own classrooms. They are always questioning, wondering, and examining their own pedagogy and the learning of their students.

Pathways to Promise

While neither our research nor our work with at-risk students is by any means complete, we more often see these students now as having promise. We can say without a doubt that what is absolutely essential for teachers working with these temporarily disadvantaged students is an unwillingness to give up. But it takes a lot of stamina and resilience not to quit, not to fold with frustration.

So what pathways have we learned are necessary for PAL teachers?

■ A Support System: Our PAL group meets monthly to affirm our belief in reading/writing workshop, to continue our research, to problem solve, and to affirm each other. These meetings are critical, and I cannot overly emphasize their importance. The number of teachers who call and want to join us indicates that they, along with the PAL members, are hungry for a network.

■ Professional Involvement: We have committed ourselves to spreading the word about our questions, our successes, and our failures through making presentations at state and national conferences, writing articles, and keeping up with the literature in our field. These experiences keep us stimulated, connected, and challenged.

■ Teachers and Students as Researchers: It is crucial that we continue to question, to listen to each other and our students, to observe each other, to reflect, and to reevaluate our work through and with students. As Barbara Lord, another PAL member, exclaims, "We are constantly revisiting, reflecting, and fine-tuning our methods so as not to compromise our philosophy." We are finding new ways of being teacher-researchers in our classrooms; and we are soliciting our students to join us.

■ We Are the Adults: It is easy to get caught in the web of adolescents, and their attendant mercurial adolescence, since they are our daily interaction group. We remind each other often, "We are the adults," and our students need us to remain so. We have to keep a steady, calm demeanor as we guide the behavior, skills, and growth of our students.

After four years of working, researching, reaching out to each other and our students, do we still have those haunting faces? I am afraid so. We still have students who do not succeed and about whom we feel guilty. However, at least we now know early in the year who these students are and what they are doing. No student will "fall through the cracks" in workshop. Every day it is clear who is making progress and who is not. However, the numbers of haunting faces are dwindling, and we are more confident that we are truly providing a pathway by which our students can succeed. They are moving steadily toward their promise.

References

Alexander, W., & George, P. (1981). *The exemplary middle school.* San Francisco: Holt, Rinehart & Winston.

Atwell, N. (1987). *In the middle: Writing, reading, and learning with adolescents.* Portsmouth, NH: Heinemann.

Barker, J. (Host and author). (1990). *The power of vision* in the *Discovering the future* series. [Videotape]. Burnsville, MN: ChartHouse International Learning Corporation.

Britton, J. (1970). *Language and learning.* Harmondsworth, England: Penguin.

Coryell, N. (1927). *An evaluation of extensive and intensive teaching of literature: A year's experiment in eleventh grade* (Contributions to Education No. 275). New York: Bureau of Publications, Teachers College, Columbia University.

Donelson, K., & Nilsen, A. (1989). *Literature for today's young adults* (3rd ed.). Glenview, IL: Scott, Foresman.

Erikson, E. (1968). *Identity: Youth and crisis.* New York: Norton.

Fader, D. (1976). *The new hooked on books.* New York: Berkeley.

We are more confident that we are truly providing a pathway by which our students can succeed. They are moving steadily toward their promise.

Feldman, S., & Elliott, G. (1990). *At the threshold: The developing adolescent.* Cambridge, MA: Harvard University Press.

Garbarino, J. (1985). *Adolescent development: An ecological perspective.* Columbus, OH: Merrill.

Golub, J. (Ed.). (1989). *Talking to learn.* Urbana, IL: National Council of Teachers of English.

Graves, D. H. (1983). *Writing: Teacher and children at work.* Portsmouth, NH: Heinemann.

Hillocks, G. (1986). *Research on written composition.* Urbana, IL: ERIC Clearinghouse on Reading and Communication Skills and National Institute of Education.

Kirby, D., Liner, T., & Vinz, R. (1988). *Inside out: Developmental strategies for teaching writing* (2nd ed.). Portsmouth, NH: Heinemann.

LaBrant, L. (1937). The content of a free reading program. *Educational Research Bulletin, 16,* 29–34.

Lehr, J., & Harris, H. (1988). *At-risk, low-achieving students in the classroom.* Washington, D.C.: National Education Association.

Moffett, J. (1992). *Active voice: A writing program across the curriculum* (2nd ed.). Portsmouth, NH: Heinemann.

Murray, D. (1987). *Write to learn* (2nd ed.). New York: Holt, Rinehart and Winston.

Muuss, R. (1988). *Theories of adolescence.* New York: Random House.

Presseisen, B. (Ed.). (1988). *At-risk students and thinking: Perspectives from research.* Washington, D.C. and Philadelphia, PA: Joint Publication of National Education Association and Research for Better Schools.

Rief, L. (1992). *Seeking diversity.* Portsmouth, NH: Heinemann.

Rose, M. (1990). *Lives on the boundary.* New York: Penguin.

Smith, F. (1988). *Joining the literacy club.* Portsmouth, NH: Heinemann.

Stires, S. (Ed.). (1991). *With promise: Redefining reading and writing for special students.* Portsmouth, NH: Heinemann.

Van Hoose, J., & Strahan, D. (1989). *Young adolescent development and school practices: Promoting harmony.* Columbus, OH: National Middle School Association.

Weber, K. (1974). *Yes, they can! A practical guide for teaching the adolescent slower learner.* Evanston, IL: McDougal, Littell.

Wells, S. (1990). *At-risk youth: Identification, programs, and recommendations.* Englewood, CO: Teacher Ideas Press.

Finding the Path with the Help of a Friend

I believe most teachers eat, breathe, sleep, and live their teaching—constantly reviewing and constructing the yesterdays and tomorrows of their classes. My life is so connected to teaching that I cannot remember when I did not feel a commitment to share with children and find ways to help them develop. The times when I am irritable about being consumed by teaching are usually when I am dissatisfied with my role and my connection to all my students. When a student does not accomplish any writing or reading, I cannot stop reliving his interactions in my classroom and rehearsing what I am going to try next.

Being Nonproductive

One such student was Mike. Mike would have been served in a special education resource setting due to his classification as learning disabled and Attention Deficit Hyperactivity Disorder (ADHD) if an inclusive, team-teaching model had not been in place in my class. This heterogeneous class of twenty-three sixth graders included seven learning disabled students who were served by my special programs teammate.

Mike's disability was in written expression, which to me meant that his writing was not well developed and lacked both fluency and specificity. His answers to the student survey at the beginning of the year, adapted from Nancie Atwell's *In the Middle*, seemed to corroborate his special needs classification:

Q: What does one have to do in order to be a good writer?

A: Spell the words correctly

Q: What is the easiest part of writing for you?

A: I like the part where you use your amagination.

Q: What is the hardest part of writing for you?

A: The hardest part is writing it the wright way

His answers informed me about Mike as a writer. He believed that employing correct mechanics and finding the "right way" were the goals of writing. I saw the glimmer of potential that he valued using his imagination in writing. His interest in creativity provided a pathway by which I could support his promise.

Getting Adjusted

The year was a "first" for both of us: Mike was beginning middle school, and I was beginning a year-round program. The fifth graders from the elementary school had graduated on June 30th and would become sixth graders on July 8th at the middle school. Using standardized test scores, I divided our team of one hundred students into four heterogeneous classes. We held writing workshop three days and reading workshop two days each week; each workshop lasted fifty-five minutes. During the first quarter, I planned to focus my mini-lessons on building fluency and voice. The special programs teacher, who came into the class with Mike, was also eager to apply a workshop approach to our joint class.

As we settled into the procedures for writing workshop, I watched Mike go through the fine art of paper shuffling and preparing to begin. He did not accomplish very much—just a word or two in a large chunk of time. I observed Mike as I traversed the room, trying to connect with each child. His head was bent to his paper, but his eyes were tracking the movements of his classmates. Secretly, he watched as some students eagerly began writing, while others jumped at the chance to talk and interact with each other in conference corners. He watched me monitor and respond to his

Virginia Smith

Sixth-grade language arts teacher, West Lake Middle School, Apex, North Carolina peers. When I came to his desk and questioned, "How's it going?" he would nod, look down, and plainly wait for me to go away and leave him alone. For three writing days after the minilesson, when I asked for a report on the status of his piece, Mike would reply, "First draft."

A wiry, clean-cut, eleven-year-old, Mike was quiet, polite, and distant. In the hallways, I saw an engaging grin as he sparred with his male comrades, but in class, he usually looked down rather than meet anyone's eyes. I wondered if he was half-asleep in his first class of the day, or if his morning medication dose for attention disorder was too large. I learned that Mike's older brother, also identified with special needs, was a behavior problem in mainstream seventh-grade classes. I wondered if Mike was imitating his older brother when other teachers complained that Mike was a disruptive force in their classes at times.

"I saw him. He just stuck out his foot and tripped Sam for no reason," reported his math teacher.

"I don't think I can let him do a science experiment this whole year! He doesn't pay any attention to the lab safety rules; all he does is play."

I was thankful that I did not have these behavior problems with Mike, but clearly, at his present rate, Mike would still be a novice writer by year's end. He did not disturb anyone in language arts class, but neither did he share. To me, he was at risk of academic failure from nonproductivity.

Observing Mike

I began to watch Mike more closely. I saw the more lively Mike in the cafeteria, on the playground, and at the bus lot, roughhousing and teasing with his friends. Soon he was in trouble in the halls and had to serve a day of isolation in In-School Suspension (ISS). On the day of his return to regular classes, the ISS teacher sent almost half a page of writing Mike had completed. I was pleased that he had "finished" the telling of one personal narrative. I did not want to gush over these four, very long sentences, but I wanted to let

Mike know that I was impressed that he had written so much.

"Look at this, you wrote the whole story! Did Mrs. Nickels light a fire under you?"

Grinning, Mike assured me that he had been bored and had had nothing else to do. He shared what the day had been like.

"It's so quiet. You just sit there with nothing to look at. So I got it done."

I realized how foreign this experience had been for Mike. As a sixth grader new to middle school, he had never experienced "time out" like this before. I knew the ISS teacher, who offers students close guidance, helped build his self-confidence through personal attention.

Formerly, whenever I had spoken with Mike in class, I had carried the weight of the conversation. He had answered direct questions warily. In contrast, our brief exchange about this writing from ISS was a real dialogue. I wanted to build on it. I told Mike I did not write well in a room full of people either. I spoke briefly on how much thinking time it takes for me to write.

"I do a lot of staring at the page or the computer screen. My mind wanders, circles around, then returns to the task at hand. I work in starts and stops—spurts of writing and long periods of thinking. If there are any distractions, my concentration is gone."

Mike nodded his understanding. As one writer to another, we agreed on the importance of silence. Trying hard to stay on an equal footing, I concluded, "Here's your draft. I guess you'll be conferencing with people." I did not comment on the content of his piece, only returned it to him, because Mike had not asked me to be one of his conferees. Remembering Atwell's admonitions that the teacher is more effective as a coach than as a judge, I was not going to direct him and would wait to be invited to respond to his piece.

From then on, Mike became a participant in our class. Most of his writing was done outside of class, but he conferenced repeatedly in class with Pat and David, also novice writers. He elaborated his ISS narrative into two paragraphs of about a page in length. It was the story of his older brother

As one writer to another, we agreed on the importance of silence.

tying him up, blindfolding him, and pushing him down the stairs. The first draft, "The Accident at the Stairs," began:

One summer when I was about eight or nine my brother tied my hands and feet together and walked me over to the stairs and pushed me and I flew through the air and my head hit the wall and made a big hole in it.

After reading Mike's opening, as well as other students', we discussed leads in several minilessons. We investigated leads in good books and in student pieces. Mike was listening and trying. He had also begun sharing his writing with his friends. Initially, I think he took the risk of trying and sharing because I did not push him. Once he began receiving positive feedback from his peers, he invested more effort. Seven school weeks after he began, his final copy opens, "One summer when I was about eight or nine my brother and I were playing cops and robbers."

To develop satisfying endings to our stories, we tried to concentrate on our purposes for writing. We asked each conference partner to tell the writer how he felt after hearing the ending to the piece. On his second draft, Mike had concluded with this sentence: "He got in trouble becuse he could have killed me and I got in trouble because I was playing near the stairs." He conferenced with his friend Pat, who suggested he make his story longer, "Just put what you told me." After content conferencing, he added two additional sentences: "I am very lucky I didn't break my neck. That was the last day that babysitter watched us." When interviewed a year later, Mike picked this piece out as his best piece, even when he found evidence of better writing in later pieces (see p.16).

Building on Success

Even though I was seeing major progress in seven weeks, I was saddened to see that Mike was still in trouble elsewhere. He often did not have his homework, played instead of worked, and belonged to a group of boys all at risk of academic failure. This behavior discrepancy between language arts and other classes may have been caused by the time of day. Mike was in first period language arts when his ADHD medication was at full strength. But maybe Mike also had found success with his own voice using his "imagination." Mike said later that he liked workshop because he liked working with his friends and he "didn't have to listen to the teacher all the time." Whatever the cause, Mike continued to break enough rules outside the language arts class to end up in ISS regularly from one to three days at a time. When I questioned Mike about the fight or prank, he would look down, shrug, and appear resigned to serving his time. From his viewpoint, he had only been kidding around, or someone else had started it and pushed him into an angry rebuttal. Since ISS days were becoming inevitable, I wanted Mike to use that isolation for writing, so I nudged him to think about his needs as a writer.

"Remember what you said about writing in ISS?"

"Yeah. I write good there 'cause there isn't anything else to do."

"That's interesting, isn't it? That really helps you get a lot of work done. Have you thought about what you're going to write when you're in there?"

"Naw. But I think I'm going to start a new personal narrative. 'Cause I'll have plenty of time."

In my heart, I was delighted that he thought he could complete a piece in the upcoming three days. I tried to let Mike know that I was worried about him, but confident enough in his ability to joke about his suspension.

"That's a good plan. I look forward to reading it when you get out. This is a very creative way to find silent time for writing, Mike! I hope you won't have to go to ISS for three days every time you want to start a new piece. I promise I'll keep first period quieter when you come back."

After our first vacation, Mike's next personal narrative was entitled "Emerald Point," the name of a nearby waterslide park he had visited. This piece was longer and showed considerably more detail. While the run-on

Once he began receiving positive feedback from his peers, he invested more effort.

sentences and fragments remained, I knew these would diminish with time and practice. Now, instead of one long, never-ending paragraph, Mike had chunked his narrative into four paragraphs. There was clearly a beginning, middle, and end to his story. I was delighted to see that he had found topics of interest to him and, as a result, improved his fluency and control.

Writing Exposition

Toward the end of first quarter, the social studies teacher told me in our weekly team meeting that she wanted the children to research an assigned European country and write a report based on five themes of geography. While I was not sure that our less proficient writers could accomplish this task, I certainly wanted to help them try. She gave Mike and his teammates a rubric that outlined her requirements for a report of at least seven paragraphs, one for each of the five themes and an introduction and conclusion. He had to investigate at least three sources of information.

Naturally, I wanted to make this interdisciplinary unit successful despite my misgivings about most of the children's ability to write an expository research paper. My special programs colleague and I focused our lessons on how to research, take notes, and form a report. The personal narratives the students had in progress were set aside.

For note taking, the special programs teacher provided a successful, valuable scaffold for the children. There was not enough space to copy more than words or phrases, so plagiarism was greatly inhibited. On reading workshop days and in social studies class, Mike researched Norway and recorded his findings. Predictably, when he began to try to write a rough draft of his report, he was stymied. He copied disjointed facts from his notes. Again the special programs teacher relieved his frustration with topic sentence guidelines and examples. Unfortunately, these structures reduced the newly emerging voices of Mike and the other novice writers.

Drafting in the computer lab on writing workshop days, researching and composing

> *Real writers do not write finished essays in fifty minutes, yet this was how all of our students would be judged.*

on reading days, our children struggled to complete the papers by the three-week deadline. The results were mixed and not very satisfactory; most students were not ready as writers to try an expository piece. When the children drafted their reports, the apprentice writers who had been able to construct personal narratives satisfactorily could not apply their writing techniques to this more formal report format.

Despite Mike's improvement at the beginning of the year, his social studies report on Norway began as a listing of facts from his notes. He did not have any thoughts or feelings to include about this topic he had studied. His knowledge of Norway was too minimal to allow for more than a recording of basic information. He struggled with the organization, finally latching onto what he considered to be a useful transitory phrase. In the final copy he turned in to his social studies teacher, six topic sentences begin, "Now I will tell you about . . . ."

The Cost of Standardized Test Success

While we could see that the writing formulas we were teaching were keeping our less fluent writers from finding their writing voices, our state writing assessment loomed on the horizon. Real writers do not write finished essays in fifty minutes, yet this was how all of our students would be judged. We bowed to the pressure, and in second quarter wrote framed paragraph exercises, spool papers, and handy lists of transition words. To help our writer answer open-ended questions on the end-of-course tests, we practiced writing topic sentences to essay questions. We maintained the form of writing workshop but took away the ownership.

Mike, along with 74% of the students in writing workshop that year, achieved the proficiency level on the state exam. Each essay contained a thesis sentence; each paragraph began with a topic sentence complete with transition word. Yet the cost to inexperienced writers was high. Focusing on the product rather than the process stymied their emerging confidence. Mike, along with others, latched onto those memorized and homogenized frames and became dependent on them. The same formulas were repeated verbatim in all kinds of writing when they returned to their own topics.

By the beginning of third quarter, the students' attitudes had changed. Their writing had deteriorated along with their enthusiasm. In truth, I was just as dissatisfied as the children. It felt as if we were on a treadmill. In first period, Pat complained every day, "I'm tired of writing! This is boring!"

I read *In the Middle* again. I tried to tell myself that Nancie Atwell's students were better than mine since they cared about their writing, but I knew it was not true. I decided to hold a class meeting. I asked, "What can I do that would facilitate your working in this class?" The results were unanimous: "You don't let us do what we want. You take up too much time with the lesson—it is *not* a minilesson anymore."

I realized that, along with taking away their time and ownership when we had focused on essay writing, I had also constructed forms, checklists, and deadlines to make them accountable. When we returned to allowing free choice of topics and genres, the students had stopped looking for real writing purposes in their lives. Our collective enthusiasm was lost.

Returning Power

After our meeting, I recognized the students' need for more power. They began to expand their topic lists as they found real purposes for writing. New topics arose from class discussions and the daily newspaper. We learned that the school board was considering an earlier starting time for the next school year. Letters to the editor were drafted overnight in a flurry of rebuttal!

The students were studying the Holocaust in social studies when *Schindler's List* debuted at the movies. Eloquent poetry followed. We began a whole class reading of *Number the Stars*, and then learned about *Zlata's Diary* when a student brought in an article from *Newsweek*. Avid letters were sent to authors. Mike and Pat began a compli-mentary letter to a local video game business, while their peers turned to other genres. We all regained our lost vitality, and I began to understand the true importance of audience and purpose.

Determined to revalue good writing, I asked the students to self-evaluate their writing folders, and then to evaluate a peer with a form provided to assist them. Mike helped Pat identify improvements, even when slight. He read through his own writing and designated his piece, "Emerald Point," as the best in his writing folder because it was "very descriptive." I remembered the revisions Mike had written after his conference with me. Trying to show the reader the "wave-maker" at the amusement park, he wrote: "Where the wave comes from, there is a wall on each side and then the walls just goes out and makes a corner." I indicated on his piece that I could not see what he meant. In our subsequent conference, Mike replied that Pat had said it was fine. I pushed further and explained that I could not see it at all in my mind's eye because I was a reader who had never been there. On his final copy, Mike revised but continued to struggle: "Where the wave comes from, the water fills up in a wall and the water comes out. To keep the wave together, two walls do not fill up with water."

Mike did not need a teacher to tell him how he had improved. Using the form's scale, he self-scored his greatest gains of the year in organization and voice. He thought he was progressing with sentence fluency, but was less adept at word choice and generating ideas. I agreed completely. (See Classroom Connections.)

After the end of the year, I audiotaped an interview with Mike. Again he reflected on his writing folder, which was being forwarded to seventh grade. His development seemed clear to him. This time he decided that his first piece of writing, "The Accident at the Stairs," was really his best.

"Why is that your best?"

"Well, I worked really hard on it. At first it was just a paragraph."

"I remember you thinking about it and working on it for a long time, too. What

I decided to hold a class meeting. I asked, "What can I do that would facilitate your working in this class?"

changes would you make to this piece if you were going to rewrite it now, Mike?"

"I would describe it more. In another paragraph I'd add how when my friend comes over he always laughs at the hole in the wall and says it looks like it fits my head."

When I asked Mike to find a piece that he liked from later in the year, he pulled out "When I Was Afraid." I placed the two pieces side by side.

"Looking at these two together, how would you compare them?"

"I spent more time on the first one. But I put more about what I thought in 'When I Was Afraid.' And I had more description."

"Could you find an example that you think is descriptive?"

He turned to his final copy and read, "'I looked down and my whole hand was covered with blood.' I think that's descriptive."

"What color was that blood?"

"Red."

He smiled, knowing what was coming next.

"Same color as mine. If you were going to revise this, how would you show your reader how your hand had been covered?"

He thought for a few seconds. "I'd say that my friend's mouth was open staring at my wet red hand. My whole palm was covered in blood. And the cut was on my index finger."

"That certainly gives me a more vivid picture. Are there other places in this piece where your writing is descriptive, Mike?"

"Here. 'I thought I was going to die because I had never seen that much blood before. I was going into shock.' There are my thoughts and feelings."

"The first time you see a whole lot of blood it really is scary. What did you mean when you wrote 'I was going into shock'?"

"I didn't know what was happening. I was shaking and everything."

"That would be interesting to put that in there too, explaining to your reader what shock is. I agree with you.

"You know, Mike, it is interesting that this second piece is a lot longer than your first piece. Yet you said that you didn't spend as much time writing this [second] one."

"Yeah. I probably just put more into 'When I Was Afraid.' I stretched it out and added more details."

"Why is your first piece, 'The Accident at the Stairs,' your favorite?"

He shrugged. "I don't know. I guess it's just important. And my brother got into trouble."

I could imagine the importance of the memory to Mike. He had lived through the ordeal and his bullying brother had been punished. He appeared to be imitating his brother's belligerence at times, but maybe he could learn to make different choices.

"Mike, what did you like most about reading/writing workshop?"

"Content conferences and you don't have to listen to the teacher all the time. Pat gave me good suggestions. I could trust him."

Friends. If Mike can keep good friends who choose to stay on the pathway to literacy, maybe he will too. Clearly Mike has figured out that better writing is more extended writing that includes specific details. With time, practice, and quality response, he will come to understand that he can add more depth to his writing and not just extend it with details. While not as accomplished as the majority of new seventh graders, Mike no longer seems at risk of academic failure except for his compulsive, combatant behaviors. He progressed so far in one year that I doubt he will keep that label when he is reevaluated for special programs service. I hope that his accomplishments and his friends give him the courage to walk down a new path and to see the promise his future holds.

> I hope that his accomplishments and his friends give him the courage to walk down a new path and to see the promise his future holds.

References

Atwell, N. (1987). *In the middle: Writing, reading, and learning with adolescents.* Portsmouth, NH: Heinemann.

Filipovic, Zlata. (1994). *Zlata's diary: A child's life in Sarajevo.* New York: Scholastic.

Lowry, Lois. (1989). *Number the stars.* New York: Dell/Yearling.

Lingering Questions

1. How can I teach young writers to use expository essay components that our state test evaluators seek without limiting the development of their fluency, voice, and confidence?

2. What if I had fewer students? Would it make a difference to Mike if I could spend more time with him? Or does he benefit primarily from peers' guidance?

If I Could Do It Again

1. I will never again try a research paper with sixth graders until second semester. Instead of an expository form, I will use Ken Macrorie's "I-Search" process.

2. This year, while students will have chances to write essays on topics they themselves value, I will not focus on our state "test writing" skills and prompts until time for the exam draws closer.

Mike's Self-Evaluation Sheet

STUDENT **Mike**_____ GRADE/TRACK`_____ TEACHER_____

Your writing portfolio shows your development as a writer since the beginning of the school year. Look at your writing carefully and thoughtfully to determine how well you demonstrate your skill in the categories below. Follow these directions:

1. Organize your writing in chronological order.
2. Skim/read over each piece to fill in the following grid.

Key:

1	3	5
Not Yet Demonstrated	In Progress	Consistently Demonstrates Mastery

Pieces that Demonstrate Ability to Write for Different Purposes

Title(s)	I	II	III	IV
Report Writing: Social Studies Report	3			
Narrative Writing: ~~accident at the Stairs~~ ~~Emerald~~ accident at the stairs	3			
Creative Writing: Roll of thunder hear my cry			3	
Clarification Writing: ~~Roll of thunder hear my cry~~ Roll of thunder hear my cry			3	
Descriptive Writing: Emerald Point		3		
Letter Writing: Literary leters	4	4		

Your pieces (including plans, research notes, drawings, drafts, and final copies) also indicate your application of the following writing traits:

		I	II	III	IV
A.	Ideas/Content:	3	4	3	
B.	Organization:	3	5	5	
C.	Voice/Tone:	1	3	5	
D.	Sense of Audience:	3	4	4	
E.	Effective Word Choice:	1	5	3	
F.	Sentence Fluency:	1	2	4	
G.	Writing Conventions:				
	1. Uses complete sentences and punctuation.	4	4	4	
	2. Revises spelling errors.	5	5	5	
	3. Writes legibly and organizes work on the page.	5	5	5	

"Sometimes I Wish I'd Never Did It": Removing Communication Road Blocks from At-Risk Students

"That's a lousy story. You don't know what you're talking about. You talk too much anyway."

—David

It was mid-September, the fourth week of school, and Rhonda was very excitedly and proudly reading aloud her piece about catching a blue fish. She and her classmates were participating in group share, and she asked them if they could see the colors of the sky, the water, and the fish in her personal narrative. The students were beginning to respond to her request for descriptive words when, without waiting to be called on, David blurted out his negative comments. His response crushed Rhonda, destroyed the mood of the whole class, and ruined group share for about three months.

The entry in my teaching journal for that day says, "I feel angry!" Upon further reflections that week, I realized this was not the first time a student had made damaging comments to another student. When they come to school, many middle grades students do not know how to develop relationships in a classroom. This is especially true of at-risk students: students who are at risk of failure in school because of problems in their lives. These problems range from poor skills to low self-esteem, from transient or alcoholic homes to peer problems, from pregnancy to abuse. These students call each other names and disrupt the tone of discussions, allow their own negative feelings to get in everyone's way, and act out to attract attention.

However, this behavior often occurs with other students as well. Many do not know how to hold a successful content conference about their writing. Listeners may often not ask questions at all, or ask the writer questions that do not help clarify a writing problem. I have overheard such comments as "Stupid" and "That's dumb." Body language also reveals students' resistance: poor eye contact, playing with their shoes, sitting far away from each other. Once when I heard Aquilla correct David's double negatives, he replied, "I don't need you, no way." In my observations, I have noted two extremes: 1) students who are afraid to hurt another writer's feelings by questioning or disagreeing and 2) those who jump right in and tell the writer exactly how to correct a piece. Their familiar ways of relating verbally to each other produce road blocks to classroom activities. Ironically, when David introduced himself to the class the first week of school, he did not produce road blocks for himself. "I have two younger brothers that are twins. We fight a lot. My mom divorced my dad a long time ago. I like to play video games and hang out." I thought he was heartwarming in his honesty about moving all the way from a big city in Ohio. He fit in with the other twenty-three students, especially those who were socially or academically at risk: shy, lanky Hannah from a small country town in West Virginia; Jason, who had just moved from New Jersey to live with his grandmother because his mother was once again in a rehabilitation center; and aggressive Aquilla, who wanted to mother and boss everyone.

While David's negative comments to Rhonda temporarily dashed my hopes of workshop's success, I did not give up. For two years I had been successfully implementing the reading/writing workshop as described in Nancie Atwell's *In the Middle: Writing, Reading, and Learning with Adolescents*. My four language arts classes in this Durham middle school met each day for fifty-five minutes; we held writing workshop Mondays through Wednesdays and reading workshop on Thursdays and Fridays. But how could I

Sue Coty

Seventh-grade communication skills teacher, Githens Middle School, Durham, North Carolina

expect students to share their writing in small conferences or large groups if the class was not a safe place, one free of harsh criticism? What of Hannah, who wrote, "I love to write. It helps me get away. I really don't have to worry about what I'm writing or anyone criticizing me because it's *my* writing." Would she ever feel safe enough to share her poetry if other students continued to block communication? How could I expect the students to feel secure if David continued to use inappropriate language and bring up condoms and sex during group share? I asked myself what would happen if I focused more directly on communication? Would the experience affect students' interactions in workshop? If I actually taught them, especially David, how to communicate effectively by teaching them how to speak creatively and responsively, would I enable them to participate more effectively in our reading/writing workshop?

Communicating Effectively

With David and Hannah in mind, I made some changes. I began teaching effective communication by setting aside Wednesdays as our talking and speaking day and by rereading Gene Stanford's book *Developing Effective Classroom Groups*. This practical guide gives both theory and strategies of group dynamics to help teachers convert a class of individuals into an effective learning group. The book is full of structured experiences that match each stage in group development: orientation, group responsibility, responding to others, cooperation, consensus, confronting problems, coping with conflict, productivity, and terminating the group. I wanted my individual middle schoolers to become a caring and cohesive group that would talk, read, write, and learn together both as a whole class and in their peer conferencing. Since each chapter of Stanford's book includes teacher behavior, I also reevaluated my own communication skills because I knew I must practice what I preached.

We had already begun our year by doing self-introductions the first week of school. I decided to use more of these orientation activities and implemented group responsibil-

ity activities on successive Wednesdays. Through their speaking and my careful listening, I gained valuable insight into the students' lives, enabling me to adjust my teaching to help them better. When I discovered that Jason had lied to the class about his family background, I learned to speak privately with him about the consequences of his behavior. I also found out that Aquilla was denied a listening parent at home so she tried to compensate at school. Understanding her background helped me offer her other ways of expressing her opinions, which she felt were the most important in the class.

These self-disclosure exercises were hardest for my at-risk students. Some students were shy, and others cocky. They squirmed, wanting to avoid the activity. Mario even refused to participate, and Paul ridiculed the activity or the topics. I began the process of accepting the blame when they were dissatisfied with my topics and gave them the assurance of being heard. We made lists of the topics they preferred to discuss, and I integrated the necessary skills when we talked about the question, "Is cheating ever justified?" Many students in each class did not understand the word *justified*, so we had a vocabulary lesson.

I made it a practice to videotape Wednesday activities so that I could view the results on the weekend. When all the students had to speak during the discussion of cheating being justified, I noted in my journal the effect of David's words on the whole group: "It was as though David's honesty had given the other students permission to be just as honest." He spoke of coming to our southern town from a large city in the north ". . . where cheating was okay. I cheated in my Spanish class. I had to." He told the story of three of his friends and how one time two had cheated and one had not. The two got money for their efforts. David felt badly for the guy who ". . . didn't get no cash. I just can't go without that cash. Walking around with that empty palm. [Shaking his head] Walking around with no money." Immediately after his comments, Aquilla told us that she had cheated in order to avoid a hard time with her stepfather.

> *Through their speaking and my careful listening, I gained valuable insight into the students' lives, enabling me to adjust my teaching to help them better.*

Clip and File

Reviews of Books for Middle Level Readers

This column was organized by Amelia McLeod, Clayton Middle School, Clayton, North Carolina. Teachers of student reviewers at Clayton Middle School are Amelia McLeod and Donna Breniman.

Journey to Jo'Burg:
A South African Story
Beverley Naidoo

HarperCollins/Trophy, 1988, 96 pp., $3.95
ISBN 0-06-440237-1

Thirteen-year-old Naledi and her little brother Tiro don't get to see their mother very often because she works in faraway Johannesburg. They live with their grandmother in a village 300 kilometers away. When their younger sister gets sick, they decide to find their mother so she can help. Their journey is difficult and they face some dangers. Finally, they find their mother and begin the return trip. Will they get home in time to save their sister?

Journey to Jo'Burg has some history in the story and the reader may have to reread some parts to fully understand the book. We liked the book because Tiro and Naledi fight just like real brothers and sisters. The book made us feel sad because the mother had to work far away from her family. We could relate to Naledi because we can handle trouble, too!

Alana Herod and Sandra Rand, Grade 7
Clayton Middle School, Clayton, North Carolina

Don't Look Behind You
Lois Duncan

Dell, 1990, 179 pp., $3.50
ISBN 0-440-20729-0

Why does April have to leave all of her friends, her tennis career, and her boyfriend? Her father is placed in the witness protection program and April must leave everything behind her. Relocated just two days before her Senior Prom, April, full of resentment, jeopardizes the family safety when she tries to contact her boyfriend and grandmother. Because she doesn't consider her actions, someone is murdered. Read to find out who!

This book is very fast paced and suspenseful. April is a typical teenager who does what she wants and doesn't consider her family's safety. I recommend this book to any middle school student who likes murder, intrigue, and an uncertain ending.

Lindsay Resnick, Grade 7
Clayton Middle School, Clayton, North Carolina

The Overnight
R. L. Stine

Pocket Books, 1991, 148 pp., $3.99
ISBN 0-671-74650-2

Hey, this is for all of you who love to read. I just got the word on a new book and I encourage you to challenge your minds by reading it.

After Mr. Alger cancels the overnight trip the group had planned, they decide to go without him. "Maia, what could go wrong? I promise you that everything will be fine." At least that's what Della thinks. Then someone commits murder and things go haywire. *The Overnight*, a shocking thriller about a group of teenagers who start an overnight club, will leave you wondering what will happen next. Read the book to find out what.

I loved *The Overnight* because I'm the type of person that loves mysteries and thrillers, especially by R. L. Stine. I was introduced to his books just this year, and have read four nonstop.

Mickela Nicholson, Grade 7
Clayton Middle School, Clayton, North Carolina

The Sign of the Beaver
Elizabeth George Speare

Dell/Yearling, 1993, 135 pp., $1.99
ISBN 0-440-21623-0

The Sign of the Beaver is the story of Matt who, left behind in the wilderness, is befriended by a local Indian tribe. Matt is left by his father to protect their cabin while he makes the journey to bring the rest of the family to their new home. While his dad is gone, Matt faces many difficult times, but learns from the Indians the tricks of the forest and how to make traps. As winter approaches, Matt is faced with the choice of going north with the Indians or staying back at the cabin to wait for his overdue family. Will Matt go or stay? Read *The Sign of the Beaver* to find out.

I thought this book was very interesting. People who are interested in adventure and nature will love this book.

Paul Uzzle, Grade 7
Clayton Middle School, Clayton, North Carolina

Roll of Thunder, Hear My Cry
Mildred D. Taylor

Puffin, 1991, 276 pp., $3.99
ISBN 0-14-034893-X

Nothing is as important to the Logan Family as their land. They would sacrifice almost anything for their land. When Mrs. Logan is fired from her teaching job, the family must think of another way to raise money to pay for the land. Cassie, the main character, is strong and brave throughout the book. Some episodes of prejudice occur and Cassie does not understand why whites treat colored people differently.

I recommend this book to students who enjoy reading great books. The author, Mildred D. Taylor, is one of the best writers in the world. This book will make you cry and wonder why times were like they were back then. I didn't want to read this book at first, but now I want to read the rest of the books in the Logan series.

Tara Williams, Grade 7
Clayton Middle School, Clayton, North Carolina

Malcolm X: By Any Means Necessary
Walter Dean Myers

Scholastic, 1993, 224 pp., $13.95
ISBN 0-590-46484-1

Malcolm X: By Any Means Necessary tells the story of how Malcolm X became a great leader. It tells how he dealt with the death of his father, the slow deterioration of his mother, and how he hustled tips in Boston nightclubs. The book also tells about how Malcolm X transforms from a prisoner to a faithful member of the Nation of Islam. We also find out about little-known facts, such as his name change from Malcolm Little to Malcolm X, and then to El Hajj Malik al Shabazz.

Walter Dean Myers has showcased his brilliance in this book. People who like detailed biographies will love *Malcolm X: By Any Means Necessary*. I really liked the way Myers gave a historical perspective to the life of Malcolm X.

Stephanie R. Vinson, Grade 7
Clayton Middle School, Clayton, North Carolina

The Year Mom Won the Pennant
Matt Christopher

Little Brown, 1986, 160 pp., $3.95
ISBN 0-316-13988-2

Would you let your mom coach your baseball team? Well, in this book, Nick Vassey's mom coaches the Thunderbirds when no one else would. Follow the Thunderbird's season to an exciting championship game and meet many of Nick's friends along the way. The team's ability is questioned when the pennant-winning coach for the past three years makes a bet with Nick's dad. If you like baseball, you will like this book because it has a lot of baseball action.

Matt Christopher, the author, has written over twenty sports books. I would recommend this book for both boys and girls in third through seventh grades.

Chris O'Neal, Grade 7
Clayton Middle School, Clayton, North Carolina

The Boy Who Lost His Face
Louis Sachar

Knopf, 1991, 208 pp., $3.95
ISBN 0-679-0160-X

David wants to fit in with some of the most popular boys in school. Unfortunately, he joins the group in a prank targeting an old lady. David really gets worried after the prank goes wrong and is convinced the old lady has cursed him. Things happen to David that he can't explain. Meanwhile, David is turning into the world's biggest loser. His only friends are weirdos, and he can't seem to do anything right—at home or at school. When he finally gets the nerve to ask out a girl he likes, his pants suddenly fall down mid-sentence. Is it because of the old lady's curse? Or is he simply a total jerk?

I liked the book because it is funny and interesting. It really made me laugh. The book reminds me of me.

Shanna Withers, Grade 7
Clayton Middle School, Clayton, North Carolina

The River
Gary Paulsen

Dell, 1993, 132 pp. $3.99
ISBN 0-440-40753-2

The River, a thrilling sequel to *Hatchet*, is just as breathtaking as *Hatchet* itself. Derek, a government psychologist, shows up at Brian's door asking Brian to accompany him into the wilderness to teach him how to survive. Brian knew he could do this task, but did he want to? A couple of weeks later he found himself heading north in a tiny plane with Derek. Everything is fine until a huge storm blows in and Derek is knocked unconscious. Brian knows that Derek needs medical attention. He must build a small raft and begin a journey that he will never forget. The details of their survival are so intense that you feel like you are right beside Brian the whole time. Full of instruction, boys and girls of all ages will like the story.

Amber Southerland, Grade 7
Clayton Middle School, Clayton, North Carolina

There's a Girl in My Hammerlock
Jerry Spinelli

S&S Trade, 1993, 208 pp., $3.95
ISBN 0-671-86695-8

Who ever heard of a girl on the wrestling team? In *There's a Girl in My Hammerlock*, Maisie decides to try out for the wrestling team after being cut from the cheerleading squad. Of course people pick on her, and her best friend won't talk to her. After a while, things start to look up. Eric, the guy she is trying to impress, finally asks her out; she makes new friends, and even becomes a hero.

Jerry Spinelli is a great author. He writes about things that can actually happen in real life. I think this book would be great for kids who have a low self-esteem, because it teaches you that you can do anything you want, if you try hard enough.

Jennifer Bennett, Grade 7
Clayton Middle School, Clayton, North Carolina

The Drowning of Stephan Jones
Bette Greene

Bantam, 1992, 217 pp., $3.99
ISBN 0-553-29793-7

"Frank wondered how many places there were where people could come together with nothing more or less to bind them together than the joy of being human. Here it really was true what they said—even the misfits *fit*. The two felt wrapped in this special privileged glow until they reached the front door of the Forgotten Treasures, when their bubble of contentment popped and all their warm and wonderful feelings ended with a sudden crash. Across the door and window of their shop, black spray paint sloppily spelled out one seven-letter word: FAGGOTS!!!"

This excerpt starts out lifting me up and making me smile, and then smashes me onto the cold surface of reality, tears stinging my eyes. Although this is a work of fiction, it was inspired by the drowning of a young man harassed by other young men. What makes this such an incredible book is the anger that builds up inside of you as you are reading. If you want a book that will make your head spin, this book will make you dizzy. It's like having reality slap you across the face.

Rachel Gooze, Grade 8
Oyster River Middle School, Durham, New Hampshire

Downriver
Will Hobbs

Bantam, 1992, 208 pp., $3.50
ISBN 0-553-29717-1

Like Gary Paulsen, Will Hobbs writes adventure stories with descriptions that pull you into the pages. In *Downriver*, a story set in the Grand Canyon, he writes, "We passed under the bridge, a graceful arch composed of hundreds of steel girders, towering above us in the world of stone and sky like a monumental work of art. There was an eerie quality about it, as if it were the vestige of an ancient civilization."

I especially like *Downriver* because it has a lot of information and detail about rafting and lifesaving skills. I also like how the main characters sort out their difficulties and have a "who cares" attitude toward the police who try to capture them. (Makes you wonder why the police are after them on the Colorado River . . . .)

Hobbs' words keep the story moving and alive. "It was amazing how high our energy level shot up with the arrival of those helicopters. Our quiet, brooding camp came alive like a nest of fire ants stirred with a stick."

I've read all of Hobbs' books and can't wait for the next one to be out!

David Tanguay, Grade 7
Oyster River Middle School, Durham, New Hampshire

Clip and File

Reviews of Books for Middle Level Teachers

Reviews: Lanny van Allen, Texas Education Agency, Austin, Texas; Robert Probst, Georgia State University; Tom Romano, Utah State University

---

Seeking Diversity:
Language Arts with Adolescents
Linda Rief

Heinemann, 1992, 300 pp., $21.00

ISBN 0-435-08598-0

Linda Rief invites us into her eighth-grade class where she hopes her students will develop "literate passions." Influenced by Murray, Graves, Newkirk, and Atwell, Rief's literacy workshop reflects a whole language, process-oriented approach; students write on self-selected topics and read what interests them. She sometimes breaks with established models, however, by tackling whole-class projects, or guiding and directing her students "by what I do and what I choose to immerse them in for reading and writing." Rief exposes her class to literature and genres they might not choose for themselves, stretching them to accept a broader definition of "literature." Rief believes "that the ultimate purpose of evaluation is to enable students to evaluate themselves," so her class evaluates writing from former classes and develops criteria for effective writing.

In order for any classroom's diverse population to progress toward a sense of quality and a broadening of mind, expectations must be high and individual goals must be recognized. Linda Rief does more than show her students the way; she joins them in their journey.

In the Middle: Writing, Reading, and
Learning with Adolescents
Nancie Atwell

Heinemann, 1987, 295 pp., $19.00

ISBN 0-86709-163-0

Nancie Atwell came from behind the desk into what she called "a new territory my students and I could inhabit together." *In the Middle* describes Atwell's process of "uncovering and questioning my assumptions," recognizing that what she was working so hard to create was *not* working. After working with Murray, Graves, Calkins, Sowers, and Giacobbe in the Boothbay Writing Project, Atwell (over time) abandoned lectures, assignments, tests, and dittos, and came from behind the Big Desk to *write with, observe, and learn* from young writers. A detailed, fast-paced, and inspiring account of how Atwell arrived at the workshop approach, the appropriateness of this approach for young adolescents, the details of class time, minilessons, grading time, and other things teachers want to know, have been given (as in Gift) by Atwell in this book. In spite of this program's success, Atwell encourages teachers to venture out, explore, risk, and adapt it to their own student populations.

This book (do not lend anyone your copy—you'll never get it back!) has probably made more difference to more teachers and to instruction than any publication in the last century, and I'm not exaggerating!

Just Teach Me, Mrs. K: Talking, Reading,
and Writing with Resistant Adolescent Learners
Mary M. Krogness

Heinemann, 1994, 304 pp., $21.50

ISBN 0-435-08815-7

I unfastened my seat belt, bolted out of my seat, seized the mike, and faced the passengers reading Hillerman and Steele. "You folks want stimulating? Read this book by Mary Krogness." (They whisper, "Mary who?") With her lively plot and great cast of characters, you'll say, "Now there's a real professional." Well, it's *not* fiction, but rather a first-person account of a true challenge: Teaching—working to find out what motivates adolescents who have to go to school but don't want to be there. (They snicker, "What else is new?") Krogness is committed to making school a positive experience, starting *where students are*. They learn to communicate, to appreciate others' stories, to talk about language, to establish rules for working in groups. They read strong and appropriate books, keep journals, and write poetry and real job applications. And Krogness takes them to new places—theatre, Red Lobster, and success—success based on mutual respect between students and teacher.

I felt a nudge—Coffee? Tea? I had fallen asleep, but felt energized thinking of this professional teacher all of us would like to be like, one who knows that classroom instruction is where true reform takes place.

Children of Promise: Literate Activity in
Linguistically and Culturally Diverse Classrooms
Shirley Brice Heath and Leslie Mangiola

NEA, 1991, 62 pp., $8.95

ISBN 0-8106-1844-3

Children of Promise addresses the difficult challenge of improving literacy learning for all children, especially those who speak languages or dialects other than standard English. Authors Mangiola, a classroom teacher, and Heath, a university researcher, examine three different but related studies, two involving cross-age tutoring and one inviting ESL students to examine the linguistic characteristics of their own communities. They believe that students of diverse cultural backgrounds, who may be perceived as problematic, might actually enrich the language classroom for all students. The authors describe the literacy practices within these classrooms and discuss some of the principles of learning and language that underlie them. In so doing, they examine how students, teachers, and researchers listen, observe, and learn from one another. The studies, briefly and readably reported, argue powerfully for curricula that respect cultural differences rather than try to erase them, and that encourage students to "focus on *language as both instrument and object of study*." The book offers a brief and useful bibliography and recommendations for those who want to implement similar projects.

Others told stories of why it is important to cheat, or instances when they had cheated, but Hannah only shook her head and said she thought it was wrong to cheat.

To draw my students into a personal awareness of our communication processes, I asked them to reflect after each Wednesday's activity. They evaluated their involvement by answering questionnaires or writing in their journals. Then we held class discussions. During one of these animated discussions, the students pointed out that some people, like Hannah, were quiet and needed encouragement to participate. We discussed possible reasons why some people are reticent, and this discussion naturally bridged to our remembering peers' behavior during conference and group share times in writing workshop. Willie admitted, "I am afraid to speak out in group share." Mona shrugged her shoulders and said, "I don't know what to say."

During our Wednesday activities and our workshop times, we brainstormed ways to draw out another person—how one person could encourage another to talk and continue talking. We practiced our body language, nodding heads, and asking questions. This discussion led into the next week's exercise of drawing out a speaker.

The following Wednesday, I partnered the students with someone other than a good friend. They had to use our list of ways to draw out a speaker and take turns keeping their partner talking for three to five minutes. I observed in my journal:

This activity caused discomfort and complaints. Jason mocked talkative Aquilla by continually nodding his head. David played with his money, stood up, and looked around the room.

I asked the students, "What's going on here?" After some discussion in which they said, "Your topic is lousy. I want to talk to my friend," I agreed to their requests to choose their own partners and the topic. We tried again; the students were more comfortable with chosen partners, easily maintaining eye contact and keeping their partners talking. I noted in my journal:

Jason leaned up close to his partner; David told Willie, "Most of these teachers here are pretty dumb. I can get around them most of the time without getting into too much trouble. I do like to hang out at lunch, though."

I began to notice small changes. During late fall, David and I had agreed that his personal writing goal would be: "Say only positive comments in group share." He kept our agreement and privately told me his negative thoughts about other students and their writings, often while walking to lunch. Rhonda, who had been burned early in September, still refused to share her own writing with anyone other than her friends. But the students exhibited positive behaviors and better communication skills during our Wednesdays. In my journal, I noted two points:

The two class periods with fewer at-risk students were orderly and the groups went quietly and efficiently to work, while the two classes with more at-risk students showed their usual reluctance when asked to communicate in a manner not familiar to them. But, after their rough beginning in each communication task, my at-risk students became more comfortable and involved.

Learning to Listen

It was December when I came upon a *big* road block. We had practiced group responsibilities during a Wednesday discussion of "Should students decide the amount of homework they are assigned?" While one student videotaped the class, I kept records of how many times each student fulfilled any of the responsibilities/roles as described in *Write Source 2000:* listening, observing, cooperating, responding, clarifying, and connecting. That weekend when I viewed the tapes, I was struck by how little the students really listened to their classmates. They did not make connections between their own ideas and another student's thoughts; they just kept adding unrelated ideas to the discussion and ignoring the comments of the previous speaker(s). Most students spent their time planning ahead for their own comments. (I had also noted this behavior in group share at the end of writing workshop days when one student would repeat what another had said without listening first.) I wanted them to

During one of these animated discussions, the students pointed out that some people, like Hannah, were quiet and needed encouragement to participate.

treat each other's contributions with respect and serious consideration, to interact directly with another student, and to value another's comments and ideas. I also remembered what Atwell had written about the importance of modeling and that students need practice to make an action their own.

I decided to show the tapes to the students and point out when they had not listened to each other. We talked about the value of not repeating or interrupting, and I modeled ways to respond in discussions. Then they practiced again after agreeing to follow Stanford's rules of contributing: 1) they would look directly at the previous speaker and tell him/her in what ways they agreed or disagreed with the stated opinion; and 2) they could comment or add to the previous opinion, but must not simply tell the group their own opinion.

Making Conversations Real

During our evaluation and discussion time after the topic, "Should students decide the amount of homework they are assigned?", the classes certainly let me know of their displeasure with this activity. They wrote that they did not like the restriction of only commenting about or adding to the previous speaker. Mario said, "Our discussion was stiff and the quiet people did not speak up."

Finally, during fifth period, I moaned, "Why is this so hard? Maybe you're not used to talking to each other."

David scoffed, "We talk together all the time!" Some students laughed.

Then Hannah said, "But we don't talk about school stuff."

A light bulb went on in my head. She was exactly right, and she understood what I was trying to get them to do. These conversations were artificial. Hannah was reflecting on our process; she was aware of our problem. I jumped up in excitement and immediately decided to incorporate more opportunities for students to practice discussing school "stuff."

For the rest of the year, we continued to expand our Wednesday communication skills but with topics centered on our writing

workshop activities. I also looked for students' use of these communication skills in our reading and writing workshops. I was delighted when one day in group share Jason tried to convince the class to agree with his interpretation of Hannah's poem. In that interaction, Jason never called anyone "stupid," and he accepted without hostility that his viewpoint did not mesh with the others'. This behavior was a contrast to his negative comments and pouting during the first months of school.

At another time, when David and Aquilla were conferencing in the corner about his piece, I listened. David took Aquilla's viewpoint into account and said, "I disagree with you." She then demanded that he explain why. David showed his ability to express his thoughts and feelings without resorting to yelling or name calling. In my own journal reflections, I noted:

Some of the students have learned to use agreement and disagreement as a method for linking ideas. Watching themselves on videotape and writing their own reflections about our activities have stimulated their awareness of themselves as speakers and group members.

Witnessing Change

By the end of the year, David did not "hit" on anyone during group share. During a Wednesday videotaping in March, when the students were discussing reading and writing workshops and our effective communication day, David told us, "I liked hitting on Rhonda. But I feel bad about doing that to Rhonda. Sometimes I wish I'd never did it." He was also able to ask Aquilla for help editing his pieces. When she or another peer corrected his speech, he would say the sentence again and include the corrections. He was still obviously uncomfortable at times when working in small groups, but he would contribute to his teams' discussions when encouraged. He still tried to leave to go to the bathroom whenever our activities were threatening to him.

I was really worried that David would not attend and participate in our "Writers All" production in June. This was a time when the students performed some of their pieces before an audience of their peers and parents. David was fine in the classroom while he and his team chose which pieces to perform, planned their parts, and rehearsed. However, during the dress rehearsal on stage, our audience included our entire team of 120 students. David left the auditorium without permission and was supposedly in the bathroom the entire time his team performed on stage. He never said, "I'm scared," but his behavior certainly showed it. On the night of our show, I bribed him with a box of cookies to come to the performance. His voice shook during his few lines of Hannah's short play, but he did his part. He even let me hug him when it was all over.

During the year, Hannah never needed physical hugs from me. She thrived on finding a teacher who listened and responded both to her journal and her individual writings while quietly nudging her to share some of her West Virginia values and thoughts with the whole class on Wednesdays. She began by shyly stating that cheating was wrong, and at the end of the year wrote:

Another reason I like this is it helps you matture on how you talk. Most people get impressed on how you talk. When your in a crowd and don't want to be embarrsed this helps you jump in and say it instead of not being noticed. This is what I like best.

Students learned to respect Hannah's quiet and perceptive comments in group share, and she had the major part of a school year to evaluate others' opinions and values during our discussions. Hannah had observed Branon, a popular and confident cheerleader in our class; she wrote to Branon in one of her final literary journal letters. If Hannah had been in a classroom that had little or no interaction and discussion among all students, including those at-risk, or a classroom in which effective communication was not taught, she might not have felt safe enough to write the following letter to Branon:

My book *The Outside Child* is about a girl named Jane who dosn't have many friends. Actually she only has 1. I think you should read this book because I see how you are so popular, and always have friends.

If you read this book you will see how hard it is for a new commer to fit in and be excepted. In the story Jane is not a bad person its just she lives with her aunts and people don't like the way she looks.
Also I notice how you have little fights with your friends. Just think if you were Jane and didn't have any friends.
Branon, I'm not harping on you I just want you to understand where I'm coming from. A friend is the most valueable thing in the world and they don't come everyday. I hope you read this book.

Branon responded to Hannah in her own two-page letter. Here is an excerpt:

. . . Sometimes my friends can be real stuck up and I really don't want to be like that or come across to people like that. I feel sorry for people who don't have many friends and I try real hard to be nice to them and talk to them, but sometimes my friends will ask me, "Why are you talking to them?" Like it's really bad. That really hurts my feelings. Was it really hard when you first came to Githens? What was it like?

Maybe Branon gained some confidence for herself from our Wednesday activities. She ended her response to Hannah with:

. . . I used to think I had to agree with everyone else to "fit in." Now I know that it's OK to have my own opinion and to disagree with people.

Rereading Hannah's and Branon's exchange, as well as my notes on David and his development into a positive communicator, still brings tears to my eyes. It also convinces me anew of the importance of meeting the problems of at-risk students head on. If I do not acknowledge, respond to, and guide these students toward their own promise, who will?

> *If I do not acknowledge, respond to, and guide these students toward their own promise, who will?*

Works Cited

Atwell, N. (1987). *In the middle: Writing, reading, and learning with adolescents.* Portsmouth, NH: Heinemann.

Sebranek, P., Meyer, V., & Kemper, D. (1990). *Write source 2000: A guide to writing, thinking, & learning.* Burlington, WI: The Write Source.

Stanford, G. (1977, out of print). *Developing effective classroom groups: A practical guide for teachers.*

Observer's Form

Date_____ Topic_____ Name_____

Name of Group Member	Membership Role							
	Call Others by Name	State Agree or Disagree	Organize Discussion	Contribute Ideas	Encourage Others	Make Connections	Speak Loudly	Look at Speaker

Adapted from *Developing Effective Classroom Groups: A Practical Guide for Teachers* by Gene Stanford. Used with permission.

Content Conference Guidelines

Reader

1. Make no apologies about your writing.

2. Read *your* piece aloud slowly and clearly so your listener can hear you.

3. While your listener responds, do not comment, discuss, or argue. You may only listen to the comments and take notes. You may place wavy lines under parts the listener likes.

Listener

1. While the reader is reading, you may write down comments.

2. You must listen and respond.

3. Speak to the writer and make eye contact.

4. Respond with *POSITIVE COMMENTS ONLY!* Praise by being involved in the piece.

5. Follow this sequence in responding:

    A. Summarize the piece you heard.

    B. Comment on the parts you liked; point to specific words, phrases, sentences, sections that you liked so the author can underline.

    C. Describe how the piece made you feel.

    D. Tell the writer what you would like to know more about.

    E. Ask questions about anything you don't understand.

6. If you're feeling:

If you're feeling:	Ask these questions:
I'm confused.	What do you want me to know? Can you tell me more about _____? Can you use more exact words?
This paper tells about a lot of different things.	What is the most important part? Can you save some ideas for another composition?
This ending doesn't fit the story.	What problem is the story about? What would be a good solution?
This story is sort of boring.	Could you add more dialogue? Could you give more details about . . . ?
I can't picture the characters.	What did . . . look like?

(Concepts extracted from the writings of Peter Elbow, Ken Macrorie, Carol Pope, and Nancie Atwell.)

Lingering Questions

1. State curricula and school administrators continue to mandate further requirements for English/language arts classes. How can a classroom teacher fulfill those commands (expectations) and also have time to conduct specific learning activities designed to bring about changes in students' attitudes and communication skills?

2. When class size is increased to 28–30 students, how can the teacher find time to give individual attention to so many students?

3. Do I need to do effective communication every year or do I adjust my plans from observations early in the school year?

Staying the Course by Seeing Promise

Carole Jacobs

Seventh-grade language arts teacher, Athey Creek Middle School, West Linn, Oregon

As a middle school teacher, I have always been concerned about those students who are at risk of academic failure—the ones who have no home support, who just give up, fall quietly through the cracks, or who become classroom disrupters. In the days when I required all students to read and write the same assignments, I met many such students. Junie, one of my students who lacked home support, grinned at me every day when I gave him the novel he had left in his seat the day before. I knew he would not read the assignment even if he had taken the book home, but I kept pushing. At home, he slept not in a bed but on the couch and, at the age of twelve, he had helped deliver his youngest sister when his mother could not get to the hospital in time. After school, he also had to care for his younger siblings and fix their meals. It came as no surprise that because of all his home responsibilities, at school he preferred tossing spitballs to writing.

Unlike Junie, Mary always took her book home but, at the end of the year, confessed that she had never read a word. She had answered the study questions as we discussed them in class, and managed to barely pass the tests because they were geared to the study questions. She did not even have to read the selections. Even more distressing than the disruptive students or the ones who squeaked by were kids like Barbie, who grimaced at me in anguish over not understanding the day's lesson on prepositions or verbs. Barbie tried so hard, but often left class mumbling and hanging her head, sometimes in tears. Failure and dejection were written all over her face.

Something was wrong! The whole-class approach was not working for these students. I knew they were intelligent; they got along beautifully in their own social milieu, but they were not successful in language arts. How could I reach them?

Reflections

Six years ago, I read Nancie Atwell's *In the Middle* and discovered reading/writing workshop. I was excited to have found a way by which I could organize my classroom so that I could build on the strengths of each student, help each student grow, and set all my students up for success. I knew I had been losing many of my at-risk students—the Junies, Marys, and Barbies—who saw no value in school, who often went home to chaotic situations, or who struggled with reading and writing processing problems. As I read Atwell's text, I began to think of my students differently. Perhaps Sharky's raucous outbursts that distracted herself and others from work could make a valuable contribution to the class; she needed a more appropriate and effective method of communication, one that would bring her success and lend itself to cooperative learning. And Davy, who could not handle the vocabulary or identify with the characters in *The Good Earth*, could read a book of his choice, perhaps a sports novel by Matt Christopher. He could be both interested and successful.

I set about to restructure my classroom. On Monday, Tuesday, and Wednesday we wrote; on Thursday and Friday we read. The students and I negotiated their goals individually at the beginning of each quarter, and I guided them toward the attainment of these goals. Many students who had formerly been at-risk of failure found success for the first time in the workshop; others fought this new way of being students. After all, they had resigned themselves to never doing well in school and were just filling seats, waiting for the time they could drop out. They found failure a known quantity and were afraid to risk success. Only when they began to trust me and my confidence in them, would they believe again in their own promise.

Observations

One student who developed confidence and skill in a workshop environment was Fred, an eighth grader who had a language processing problem. He was identified Learning Disabled (LD) and had an Individualized Education Plan that focused on his becoming an independent reader and writer, working especially on organization and structure in his composing. He had spent his previous years in pull-out language arts classes and had worked with the speech therapist for the processing problem. His mother complained that Fred often began his disjointed conversations in the middle of an idea. I found that he transferred this same approach to his writing. In September, he wrote:

I don't like bush because he his raising taxes and want help the poor people that can't afford food are shelter in N.C. He is raising the taxes for middle class people because he his rich and don't care.

I don't understand even why he sent people over to Kwait besides to save the oil from Iraq. But other wise what if somebody came to N.C and sent a bomb and wanted to have a war with us and we are over the sea's He could keep people over here to save N.C or help people in Somalia, give them food, shelter and get them a life. And also people on the streets in N.C who don't have a life.

This early writing sample reinforced the diagnosis of his IEP. I could see that Fred certainly had an interest in political issues, had strong opinions, and wanted to express his ideas. We did, indeed, need to work on focusing and organizing those ideas.

One of the first milestones Fred reached was a short, mouth-watering descriptive piece that included the phrase, "steaming biscuits dripping with sizzling butter calling him to breakfast." When his classmates and I began to drool over his imagery, he began to see that his struggle to communicate could bring him success with his readers. He was motivated to work harder, and he sought my guidance more readily. I always began by pointing out his vivid images and then began to query him. "What happened first? Then what? Can you add any more? How might you end this piece?" With my and his peers' feedback, Fred was seeing himself as a writer. He believed he could write well, so he wrote every day and, again with peer and teacher conferencing and affirmation, carried several stories to completion. Near the end of school in April, Fred submitted the following piece.

When our family moved into the green and white house in Cary, we were very excited. We rushed up the stairs to the porch heading to the door to open it. Our neighbors met us at the door to show us around because they owned it. My brother and I went to pick out our room and got a big closet for our clothes and toys. Our neighbors showed us a hole in the wall with toys and gold behind it. We started digging for the toys, but the toys were too far away. We then got the flashlight to check it out and couldn't see anything. The next week we started to get one of our toys to dig farther into the hole more, but then our mom walked in and caught us. When we told our mom, she laughed, got our dad to cover it and told us the truth about the hole Someone had slammed the door and busted a hole in the wall.

Clearly, Fred was moving toward promise and was no longer at risk of academic failure. Even though he was still classified as LD, we were able to modify the goals

Only when they began to trust me and my confidence in them, would they believe again in their own promise.

in his IEP, and he was decidedly pleased with himself. His mother remarked to me that she no longer had to make Fred start over in conversations. He was effectively organizing and communicating his thoughts orally as well as in writing. She could tell a big difference and was delighted.

Reality Checks

My daily status-of-the-class report (Atwell, 1987), reveals exactly where each student is in the development of a piece of writing. When I call their names, each student responds with the day's topic, draft number, or need (e.g., "Peer Conference," "Teacher Edit"). I can see at a glance who needs an extra push. Ray, for example, always responded with "left my work at home." When I talked with him, he would say he was working on a piece, but it was at home so he could not work that day. As I got to know Ray better, I discovered that after the breakup of his parents' marriage, he had moved with his mother from a big city because she felt his life was in danger. He resented his mother for moving him from his friends; he was angry and was not about to cooperate with any school or teacher. More important life experiences were on his mind.

After much oral discussion with Ray, he revealed to me that he had seen a friend murdered on the street, and he was interested in writing a story of mob violence. We discussed this idea in detail after Ray became excited by his social studies teacher's story of an ancestor who reputedly had mob connections. However, the work never made it to the classroom. While everyone else was writing, Ray would sit staring at his bare desk top. When I insisted on his having his writing tools out, he would dutifully assemble the tools and resume staring at the desk through the paper and pen.

I tried numerous strategies and scaffolds to support Ray. He and I had set reasonable goals, both short-term and long-term. I arranged for an administration mentor for him, and together his mentor and I even arranged for an at-home tutor. Ray still turned in nothing. I tried a positive

reinforcement approach by saying, "I know you will get your work in tomorrow," but the next day came, and no writing appeared. Nothing worked! I could not pretend that I didn't know what was going on or kid myself into believing that he was really doing the work. The daily reminder was right there in black and white on the status report.

Quite by accident, I discovered that Ray was working on a poem about his favorite city.

Chicago is a place of excitement and joy,
Brothers on the corner yelling, "Get that boy."
It's a place with murderers and thugs;
At night the freaks come out and start selling drugs.
This city like every city has its good things,
Like clothing saying, "It's a black thing."
You go in the supermarket - shoplifters galore,
Like bag ladies stealing bread or more
Cause they got hungry kids waiting outside.
Sometimes they send the kids to steal,
So they won't lose their pride.

Although Ray was angry and did not want to work with me, he did write some. His poetry shows that he missed life in the city, that he had compassion for others, and that he had some skill as a poet. He has good language control and a sense of rhythm and rhyme patterns. My awareness of his potential increased when he scored a 3 out of 4 on the state writing test, improved his California Achievement Test reading score by 30 points, and his language expression score by 4 points! Ray had reading and writing abilities, even if he shared little of his talent in school.

Ray issued me a "wake-up call." Even though some students may not be producing according to my expectations in class, they may have abilities they keep to themselves. I try to remember Ray when I have others like him in my classes.

King of Africa

While Ray did not choose to write in workshop time, most students do, and many of their stories are compelling. One of my most vivid memories is of Andy, who turned sixteen during his eighth-grade year and did not think he should be stuck with "these little kids" in middle school. He had moved to our area from a dangerous situation in a big city. He had a scar from a knife wound on his face and was living with a stepfather he had not seen in years. The stepfather worked long hours and was rarely at home. Andy slunk through the halls as only a tough guy can and refused to read or write. All the girls were in love with him, and many of the boys imitated his style of dress. Although he was admired by the other students, he considered himself too old to work with others in the class and would confer only with me. His handwriting was beautiful and, when he began to write, each page was full of perfectly formed letters, sentences, paragraphs, and margins. Andy wanted everything he produced to be perfect the first time. Since Andy was African-American and frequently voiced his racial pride, I suggested that he write about what it would be like to live in Africa. That idea sparked his interest; one of the first pieces he wrote was about being reincarnated as a king of Africa.

I wouldn't be a mean king and would try to give my people as much as possible so that no one would really be poor in wealth nor health. I would have about a good ten or twenty wives because I love women. Nobody else could have more than two.

His view intrigued me, so I playfully asked him if I could live in his kingdom and maybe have three or four husbands. He grinned, genuinely delighted at the question, and began to talk more readily with me. As I came to know him better and discussed further his personal interests, I discovered that he was a budding graphic artist, not only on the top of his desk, but also in art class. I brought from home a book of M. C. Escher prints. He could not resist the large, coffee-table sized book that was full of black-and-white photographs and prose. He was intrigued, spending hours poring over the prints and Escher's own comments about his work, processes, and perspectives. Andy's writing pieces, built from his literary log of responses to his reading, became reflections on Escher's prints. The following is part of his piece on Escher's "Relativity":

I especially enjoy looking at this drawing because it challenges the mind. I don't think it's a boring picture because actually it seems to show movement from all over. This picture is something that could never be drawn by me simply because it takes a great amount of time to do and is so complex to think about. . . . It shows the dream of a twilight image. Also, I think this picture gives a mystical sort of strange look of death. I would really love to have the picture blown up shaded with a dark/blue or black/grayish like color, framed and hanging on my wall.

And this was a student who couldn't pass the seventh grade by the age of 15? I was thrilled by his analysis of the art as well as by his facility with language. It was a combination of our determining and building on his interests, as well as the reading/writing workshop, that allowed Andy to follow his own intention, read what intrigued him, and write about his interaction with the text and the art.

Collaboration

While reading/writing workshop encourages highly individualized pursuits, such as Andy's, it also provides an environment conducive to students' collaboration. One story of successful collaboration is that of Sheronda and Vonnie. Sheronda came to eighth grade with many creative ideas but little evidence of writing skill. When given writing time, she did not even write a sentence, let alone a paragraph. When our team members discussed her nonproductivity, her impulsivity, and her nonsequiturs in class, we worried about the possibility of neurological damage. At one point, early in her sojourn in my class, she surprised me by talking out loudly during a minilesson. She muttered incoherently for several minutes. When I asked her to stop talking, she stared off into space and talked about the fact that she was not talking to herself. When I later asked her what had caused her uncharacteristic behavior, she grinned knowingly and said, "Yeah, I know." I wondered if she even connected with my question or with our present reality. These clues prompted us to have her tested, and we found that she had a severe language processing problem and a language delay.

> As I came to know him better and discussed further his personal interests, I discovered that he was a budding graphic artist, not only on the top of his desk, but also in art class.

As with many of our at-risk children, family problems also became obvious over time. Sheronda's father was not present in the home, and the brother she idolized was often in trouble with police. When her mother finally attended a parent conference, she, too, was disoriented and had difficulty understanding the discussion. We were, however, pleased that she cared enough about Sheronda to attend the conference at all.

In spite of all her personal and language processing challenges, Sheronda wanted to write. She would write pages and pages of ideas—all one disconnected paragraph. Some ideas made sense; others did not. Here is an excerpt:

She also loved her bringing up becuse she had two parents how loved her. If somone would of ask her if she wanted to be born she'd said 'no!' She loves her life and what she has accomplished.

While loving your life and at the same time not wanting to have been born is an obvious dichotomy, I could see a story in Sheronda's piece wanting to emerge.

When I pulled up my chair beside Sheronda's desk, I looked into her eyes and asked, "Will you explain to me what you are saying here?" She was at first frustrated that I did not understand, so I moved ahead in the piece and praised her use of such vivid words as *tarnished, yanked,* and *clutching.* I knew she had creative ideas and language in her head; it was just difficult for her to put everything together.

After several weeks of working one-on-one with Sheronda, I asked Vonnie, who was an accomplished, gifted writer, to become a conferring partner for Sheronda. Suddenly exciting things began to happen. Vonnie was enthusiastic about the creative ideas that Sheronda, a child with a diagnosed language delay, shared with her and thanked me for putting them together. She could see past Sheronda's disconnectedness and help her put her ideas into order. Sheronda, meanwhile, began writing in punctuated sentences and paragraphs, her thoughts organized and at times chiseled, rather than scrawled, on the page. The following is part of "Halloween Scare," a piece written just a few weeks after the passage about "parents":

> *Sheronda glowed in the fact that her response was helping the class-appointed "best" writer in the class. Sheronda was moving toward her promise.*

I drew myself to the entrance, moving closer to the noise steadily. I looked around to see the lumps of grass, damp, soggy-looking ground, and the cold, concrete markers. Then I looked up at the black filled sky with spots of sparkling white. . . . As I threw my head in the air and looked back a second, a tarnished-looking body pulled itself out of its grave with the help of my leg. It was gasping for air as if it was alive. My scream grew even larger, my tug for the freedom of my leg even larger . . .

As I continued screaming, it released my leg and grabbed for my arm. It drew its other arm, and before I knew it, it tore into me with its sharp but strong and rugged deteriorated nails. It ground its old, large hands into the core of my body, tearing my insides apart. My torn body dropped to the ground as my blood poured out of the large wounds - onto the graves beneath and beside me.

Sheronda's writing was now coherent, and she was thinking of herself as a competent writer. She was gaining self-assurance with her success, not only as a writer but also a responder to Vonnie's writing. In fact, Vonnie often announced that Sheronda helped her improve her pieces. Sheronda glowed in the fact that her response was helping the class-appointed "best" writer in the class. Sheronda was moving toward her promise.

Discovery

Keeping track of such at-risk students' stories as those of Fred, Andy, and Sheronda has reinforced my commitment to using a workshop approach in my classroom. I will continue to offer students choice in their writing and reading topics, to provide writing and conferencing time in class, and to help them develop self-confidence as language users. Each of these students, in the course of only one year, moved from being at risk of academic failure to being on the path to promise and success. The pride my students take in their own growth has kept me reflecting and revising workshop as we learn together; it has also helped me assuage the ghost of those students like Junie, Mary, and Barbie who were in my class before I found my own new pathway to their promise.

Reference

Atwell, N. (1987). *In the middle: Writing, reading, and learning with adolescents.* Portsmouth, NH: Heinemann.

Lingering Questions

1. I wonder about my at-risk students when they leave my classroom. Will they adjust and succeed in situations that focus on whole-class instruction rather than individualized approaches? How will they do in high school? Will they and their teachers think I have not been sufficiently "academic" in my work with them?

2. I always wonder and worry, of course, about the students I never reach, like Ray. Will someone else be able to support and guide them where I have failed? What could I have done better? Did I make mistakes that will limit their future options?

Goals Sheet

Quarter - 1 2 3 4   Name _____

	Date	Plan	Topic	GS Interaction	Date	Page	Book	Journal	Pts.
1									
2									
3									
4									
5									
6									
7									
8									
9									

Final	Publish	Title & Type - Date	Writing Process				Skills Taught
			Student Record Form	2	3	4 5	
			Planning	2	3	4 5	
			Cont. Conf.	2	3	4 5	
			Several Drafts - revision	2	3	4 5	
			Editing: self	2	3	4 5	
			peer	2	3	4 5	
			All steps included Yes No				
			Readability & Presentation				

Adapted from concepts presented by Nancie Atwell in *In the Middle: Writing, Reading, and Learning with Adolescents.*

Selected Readings

†*Atwell, N. (1987). *In the middle: Writing, reading, and learning with adolescents.* Portsmouth, NH: Heinemann.

Atwell, N. (1988, 1990, 1991). *Workshop 1; workshop 2; workshop 3.* Portsmouth, NH: Heinemann.

Atwell, N. (1990). *Coming to know: Writing to learn in the intermediate grades.* Portsmouth, NH: Heinemann.

Atwell, N. (1991). *Side by side: Essays on teaching to learn.* Portsmouth, NH: Heinemann.

Calkins, L. M. (1994). *The art of teaching writing.* Portsmouth, NH: Heinemann.

†Fader, D. (1976). *The new hooked on books.* New York: Berkeley Publishing.

Glasser, W. (1986). *Control theory in the classroom.* New York: HarperCollins.

†Glasser, W. (1990). *The quality school: Managing students without coercion.* New York: HarperCollins.

Glasser, W. (1993). *The quality school teacher.* New York: HarperCollins.

*Heath, S. B., & Mangiola, L. (1991). *Children of promise: Literate activity in linguistically and culturally diverse classrooms.* Washington, D.C.: NEA.

†Kirby, D., & Liner, T. (1988). *Inside out: Developmental strategies for teaching writing (2nd ed.).* Portsmouth, NH: Heinemann.

†Kozol, J. (1991). *Savage inequalities: Children in America's schools.* New York: Crown Publishing Group.

*Krogness, M. (1994). *Just teach me, Mrs. K.: Talking, reading, and writing with resistant adolescent learners.* Portsmouth, NH: Heinemann.

Lane, B. (1993). *After "the end": Teaching and learning creative revision.* Portsmouth, NH: Heinemann.

†Lehr, J., & Harris, H. (1988). *At-risk, low-achieving students in the classroom.* Washington, D. C.: National Education Agency.

Mayher, J. (1989). *Uncommon sense: Theoretical practice in language education.* Portsmouth, NH: Heinemann.

†Phelan, P. (Ed.). (1989). *Talking to learn: Classroom practices in teaching English (Vol. 24).* Urbana, IL: National Council of Teachers of English.

†*Rief, L. (1992). *Seeking diversity: Language arts with adolescents.* Portsmouth, NH: Heinemann.

†Rose, M. (1989). *Lives on the boundary: A moving account of the struggles and achievements of America's educational underclass.* New York: Viking Penguin.

†Rubin, D., & Dodd, D. (1987). *Talking into writing: Exercises for basic writers.* Urbana, IL: National Council of Teachers of English.

Self, J. (Ed.). (1987). *Plain talk about learning and writing across the curriculum.* Richmond, VA: Virginia Department of Education.

Smith, F. (1988). *Joining the literacy club: Further essays into education.* Portsmouth, NH: Heinemann.

Stires, S. (1991). *With promise: Redefining reading and writing needs for special students.* Portsmouth, NH: Heinemann.

Stuckey, J. E. (1990). *The violence of literacy.* Portsmouth, NH: Heinemann.

Trelease, J. (1985). *The read-aloud handbook.* New York: Viking Penguin.

* Books reviewed in journal
† Good beginning books

Our thanks to Adrienne Tropp for compiling this bibliography.

Voices from the Middle

Volume 2 • Number 1 • February 1995

There dwelt a terrible woman called Medusa, the Gorgon. The hair of the Gorgon was a mass of living snakes; and she was so hideous to behold, that just to look upon her turned one to stone. Perseus was commanded to bring home the head of this woman; and although he set out obediently, he did not know at all where to find her. But while he was wandering helplessly about, the god Hermes and the goddess Athena came to his aid, and gave him courage for his dreadful task. They told him that he must have a pair of winged sandals to help him on his way, and also a helmet which would make him invisible. These wonderful things were in the cave of some water-nymphs, and he could find out where these nymphs were only by going to some dreadful old women who had but one eye and one tooth among them. These they were obliged to pass around from one to the

other as they needed them. Hermes led Perseus to these old women, and then left him. At first Perseus could not get them to tell him what he wished to learn. But when he stole their one eye as they passed it from one to another to look at him, they were glad enough to tell him what he wanted, in order to get back their eye again. When at last Perseus reached the cave of the nymphs, he easily obtained the sandals and the helmet. Putting these on, he soon reached the cave of Medusa, and found her lying asleep on the ground. But he did not dare to approach her face to face, for fear lest he should be turned to stone. Then it was that the goddess Athena came to his aid, and gave him her bright shield to use as a mirror. Holding this before him, Perseus walked backward, looking not upon Medusa, but only upon her reflection in the shield. . . .

Portfolio Cultures

A Publication of the National Council of Teachers of English

Contents

Cover art by Raymar Rainey, 7th grade, Schiller Classical Academy, Pittsburgh, PA

Design: Doug Burnett

Editing and Production: Carol E. Schanche

Message from the Editors

New Hampshire is Robert Frost country. Stone walls meander through the woods, defining property lines. Fallen leaves crumble underfoot on Sunday morning walks. Patches of snow lie frozen on the north side of the road despite the unseasonably warm December temperatures.

Where we live partially defines who we are. The stone walls in New Hampshire were put there by men and women hundreds of years ago marking their property. Defining the amount of land one owned, defined the owner. Defining who we are today though goes well beyond establishing what we own, or where we live. It has to do with the roles we choose in life, the friends we pick, the music we listen to, the literature we read, the way we act toward other people. It has to do with how we use time and space, how we listen, what we say, what we do with what we see. Truly defining ourselves has to do with what we think, what we believe, what we value, both personally and professionally.

The theme of this year's annual NCTE convention was *Defining Ourselves in a Changing World*. It's a theme we cannot, and should not, let go of. Who are we? Where do we fit in this changing world? Who are our students? Where do they fit? What should our students know and be able to do? What do we value most? What is everything we do *for*? We have to ask these questions of ourselves, and we have to encourage our students to ask these questions of themselves. The questions are asked with intent. Our answers should broaden the conversation. We should be open to surprise.

Defining Ourselves seems particularly relevant to those of us who work with middle level students. For years we have struggled to find our identity, somewhere between elementary and high school, and it is only late-

ly that we have begun to recognize the extraordinary challenges we face and the unique opportunities we have to contribute to our students' learning. Adolescents themselves face a unique set of challenges as they attempt to define themselves academically, socially, emotionally, and physically. Step into any middle level classroom throughout the country and see just how diverse, and difficult, these individual attempts are at defining oneself. Notice the clothes, the language, the hairstyles, the music, the friends. In defining themselves, some of our students whisper, some of them shout.

There were voices at this conference that will continue to whisper and shout at us as educators: the voices of Georgia Heard, Nikki Giovanni, Elliot Eisner, Cornell West, Carol Edelsky, Donald Graves, Chaim Potok, and Katherine Paterson. Paterson, who defines herself through stories, asked us to be ourselves. "In a cynical world starved for goodness, teachers must take off the shrink-wrapped jargon of academia and be themselves, the mythical heroes of our children's journeys." Nikki Giovanni reminded us that "we are all the product of somebody's dream" and that we as teachers are "on the front lines" in the fight to preserve democracy in our society.

Carol Edelsky, keynote speaker for the Day of Whole Language, also stressed issues of democracy and social justice in her eloquent description of what a critical curriculum might look like in years to come. Before teachers can help children take a look at the status quo and ask questions about whether or not things are fair and just, she explained, we must have a critical perspective ourselves. "Assuming you want one, how can you get one?" she asked. Edelsky urged us to become event watchers as well as kid watchers, and to

Maureen Barbieri

Middle School Teacher, Greenville, South Carolina

Linda Rief

Middle School Teacher, Durham, New Hampshire

develop the habit of questioning systems we have always taken for granted. "Why is it like that?" "Is it fair?" "Whose story is this?" are often the beginnings of important thinking that may, in turn, lead to important conversation and activism.

At the CEL luncheon, Elliot Eisner reminded us that imagination, passion, and vision are fundamental to education. It is the imagination, passion, and vision of writers that "awaken our sensibilities to things that often pass us by . . . . the outcome of a work of art," he continued, "is a surprise to the maker, and in the surprise the work of art remakes the maker. The great function of art is not only to provide another world for others, but to redefine ourselves because we are in the process of entering possibilities, entering worlds, finding things that we didn't know were there when we started." Eisner urged us not to forget why we came into education. We cannot forget what literature and writing and the arts are about and the ways in which they enable people to see things anew and afresh.

In the picture book *i live in music* by Ntozake Shange, the illustrator Romare Bearden writes in an afterword, "I think the artist has to be something like a whale, swimming with his mouth wide open, absorbing everything until he has what he really needs. When he finds that, he can start to make limitations. And then he really begins to grow."

Megan Guy, an eighth grader at Oyster River Middle School in Durham, New Hampshire, recently wrote a quick write in response to Bearden's words. Throughout the week, she revised her thoughts again and again until she had crafted a piece of writing that had begun as a two-minute journal response. She wrote:

Art comes from everything around us. Whether I'm working with a paintbrush, musical notes, or simply words, everything I see, hear, and feel goes into my work. Though it may seem unimportant at the time, things around us become a part of us and influence all that we do.

Many people don't realize the truth in this. Some go through life hurrying from one thing to the next, never taking the time to enjoy life's little pleasures. I make a point of running through leaf piles whenever I see them. I love the crunching

> Megan found out things about herself she didn't know were there before she started.

noise they make under my feet, the crisp, brittle feeling that they have, the smell that I know can belong to autumn alone.

And what better way is there to spend a warm summer day than laying on your back watching the clouds drift by overhead? I love just relaxing on the soft grass with the sweetness of the breeze and the clouds for company. Letting my mind wander, finding all kinds of creatures in the slow moving whiteness. Sometimes a butterfly soars by on a puff of wind and I get up to chase after it, following the elusive insect for what seems like hours, until I lose sight of it in a ray of sun.

Maybe one of the greatest little pleasures of all is puddle jumping. So many people forget the joy of stomping in a puddle, when you can still smell the freshness of the rain and the dampness of the air. It's especially fun with friends, because then you can try to soak each other as well as yourself. I love the sound of water sloshing around in my shoes with each step. The feeling of being totally soaked. It's by far one of my favorite things about April.

These sights, sounds, smells, and feelings all become a part of me. Even though I don't realize it sometimes, they all work their way into all that I do, and all that I am. It makes all of my art—writing in particular—seem real. If I can capture the smell of the leaves, the feeling of the sun on my face, the splash of a puddle, I have made my writing come alive. The reader can experience the same feelings that I had on that rainy day in April.

What I'm saying is that we all need to be more like the whale. Absorb things from the world around us. Notice details. Feed on them, use them to grow. Chase butterflies. See how high we can go on swings. Remember the taste of an apple fresh from the tree. Little things. Things that the busy, preoccupied side of each of us doesn't notice. But things that the whale in us does.

Megan found out things about herself she didn't know were there before she started. She complained for two weeks that she had nothing to write about. Yet, through this piece of writing, she not only provides a convincing example of all that Eisner is talking about, but redefines and surprises herself in the process. Her imagination, passion, and vision awaken our sensibilities to all the things that often pass us by. These are often the things that "become a part of us and influence all that we do." These are the unintentional things that often define us as human beings. They are the things that we value, yet they are the things we cannot measure.

Our students must be central to all we do as educators. When we attend conferences, when we read articles, when we sit in on local and national committees, we have to keep our students' voices central in all our conversations. It is through their voices that we begin to know how they define themselves. Unless we know how they define themselves as learners and human beings, how can we begin to define ourselves as educators?

Hundreds of years ago in New Hampshire, property lines were marked by stone walls. In today's world, even that simple task has become much more complicated. *Defining ourselves* is an even more complex task. Eisner reminds us both passionately and compassionately that what is fundamental in all we do is the fostering of empathetic forms of understanding that stop separating mind and body, stop separating emotion and thinking, stop separating imagination and intellect. We must realize that all must come together in an educational system that promotes complex ways of thinking, ways of inviting things that matter.

This issue of *Voices* is about students and teachers looking for ways that truly define themselves in ways that matter. Dennie Palmer Wolf's assertion that portfolios are far more than an assessment tool is one that we welcome at this point in our professional lives. When we seek to nurture a "portfolio culture," we are adopting a stance that celebrates each student's definition of herself or himself. A portfolio becomes an ongoing definition of oneself. In a portfolio culture, "worthwhile work" is the norm. In a portfolio culture, thoughtful teachers not only listen carefully, but also make informed decisions affecting the life of the classroom. In a portfolio culture, self-reflection is ongoing, rigorous, and relevant, and encourages "imagination, passion, and vision."

Listening to Nikki Giovanni at NCTE's convention, we were struck by her words when she reflected, "I am somebody's dream. We are all the product of somebody's dream, the product of a possibility." In defining ourselves through portfolio cultures, we share all the possibilities.

> *In a portfolio culture, self-reflection is ongoing, rigorous, and relevant, and encourages "imagination, passion, and vision."*

Reference

Shange, Ntozake. 1994. *i live in music*. New York, NY: Welcome Enterprises.

Portfolio Cultures: Literate Cultures

Dennie Palmer Wolf

Eunice Ann Greer

Joanna Lieberman

Harvard Graduate School of Education, PACE

For three years now, a cluster of middle school teachers and administrators, together with a clutch of researchers curious about school change, have been hanging out together shamelessly. We are all members of the PACE network, a nationwide collaborative of middle school educators investigating how to widen and deepen learning opportunities for young adolescents. At the heart of our work is the effort to build robust and varied examples of what we call "portfolio cultures." Yes, our portfolios are records of achievement and yes, we hope that they can be used reliably, at least at the school level, for public accountability. Our poorly kept secret, however, is that we are at least as interested in using portfolios as levers—levers to lift the lid on public discussions of how we can engage students in sustained, challenging, and inventive work; what we want to consider good work; and how we might promote and recognize the many varieties of excellence students display.

In the years of working together, we have learned that you cannot collect, honor, and discuss student portfolios for very long without saying, "Why, oh why, didn't we realize that you need to rethink teaching, curriculum, and learning before you rush about collecting and scoring their results?" There is no better example than that of language and literacy. Now that we have been at this work for several years, we understand what has to be in place *before* portfolios. Simply put, if you want portfolios worth their manila, then you need a school-wide, bred-in-the-bone concept of literacy that is:

1. Leaky

2. Noisy

3. Runaway

Just what does this mean?

Start with leaky. If you are looking at portfolios, you see students writing about the canopy and the floor of the rain forest; you discover how closely an eighth grader has to read a math problem in order to find just the relevant information; and you find students writing in the words of colonial journalists. You realize what a mistake it is that we think of literacy as the sole responsibility of language arts teachers. It is—or ought to be—everywhere. But you also realize that you want it to leak in just the right ways. Writing in mathematics doesn't mean a reflection sheet asking, "What did you do well?", "What was difficult?", and "What do you want to work on in the future?" stapled reflexively to each project. If we want mathematics to support literacy, then we should be asking for the kind of reading and writing that are powerful *in* mathematics. We have to think this through wisely, not quickly. Does that mean critical readings of problems to look at how the language provides clues? Does it mean writing out the inferences you think you can draw from a graph in order to examine them more closely? Does it mean being able to read someone else's work and see where they got derailed?

And then there is noisy. Just suppose you're curious and you want to talk with students whose portfolios you've read. That will take you into earshot of the portfolio cultures that generated those collections of work. Not surprisingly, those hallways and rooms are places where talk is paramount. When you enter, you are forever interrupting a presentation, a discussion, or a debate about what makes a good solution or interesting writing.

Once when we walked into Kathy Howard's eighth-grade class in Pittsburgh, students were reading their work aloud. Posted on the wall behind them was a list of their criteria for good writing. Smack in the middle of the list was "Long." A student read a very short piece about learning that his grandfather was seriously ill. So short that he had to read it over again for everyone to catch it. The room went still. Quietly, Kathy walked over to "Long" and asked, "What do you think?" A voice from the back of the room said, "What we meant was long enough."

Still another time, when we interrupted the daily schedule at O'Farrell Middle School in San Diego, students took off their free periods to be our guides. It was up to them to explain the school's unique schedule, its family system, the computerized catalogue in the library, and the point of eighth-grade graduation exhibitions. Somewhere toward the end of our group's tour, our sixth-grade guide held us back from entering a classroom: "You haven't asked very many questions, not as much as other visitors . . . or, I mean, not very many hard or interesting ones. So do you have any?" And then he gave us "wait time."

We hope that things will get noisier still. Come spring, you will be able to walk into Reizenstein Middle School in Pittsburgh and interrupt students as they create their year-end portfolios. The students may look up from their folders stuffed with math, social studies, or music. Or maybe not. You will have caught them searching for the pieces of work that give evidence that they are critical thinkers, problem solvers, creative thinkers, collaborators, and capable revisers. They are going to be laughing at how they used to write. They are also going to be figuring out what this funny sentence at the bottom of the page means: "Please include other pieces of your work that complete your portrait of yourself as a learner." But through that hub-bub, they are going to be grappling with what it means to find evidence of quality in their own work. If we are lucky, they are also going to be discovering that problem solving doesn't just occur in math class, and that revision is not just their English teacher's crusade.

And runaway? In PACE, we want literacy to do more than leak across subject matters, we want to see it leaving the classroom—in the best sense. Our three years in hallways and classrooms, interviewing and observing, has us convinced that many middle school students are in the midst of deciding whether school and the larger culture or community are "for them." Consequently, in the schools where we work, portfolio cultures are just the "heartbeat" of a much bigger learning system. Along with teachers and engaged administrators, we are looking to make school chock-full of occasions to find out that literacy can and will do work in the world. Some students apply their literacy in service-learning well inside the school.

At Ben Franklin Middle School in San Francisco, Linda Galassi's students work regularly with severely disabled students. These students have to think all the time about how to convey information and ideas they want to share in ways that will reach their disabled peers. They also regularly talk with Linda about what learning looks like for their peers with autism or multiple handicaps.

Other students are taking their literacy farther afield. For example, at Jefferson Middle School, a small group of students have become the docents at High Falls, an up-and-coming social history museum in downtown Rochester, New York. In this role, the students have created contemporary

Along with teachers and engaged administrators, we are looking to make school chock-full of occasions to find out that literacy can and will do work in the world.

commentary on social issues to accompany an exhibit of the Frederick Douglass papers. At other times, they have dressed as characters from the period of an exhibit and tried to answer visitor questions from the perspective of that time and place.

In many respects, we are trying to acknowledge and prepare for a reality that P. David Pearson (1994) identifies:

Problems in life do not come packaged as reading problems or writing problems or math problems or science problems. Real problems come in integrated packages, and they invite us to traverse the entire language and literacy landscape—indeed the entire school curriculum landscape—not just a single dimension of either (1994, p. 17).

So this issue is about portfolio cultures as a growing medium where young adolescents can develop a wide, curious, contemporary literacy. It is also about those cultures as the heartbeat of a larger learning system bursting with chances to see what literacy can do in the world. In the first section, we address how to use an entire curriculum, not just language arts alone, to help middle school students build a very broad-based literacy that is both imaginative and critical. In the second section, we see how teachers have helped students to understand how powerful their literacy is in the outside world and how reading closely and writing well signals that students are ready and able contributors to their communities. In the final section, authors look at the place of reflection and discussions of standards in the formation of a literacy that is both reflective and just a little restless.

As we worked on this issue, and other projects, late into summer nights, we began to joke. When it was all done, we said, we would answer one of those ads you see in the back of airline magazines for insignia paraphernalia. We would buy everyone who slaved away a baseball cap, or maybe a red

> *Literacy learning has to overflow into mathematics, Spanish, earth science, and community service. No stopping until it is wall-to-wall.*

satin bowling jacket, stitched in silver. The insignia would say something like "PACE? It's because we never stop." The slogan began as part of blurry late night fun, but it had—and has—quite a serious meaning. Literacy learning has to overflow into mathematics, Spanish, earth science, and community service. No stopping until it is wall-to-wall.

Acknowledgments

As we made imaginary lists of who would wear those red satin bowling jackets, we realized how many people we had to thank. The grown-up and the student authors, of course. But also we wanted to thank:

Dan Bolick and Raymar Rainey, the young artist in Dan's 7th-grade art class at Schiller Classical Academy in Pittsburgh who did the artwork on the cover;

Sally Kwak and Alex Chisholm for close reading, patience, organization, and research beyond the call of duty;

Hugh Price, Jamie Jensen, and Marla Ucelli at the Rockefeller Foundation for their support of our work on portfolio cultures;

Warren Simmons of the Annie E. Casey Foundation for funding us to work on the opportunities to learn that have to underlie portfolios;

The principals and teacher-directors at the middle schools where we work for the foresight to let teachers and students engage with this project: Joe Accongio, Mary Adler, Bert Alexander, Barbara Coates, Cassandra Countryman, Julie Elliott, Richard Gutkind, Harry Hinman, Dianne Meltesen, Richard Murphy, Kay Shambaugh, Bob Stein, Rhonda Taliaferro, and George Thompson.

Reference

Pearson, P. D. (1994). Integrated language arts: Sources of controversy and seeds of consensus. In L. M. Morrow, J. K. Smith, & L. C. Wilkinson (Eds.), *Integrated language arts: Controversy to consensus* (pp. 11–31). Boston: Allyn and Bacon.

Literacy through the Schools

Welcome to the world of learning as experienced in vibrant middle-level classrooms in different parts of the country. Meet Jarreau, Jerome, Derek, and others—all middle-level students actively engaged in this world of learning through a variety of literacy experiences in their classrooms. Get to know Judy, a teacher who believes all children deserve and will succeed in a "gifted and talented" approach to instruction. And most important, read to discover the delight in expecting success from students in different programs—and achieving it.

The classroom portraits included in this section show evidence of a literacy focus at the most interactive level: students (many), a teacher (or two), and quality literacy materials (lots). While differing in resources, products, and content, both classrooms share the purpose of literacy instruction—producing students who can articulate, respond to, interpret, challenge, extend, and analyze information gathered by print materials, oral and written communication, and other media.

This glimpse of classroom life is more than fascinating. It is the first step toward the vision of ideal literacy teaching and learning, as seen through the efforts of students and teachers at the middle level. The value of these pieces, for a practitioner like myself in a large urban school district, lies in three main areas:

1. They show the realm of the possible within the realm of the real. The classrooms painted in these portraits represent the very students for whom instructional reform is most necessary—students of diverse cultural, linguistic, and economic backgrounds, students in second language and special education programs.

2. They demonstrate that there are many ways to be right. The teachers highlighted here employ many instructional strategies, a variety of teaching styles, and multiple entrances into the student work. Students are able to adapt, extend, and interpret basic assignments to best represent their own strengths in learning and presentation skills.

3. They provide evidence of learning environments designed for students, rather than teacher prep periods, administrative supervision, or master schedules. You will see blocks of time instead of periods, partner teachers instead of self-contained classrooms, integrated subject areas instead of seat time in individual subjects.

These classroom portraits should be viewed as risk taking in progress, not as perfect, polished models. The classrooms here will continue to grow, modify, try things out. Jarreau, Jerome, Derek, and all the other students will continue to push the best-laid plans and make them better. We all need to support these classrooms, and our own just like them. Use the pieces in this section to embed such classrooms in your own systems.

Linda Carstens

San Diego City Schools

New Dimensions in Mathematical Literacy

Nancy
Sundberg

Frederick Douglass
Middle School,
Rochester,
New York

Judy Dean, the mother of one of our students and a math teacher by training, wanted to join us in First Class, a heterogeneously grouped classroom of urban sixth, seventh, and eighth graders. She wanted to conduct a workshop that she had previously done with gifted youngsters.

Great idea, share the wealth, we thought. The topic?

"Tesseracts, hypercubes, looking at the fourth dimension."

Intriguing, but . . . .

"A hands-on approach. Students would construct models with pipe cleaners, perhaps toothpicks or dowels as well."

Yes, good match, our academic program is almost entirely project based . . . .

"We'd have them work together in small groups."

A natural fit, kids spend most of their time in class in direct work with partners or teams anyway . . . .

"There's a story that goes with it. We'll have to find a copy of '. . . And He Built a Crooked House' by Heinlein, a short story."

Nice connection. It is, after all, a *math literacy* class . . . .

Judy's philosophy and pedagogy were wonderfully matched with ours. What we found worrisome, however, was how well her "workshop for gifted youngsters" would transfer. After all, how many students had she had at a time? Weren't they math whizzes with remarkable attention spans? By contrast, First Class, an innovative program of 150 students currently housed in Frederick Douglass Middle School in the Rochester (New York) City School District, is ungraded and untracked, intentionally made as heterogeneous as the population of students in our school will allow. Our particular class was made up of twenty-nine sixth, seventh, and

eighth graders: African American and Hispanic students comprised the majority, two were of Caribbean heritage, one was Turkish; three were eligible for ESOL classes, five for MAP (Major Achievement Program for the gifted), eight for special education, seven for Chapter I services, six were identified as highly "at risk"; another eight or so were in the middle (the so-called "average" group). How would her demanding ideas and complex problems play out in our setting?

Judy was undaunted. She only wanted one change. Whereas her workshops typically ran for a week, we would take two weeks. So we began one week of introductory work on two-dimensional space built around the amazing book *Flatland*, and a second week devoted to investigating tesseracts, supported by Heinlein's short story. What evolved was an exploration and trying out of ideas and suppositions that only Judy could have anticipated: a full four weeks of exploring the worlds of various dimensions—three weeks investigating the two-dimensional construct of *Flatland* and a fourth week learning about tesseracts.

Judy opened our study of Dimensions with an overview of points, lines, squares, isosceles and equilateral triangles, pentagons, hexagons, other regular polygons, and cubes. It seemed a traditional, well-constructed math class led by a talented teacher. Then came the reading of an excerpt from *Flatland*:

"Visualize a flat extended plane in which two-dimensional geometric figures—somewhat like shadows, but hard with bright, shiny borders—can move in all directions, this is Flatland and its inhabitants . . . . The houses are pentagonal. . . . On the left is a wide door for men, on the right a narrow one for women—who are much slimmer, as we shall see . . . . The inhabitants are about 11 inches long. The women have the shape of a straight line of almost no width; the men are triangles or polygons . . . . Generally speaking, the women are unhappy creatures. Their very tiny top lets them have very few brains . . . ." (Abbott, 1884, pp. 11).

The tone of the class changed dramatically. Students responded, first with amusement, then with varying degrees of indignation and outrage about how the life situations of the various characters were rooted in the geometry of their bodies:

Maybe it sounds good if you're a man who's a circle and in the top class but it's not right and you always have to find ways to protect yourself for the things you do that aren't right . . . like the way you treat your wife and I think it's just not fair . . . .

—Kedesha

Interestingly, by taking up such impassioned topics, students quickly became fluent enough with the language of Euclidean plane geometry to understand the consequences and constraints of different geometric worlds. For example, one triad, attempting to avoid collisions by inserting sidewalks in their model house, struggled with the fact that there was no "up" or "down" or "on" or "under" in two dimensions. Eventually they had to admit that there was no way the Square or Line, or even the highest class Circle, could walk "on" a sidewalk. Other triads worked on ideas for vehicles, parks, buildings, toys, and clothes, and worried about practicalities such as why there was no bathroom in the house diagrammed in the book and what the various characters did about such things. Even when students wrote scripts that were clearly rooted in the dynamics of their own personal lives, these dialogues were full of details that indicated an understanding of the underlying geometry. Here is an example from Alexandra, Ulysees, and Ebony:

Narrator:	M.C. Square's son Pentagon is a bad student but his grandson Hexagon is a great student. He wonders how one can be smart and one can be, as you say, underachieving.
M.C. Square:	I don't know how you can be so underachieving.
Narrator:	M.C. Square leaves for work and sees a Polygon.
M.C. Square:	Can I feel you?
Narrator:	This isn't being rude, it's just how inhabitants identify each other since all they can see are lines.
Mayor Octagon:	Sure.
M.C. Square:	Hi, Mayor. My son is a bad student but my grandson is a great student.
Mayor:	Don't worry about it. He will come around.
M.C. Square:	OK. (walks off quickly, then leans up against what he thought was a tree but really is a police officer) I'm sorry, Equilateral.
Equilateral:	It's OK.
Narrator:	M.C. Square went to work. And got a call from Pentagon's teacher.
Teacher:	Your child is expelled!
Narrator:	After the call, M.C. Square had an angle attack. His son went to visit him at the hospital.
Pentagon:	I am sorry, Father. If you recover, I will be a wonderful student.
Narrator:	All of a sudden, his father woke up. After that, Pentagon was a straight A student, but Hexagon became a bad student and so M.C. Square still had this problem but he didn't want to have another angle attack.

To extend our explorations, we shared a passage from *A Wrinkle in Time* where the two characters are squashed and nearly suffocated as they stop briefly on a two-dimensional planet. Kids responded with brief sketches of their own imagined experiences on such a planet:

> *Interestingly, by taking up such impassioned topics, students quickly became fluent enough with the language of Euclidean plane geometry to understand the consequences and constraints of different geometric worlds.*

. . . Suddenly the weirdest feeling came over me. It didn't hurt. It was just like I lost something. All I could see was lots of lines. One came up to me. "Kill the irregular!" it yelled and seemed to get smaller . . . . (Ben)

. . . I would feel smushed and squeezed. My organs would have to work sideways and they'd barely be working enough to survive. I would hear myself gasping for air and my heart trying to pound side-

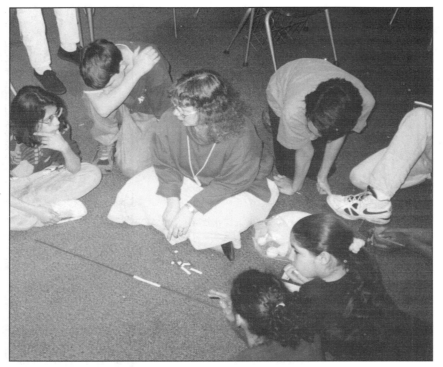

FIGURE 1. Telling the story of A. Square's visit to Lineland with a model of Lineland

ways, trying to keep me alive. I would see my thin paper-like body trying to expand somehow to pump blood through my body . . . . (Margarita)

My face was smooshed back like on the round-up at Seabreeze [a local amusement park] . . . . I looked around and saw lines around me.
    I moved up to one and it said, "Let me feel you."
    I answered, "Yes."
    And as he touched all around me, he yelled, "You are not equal angles, what shape are you?"
    I said, "I'm not a shape," but as I said that, two more lines pushed me along and I felt a poke and nothing more." (Evan)

In these ways, the mathematics became truly integral to understanding the society and the story line of the book, and the characters and their problems provided a grounding for achieving a deep-level integration of the mathematics. Not incidentally, the students' writing seemed to say as much about a grow-

ing awareness of individual responsibility, work habits, and standards, as about mathematics.

"Our model is pretty fair but I'm not satisfied because it doesn't have much detail. Now our script, that's what I like. I like it because it makes sense about Flatland and it's funny so it's fun for everyone to get to listen to.
    P.S. They'll learn about geometry from it too." (Nicky)

"The model we did turned out great. It's the only one in the class that's a double house and it looks really good. But really it's just because we all had our own ideas and nobody would compromise on the rooms and things . . . ." (Karen)

Near the end of the third week, we discussed A. Square's visit to Lineland and considered existence in one dimension. It was interesting how in this context, comparisons with life in our three-dimensional world came into sharper focus and elicited an even heavier barrage of questions and concerns. Students came to understand that in a one-dimensional world, creatures would be able to move back and forth but they could never pass one another or move to the side or see anything but a dot belonging to the next creature or object on the line. The story line of the king of Lineland and his subjects, males each having both tenor and bass voices and females having a soprano or contralto voice, again helped provide a sense of parameters and limits. The questions flowed. How did they get food, and what was it? How did they really find mates, get pregnant, have babies? What happened to their bodies when they died? Living in Lineland, the kids decided, would be far less interesting than living in Flatland. There, at least, the characters could see lines and shadings, move more, and experience more. It was clear to them that while these places might be interesting, they were nothing compared to our world of three dimensions.

At last, Judy introduced the possibility of a four-dimensional world. She began with a charting of relationships and the making of models. We read Heinlein's story of life in such a space together and for homework. Students stacked paper cubes to represent the house as designed and built by the architect in Heinlein's story, and later assembled pipe cleaners to represent it unfolded after the earthquake. This hands-on work was clearly an essential element in helping kids make sense of a dimension we can't sense or intuitively know about, a dimension that is somehow perpendicular to what we can experience in our world. The change in tone was even more dramatic than with Flatland. We all know what a house is, what it's like to walk through a doorway and enter another room or look through a window; but in Heinlein's story, nothing any of us thought we knew about houses held true.

"Now tell me what happened," suggested Teal. "I thought you two had left."
"But we did—we walked out the front door and found ourselves up here in the lounge . . . ."
Teal went into the lounge. He peered cautiously through the big view window at the end of the room. He stared, not out at the California countryside but into the ground-floor room. . . . He said nothing, but went back to the stairwell which he had left open and looked down it. The ground-floor room was still in place. Somehow it managed to be in two different places at once, on different levels . . . (Heinlein, 1978).

Here students encountered and grappled with interpreting language that described a world they could never enter, only imagine. In this way, literature became a major route to understanding the conceptual nature of some very difficult mathematics.

These two pieces didn't just illustrate an aspect of math being applied in the real world or a reinterpretation of a mathematical concept psychologically or philosophically. It was the fundamental way in. Students were working with a world that existed in language alone and the literature is what made the concepts alive and consequential. As Tom Gillett, one of my teammates, said, "There were ideas popping all over the room." Steven Daniel, my other math literacy teammate, said it best when he pointed out, "I saw students grapple with really difficult material, work at making sense of tough things. . . . I was surprised at how engaged and interested they were, with material that might seem 'above their level.' It was an

FIGURE 2. Constructing a pipe cleaner model of a tesseract

important learning/relearning." What did the students themselves perceive and have to say about their own learning during this unit?

From Jeff's thank-you letter to Judy:

I am glad you enlightened us with information about tesseracts of the fourth dimension. Next year if it is possible maybe you can teach us more mathematical studies like this because it makes our knowledge grow fast. . . . I think that the story was one of the key ways to teach this class. . . . I have learned that the fourth dimension may be beyond us but it is good to read about it and possibly write about it because you can check out every possibility and you can even make a career out of checking out the possibilities . . . .

References

Abbott, E. A. (1884). *Flatland: A romance of many dimensions by A. Square.* Now available as *Flatland: A romance of many dimensions.* (1983). New York: Harper Perennial.

Abbott, E. A., & Burger, D. (1994). *Flatland/ sphereland.* New York: Harper Reference.

Heinlein, R. A. (1978). —and he built a crooked house—. In T. Carr (Ed.), *Classic Science Fiction: The First Golden Age* (pp. 166–194). New York: Harper & Row.

Reading Shabanu: *Creating Multiple Entry Points for Diverse Readers*

Amy Benedicty

Horace Mann
Middle School,
San Francisco,
California

Goals and Challenges

How can teachers provide ways for the middle school student to complete, understand, and enjoy a 240-page, meaty novel, in this case Suzanne Staple's *Shabanu, Daughter of the Wind?* How do teachers of heterogeneous urban classes that include readers ranging from novice to expert, the vast majority non-native speakers of English, avoid boring some students and discouraging others? How do we prepare *all* students, including those from backgrounds underrepresented in higher education, to succeed in writing analytical essays, a standard expectation for college-bound students? As teachers at Horace Mann Middle School, a restructuring school in San Francisco, we have concerns about how to entice students of all literacy levels to enjoy reading, how to prepare them to pass gate-keeping tasks of literacy and writing, and how to create understanding of an unfamiliar culture beyond levels of stereotyping. These questions have guided us as we introduce *Shabanu* to inner-city seventh graders each year.

We believe in multiple entry points. We use all the components in the list below in some form each year, although we try to avoid the sort of "backgrounding overkill" that Barbara Hoetker Ash describes in "Student-Made Questions: One Way into a Literary Text" (1992).

1. The "Novel Journal," a sort of flexible workbook.

2. Class activities and integration with other content areas to build a context for understanding Shabanu's culture and to help capture students' interest.

3. A variety of reading strategies.

4. An abridged version of the novel.

The Novel Journal

The writing portion of the unit centers around a Novel Journal that allows students to keep track of, analyze, and process the events of the novel, and to write creatively in response to it. It also enables teachers to diagnose learning problems, and offers evidence that can change the way we teach the novel from year to year. As the students assemble the Novel Journal on the first day of the unit, they seem eager and curious to begin reading.

At the front of the journal, we publish the reading schedule for the seven-week unit and a menu of essay questions for the final written in-class essay exam. This way, students know that we expect them to complete the novel on time and to be able to respond to one of the exam essay questions when they finish the novel. Here are four of the eight exam essay questions from which students may choose:

■ How does Shabanu change during the course of the novel? What is the evidence for the changes? Keep in mind her actions, what she says, what others say about her, and how they treat her.

■ Identify the parts of the plot of the novel. What is the exposition, the conflict, the development, the climax, the resolution of the novel? Is there denouement and what is it?

■ Trace the theme of obedience and duty in the novel. What is obedience? Does Shabanu's definition of obedience and attitude toward it change during the novel? How does it change?

■ Compare how women and men are portrayed in the novel. What qualities and concerns do women and men share? What is different about women and men in the novel?

We offer students choice in a variety of other activities in the journal. There are "Wonderings and Wanderings," sentence starters for a response log. Homework menus include a dozen choices, including predicting what will happen in the next chapter of the book, choosing a portion of the text as a caption and illustrating it, and writing poems based on the book. Figure 1 is a copy of the "Wonderings and Wanderings" assignment sheet; Figure 2 gives Stephanie's prediction about the next chapter. Both examples present ways to help students relate the novel to their own experience.

A vocabulary menu allows students to draw cartoons to illustrate word meanings, create crossword puzzles and clues, and write *Jeopardy* questions. These activities are designed to help students with diverse learning styles draw on their preferences, and to create a bridge to the more traditional final written exam. Other journal activities include elements related to analysis of story structure and style. Chapter summaries help students keep track of the characters and action of the book. In a section called "Language Gems," students pick out examples of simile, metaphor, alliteration, and vivid verbs, and then apply these figurative techniques to their own writing. Examples from previous years are included in the journal and students vie to top, "It smelled as sad as the bathroom at

---

WONDERINGS and WANDERINGS*
(literature log)

Try exploring with the following sentence starters:

1. I wonder . . .
2. I began to think of . . .
3. I suppose . . .
4. I don't see . . .
5. I like the idea . . .
6. I know the feeling . . .
7. I noticed . . .
8. I love the way . . .
9. I was surprised . . .
10. I can't really understand . . .
11. I thought . . .
12. I can't believe . . .
13. If I had been . . .
14. I was reminded of . . .
15. Why did . . .
16. Maybe . . .
17. I wish . . .

FIGURE 1. "Wonderings and Wanderings" assignment sheet

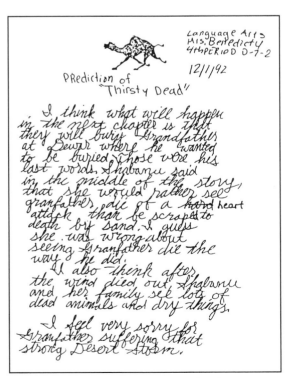

FIGURE 2. Stephanie's prediction for the next chapter of her book

*"Wonderings and Wanderings" is by Audre Allison. It was included on p. 45 of Perl, S., & Wilson, N. (1986). *Through teachers' eyes: Portraits of writing teachers at work.* Portsmouth, NH: Heinemann (out of print). © Sondra Perl and Nancy Wilson. Used with permission.

McDonalds." They enjoy knowing some of their work will appear in next year's journal to inspire students coming after them!

A plot graph, with an x-axis by chapter and a y-axis with descriptors ranging from "really boring" to "I wish it would never end," serves two purposes beyond its inherent reinforcement of math concepts. First, it allows a visual representation for words like *exposition, inciting incident, development, denouement.* Second, it allows teachers to see the places in the book that are more difficult for the children, and to plan in-class activities for these portions of the novel.

We have also added a graphic organizer for each essay question. As students read, they can gather evidence to support their essay responses. The organizer helps students structure documentation and ideas for their essays.

The unit does not end with the writing of the final in-class essay. Rather, following the exam, teachers copy examples of a range of student essays. Students generate criteria, read their classmates' work, evaluate it, revise their criteria if necessary, and make comments. Even the most skeptical students find this task absorbing. One can walk around the room and hear comments like, "Hey, this is some vocabulary!" and "Wow! If I try I can almost *see* what he's writing about." Students are then encouraged to revise and improve their essays as homework. There are also evaluations for class participation and the Novel Journal as a whole, including its homework component.

For many students, this is the first time they've had to write an analytical essay. Consider the accomplishment of Jason, a participant in a program where students with learning disabilities are mainstreamed into heterogeneous classes. He is responding to a "compare and contrast" question about Shabanu and her sister, Phulan, assisted only by his graphic organizer.

Shabanu and Phulan are both desert girls, they enjoy each other's company but they are alike in many ways and here are some of the ways. Shabanu a beautiful, curious little girl is more outgoing than her sister. She loves to help out with her dad and go out and play with her camels. When I think of

> Students generate criteria, read their classmates' work, evaluate it, revise their criteria if necessary, and make comments. Even the most skeptical students find this task absorbing.

Shabanu I will remember her like an adventurous child who loves her mama and dadi dearly and will do things to help her mother out around the house, but sometimes Shabanu can have her moments, remember when she and dadi went to the Sibi Fair and her dad sold their prize camel Guluband? Shabanu was very sad and said, "Please, please don't sell Guluband." Or when she found out that Hamir was killed and Phulan was going to marry Murad plus that she was betrothed to Rahim-Sahib a man who has more than 2 wifes. When I hear Shabanu's name I will remember her, "as wild as the wind."

Phulan on the other hand is not anything like Shabanu. Phulan is more aware about her self, she is a very beautiful, delicate thirteen year old who is very dreamy and emotional. . . .

While this student struggles with mechanics and clarity of expression, he clearly understood the plot, kept the characters straight, built vocabulary (e.g. "betrothed"), and mastered some techniques of organizing and defending his ideas with examples from the book. Additionally, he controls some subtleties of character with the simile of Shabanu being "as wild as the wind."

Here are the opening paragraphs of an essay by Derek, a newcomer from China:

Shabanu Mama Auntie were all women, but they are very different. They were in a big family a wonderful family. And they had their work to do. Sometimes they were argue each others but the still good to each others.

Mama is someone who love her children. At first they lived in a desert in Pakistan. Mama was sewing one of Phulan's wedding dresses. The dress was becoming very beautiful with silver and gold threds and small mirrors sewn to the front. And Mama and Auntie won't agreed the same thing. She work hard at home and she was good to his husband.

While hardly a polished performance, this is surely carrying Derek closer to college prep than the mundane exercises that comprise so many ESL curricula.

Using Real Artifacts to Create Visual and Tactile Experiences

Shabanu has many elements that should appeal to middle school students. Shabanu, a feisty twelve-year-old protagonist, is struggling with issues similar to ones our students deal with: her awakening sexuality, her emerging independence clashing with parental expectations, violence within and directed against the perceived social underclass she belongs to, feminism, sibling rivalry, and romantic love. But it also takes place in an environment (the Cholistan Desert in Pakistan) and among a culture (the indigenous nomadic peoples) that appear to be a long reach from the diverse experiences of our San Francisco students. For those who wonder if a novel with a female protagonist can appeal to their male readers, we assure you that the novel holds the interest of all students.

While the coming-of-age themes in the book provide a window on universal experiences, the book also offers insight into the unique beauty of the Islamic culture, and complements the Middle Eastern unit of the social studies curriculum. But additional teaching issues arise: We struggle with how to enhance students' understanding of the culture and history of the region without reinforcing stereotypes; we focus on the book's festivals and religious pilgrimages, illuminate the advantages of a religion that emphasizes surrender to the Will of Allah in a harsh and often unpredictable desert environment, and celebrate family cooperation and a circle of supportive women. All the while, we want students to see that the book captures the present moment in time of a nomadic culture that, far from being representative of contemporary Islamic societies, is being encroached on by them. Integrating social studies concepts and information provides a context for the drama, while the characters in the novel give a human face and emotions to the social studies lessons.

In many ways our students do not just read *Shabanu*, they live it. To help get into the book, we turn off the lights, burn incense, play Middle Eastern music, and visualize finding ourselves on a high desert dune. Who are we? Where are we going? What do we see in each direction as we stand there? What do we love and fear about this place? Students record their visualizations in their journal. Here is an example from Dakota, an African American girl who has lived her whole life in San Francisco:

"Chaba," my mother calls. The sand crunches under my feet as I walk to her. "Chaba," she says again, "I need you to go get me some water from the oasis."

"Okay," I say, but I don't really mean it. The walk to the oasis is long and difficult. I have to go though, we need water to survive.

I walk slowly toward the hut, letting the sand burn the cut on my foot. I get my scarf and put it on my head. The sun is too hot to stay out long without protection. Then I set off on my way to the oasis.

The road. It seems to go on forever forward. I want to stop to eat lunch but I will my feet to go on. "Stststst," I hear a snake scurry by. I don't mind him. When you live in the desert all your life, you get used to danger. . . .

To prepare for this exercise, the science teacher, Sean Donahoe, has familiarized the students with elements of the desert biome. They've seen videos about desert flora and fauna, they've struggled walking up sand dunes at the beach. He has made a database of references to science-related subjects in *Shabanu*; students can research and add to this database as a homework option.

We wrap ourselves in chadrs and turbans, paint ourselves with henna as the Mahendi women do to Shabanu's sister, Phulan, before her wedding. One class member's mother shares a slide show of the family wedding she attended recently in Syria. We draw connections to wedding-related experiences in our society—wedding showers or things going wrong with a wedding that students have observed on television or in the experiences of family and friends.

Over the years, we have gathered many sources of visual images. We look at photographs in *National Geographic* and *Aramco World* magazines and list words that come to mind. We stock classroom display shelves with library books about the Middle East. Social studies teachers show segments of *The Message*, a film biography of Mohammed (and explain to students unfamiliar with Islamic tenets why no actor portrays Mohammed), and of the pilgrimage portions of Spike Lee's *Malcolm X* . We rent videos from the local Arabic and Pakistani markets and even though most of us don't understand the words, the music and visual

We wrap ourselves in chadrs and turbans, paint ourselves with henna as the Mahendi women do to Shabanu's sister, Phulan, before her wedding.

images help us form images of Shabanu and her world. We invite guest speakers from local Muslim organizations. The difficult chapter on the religious retreat to the tomb of Channan Pir, a saint equally revered by Muslims and Hindus, takes on more meaning as students study the ongoing Muslim-Hindu conflict. In math class, the teachers show a slide collection available from the Metropolitan Museum of Art called "The Mathematics of Islamic Art," and students do ruler and compass drawings to re-create Islamic designs.

Reading Strategies

We do not have enough of any given title to allow each student to have a copy, nor do many of our children have habits or lifestyles that would assure that they would read outside of class, so the schedule allows class time to read. Following the visualizations or other activities, the teacher reads the first chapters aloud. We tell the students they are free to read ahead, but they must be reading—passive listening is not permitted. Visitors are often surprised to find a classroom of students absorbed for periods of twenty or thirty minutes in silent reading, but many of the children so rarely read that the novelty alone seems to sustain them.

When students read on their own, it becomes apparent who has the most difficulty focusing; these students invariably do better reading in pairs or small groups. For variety and for critical and climactic passages, we do "readers' theater" where students take on roles and one reads the part of Shabanu as narrator. The pace relies on the middle range of students: faster readers move ahead, interested or slower readers may check out books to take home.

Reading the Abridged Version in Addition to the Original

For the least able English readers, Nick Bartel has written an abridged version of *Shabanu.* Students read and complete work-

sheets on this shorter version. *However, when they come to Language Arts classes, all students read the original book.* This two-text reading system resolves a number of issues:

- It allows students who need extra support and processing time to use the simplified version to access plot and vocabulary.

- It assures equitable exposure to rich curriculum and avoids the dangers of having diluted curricula slow down students' reading growth.

- It overcomes arguments of interpretation inherent to any abridgment.

- It promotes high performance in class and shores up self-esteem.

In one of those glorious moments of affirmation for having chosen teaching as a vocation, we remember a new student who had begun the book with great reliance on the abridged version. We were never sure how much Jamie was getting out of reading because her spoken English was very limited. But she kept turning pages and reached the end well before many of her classmates. In the last paragraphs of the book, Shabanu's loving father beats her bloody for disobeying her family's requirement that at age thirteen, she marry a kind, well-respected, but 55-year-old man. As Jane reached the end, her indignation broke both the silence of the classroom and her own considerable reserve. We heard her scream out, "But no, this is not right! This is not right!"

We are not certain we succeed as well with every student. But the various scaffolding structures at least give us tools for diagnosing student needs and the beginnings of strategies to meet those needs. According to Steven Pinker in *The Language Instinct: How the Mind Acquires Language,* "Illiteracy is the result of insufficient teaching" (p. 189), which gives us great hope that with the right efforts, we can help children who have spoken language ability—and certainly this describes our middle school children!—to acquire literacy of the richest sort.

> *With the right efforts, we can help children who have spoken language ability—and certainly this describes our middle school children!—to acquire literacy of the richest sort.*

Acknowledgments

We are grateful for the friendly criticism and support of adult and student colleagues in the development of this unit. We are fortunate to work in a restructuring school, where class sizes are under thirty and where teachers have two hours of paid, scheduled planning time per week with creative, supportive colleagues. We are grateful for the assistance of Marty Williams of Access (a U.C. Berkeley/San Francisco Unified School District collaboration to provide rich curriculum for urban students). Among Marty's many contributions, she orchestrated the first 'visualization' and introduced us to the "Novel Journal" devised by San Francisco teachers Jennifer Sliney and Glorine Mira-Johnson. We recognize the wisdom and patience of Dennie Palmer Wolf and her colleagues at Harvard PACE in leading us to insist on high standards for student work and to recognize reflection, by teachers and students, as the essential element to achieve those results. We welcome suggestions from readers of this article.

Resources

AWAIR (Arab World and Islamic Resources and School Service), 2095 Rose St., Suite 4, Berkeley, CA 94709; (510) 704-0517; Audrey Shabbas, Executive Director. Write for their free catalog; the "Arab World Notebook" binder contains 460 pages of duplicate masters.

References

Ash, B. H. (1992). Student-made questions: One way into a literary text. *English Journal, 81*(5), 61–64.

The Mathematics of Islamic Art (slide show with activity masters). Available for purchase from The Metropolitan Museum of Art, Customer Service, 1000 Fifth Ave., New York, New York. Order No. 13-02044-1, $14.95.

Pinker, S. *The language instinct: How the mind creates language.* New York: William Morrow.

Staples, S. F. (1989). *Shabanu, daughter of the wind.* New York: Alfred Knopf. (Knopf has also developed a brochure on *Shabanu* with integrated curriculum ideas for teachers.)

The Community as a Resource for Schools

Sally
Hampton

Ft. Worth
Independent
School District

It's interesting that we prepare American students to become productive participants in their communities by shutting these students away from those communities for almost all of their educational lives. Our schools are typically autonomous entities: separate, closed, and academic. Schools and school personnel have a long history of opening their doors to students in the mornings, delivering curriculum for six hours, and then sending students home at the end of the school day with homework that is tied to the academic life of the school. Recent interest in community service notwithstanding, most school links to the community—or to any interest outside of school—are fairly tenuous and usually serve only as extensions to the curriculum.

But if one of the goals of American education is to prepare students to become responsible members of the community, it makes good sense for schools to use the community—with its problems and resources—as a lab for learning. Schools can no longer afford to overlook the community as a promising resource simply to keep learning within the school walls.

The community is a resource that enriches education in a variety of ways. It offers schools access to knowledge, facilities, and expertise far beyond what budgets usually allocate to school districts. School/community linkages also educate the general public and make people more appreciative of what many youngsters must struggle to overcome in order to learn. But in addition to these rather obvious rewards, school/community linkages offer to teachers and their students the greatest promise of all: creating the habit of active citizenship and making education alive and relevant. The relevancy issue is particularly compelling. Too often students do not understand how what they learn in school has impact beyond the classroom. It does not occur to them (or to their teachers, unfortunately) that community-based organizations work with budgets and produce brochures; that cultural and civic events take planning and managing of resources (as well as talent); that many of the problems plaguing communities offer rich occasions for literacy, mathematics, science, and social studies investigations. In short, the communities themselves (and the cities of which they are a part) offer a template for learning at once more vital and alive for students than textbooks or structured simulations.

The following articles have been written by educators who have discovered the value of teaching learning outside the classroom.

Jarreau Makes History: Whole-Class Projects as a Context for Individual Literacy

One of the sixth-grade students in my English/Social Studies block has spent the better part of a school year researching and writing about oral history. Jarreau's plans are to network with expert adults, expand his research, and write a book for young people based on his work. His project really began early in the year when my colleague, Paula Miller, and I decided that students needed to take part in a whole-class project in order to form some frame of reference for choosing and working on related individual projects. Our essential elements (state guidelines for curriculum) in social studies for sixth grade were based on the study of world cultures and the application of research skills. Our students chose Africa as their first subject of study and decided they would work toward organizing an Africa Symposium. Groups of students from our classes researched, prepared, and presented different topics for the symposium.

Having gleaned basic information from a variety of reference books, students came to class ready to discuss general facts about the regions of Africa. Paula and I, armed with a borrowed display panel for our overhead projector, took notes as the class brainstormed research questions. A few parents and one library technician wandered in to watch the new display panel and were as excited as the students to see the myriad research questions being generated and shown on the screen. At the end of the period, a hard copy was produced for each group.

Students worked in groups to categorize, choose, and refine drafts of research questions. They revised questions as they sorted through research material, and they distributed the research workload among all the groups. Students were then ready to spend time in the library. They also received permission to work in our school district's Library Media Services. They retrieved a good bit of data from the public library, but Library Media Services was an even better resource. There they mastered the use of Encarta and Proquest (computer reference software), augmented their research with magazine articles pulled from CD-ROM, prepared poster-sized visuals of their data, and rehearsed their presentations with the technical crew in Library Media Services. They interviewed adult "experts" in our community from Nigeria, Tunisia, and Malawi.

When students searched faithfully but still could not answer all of their research questions, Paula and I recognized their efforts by encouraging a representative from each group to call the embassies of the countries in question. Before beginning their telephone contacts, each group submitted phone scripts of polite questions and possible follow-up questions. Students worked with their own group and then with groups unfamiliar with their work to try out questions. Paula and I modeled a variety of likely conversation scenarios that put the caller on hold and transferred the caller from person to person. We tried to prepare students for repeating information again and again until they connected with someone willing to speak with them.

When students were ready (and you cannot imagine how many times they *thought* they were ready), Paula and I sat in on and videotaped their conversations on speaker phone. It may have been the most fun part of the project for the teachers, but it was excruciating for the students. Many students had never really sought information over the phone from an adult. With all their preparation and practice, they anticipated flying

Kay Shambaugh

Applied Learning Academy,
Ft. Worth, Texas

through the interview, only to find that they were speechless when the other party answered. Still, the embassy officials provided answers to difficult questions with all the diplomacy usually afforded visiting dignitaries.

Heady with their accomplishments outside the classroom, students prepared their research using various modes to display their new knowledge. They filled classrooms, offices, and even the snack bar with their work: posters; televisions playing videotapes, ethnic music, and dancing; examples of tribal dress and art; Hyperstudio programs on computers complete with student voices and graphics; and student experts explaining their research. Students' writing had taken many forms as well: reports on different aspects of their study, captions for pictures, invitations to experts to speak at the school, invitations to the symposium, brochures, phone scripts to embassies as well as to local vendors and school administrators, complex directions for Hyperstudio programs, reflections on their group work, letters to experts soliciting information, and memos to personnel in central administration. Adults who came were awestruck, not so much by the exhibits themselves but by the students' skills in researching and presenting the material.

In their study of Africa, students learned to access information in a variety of ways while organizing, planning, and preparing a cultural study. Their reading skills now ranged from selecting books and note taking to the more sophisticated skills of narrowing down a subject for a computer program and using general information to steer toward more specific information. When class time switched to individual and small group projects, students like Jarreau built on the scaffolding of the whole-class study and refined their skills in accessing information.

In the large-group study, Jarreau wrote short proposals and letters as well as phone scripts. He demonstrated oral communication skills in a variety of situations by completing phone calls and interviewing adults. Deadlines were commonplace in the large-group study and Jarreau prepared updates of progress from week to week. Jarreau and his classmates acquired and evaluated data routinely after learning to use two different types of library organizations.

While compiling research for his part of the Africa Symposium, Jarreau became fascinated with oral history. There seemed to be so many connections between the oral history tradition he was reading about and present-day African American culture. The histories he read were so rich with wonderful language and so satisfying to read aloud that he decided to memorize some of them. During the histories he performed, Jarreau transformed himself into a tribal storyteller and mesmerized his listeners—adults and children. His throaty voice rose and fell with the cadence of the best Southern ministers, never betraying the child under the tribal garb. A few days after the Africa Symposium, Jarreau approached me with some trepidation to ask if he could continue to study oral history. He wanted to find more than the few, isolated histories and references to the tradition that first intrigued him, and he was ready to share his new passion with others.

His study started the next day. One of the crew in Library Media had committed to assist him as he pursued the topic using two different reference programs and computer periodical catalogs. About two weeks later, a disheartened Jarreau requested a conference. He had found a few books at the public library and one book at an African American bookstore. All of it was academic writing and Jarreau reported reading the same page over and over without much success. I was sympathetic about the lack of books for young people on the subject since the books and articles did seem to be written for a much more scholarly audience, and I offered to read some of the material that night and talk with him about it the next day at lunch.

The following day, as I started trying to explain the first chapter of one of his books to him, Jarreau began to chatter excitedly. He had an idea to write a book for young people so they would not have to go through what he had. Evidently Jarreau was not enjoying our stimulating little lunch talk as much as I was. I questioned him about his

> *Adults who came were awestruck, not so much by the exhibits themselves but by the students' skills in researching and presenting the material.*

plans. How would he find the information he needed? As he explained about writing to the author of one of the books and searching for local experts, I fought to overcome the sinking feeling that Jarreau didn't need me at all. After all, weren't independence and self-direction the strategies for learning we were trying to foster?

The book that most intrigued Jarreau was published by Heinemann—the Nairobi branch. Jarreau decided to try Heinemann —the New Hampshire branch. He wrote a phone script just as he had for the Africa project and called the publisher, but had no luck with a rather brusque receptionist. I urged Jarreau to try again but he was obviously intimidated. After I called Heinemann and explained that Jarreau was eleven years old and doing research on oral history, Jarreau got back on the phone to speak with Heather Smith in public relations. Heather gave him the name and fax number of a professor in Johannesburg who was writing a book on the subject.

The next day, Jarreau met the school secretary at the door. "Could you help me send a fax?" The secretary and Jarreau spent over a week trying to fax the professor at the University of Witwatersrand. First, the area code was wrong. Then they discovered the international code was incorrect as well. Jarreau contacted a local operator and then international operators for help. Some adults were more helpful than others, but each person gave him just a bit more information. Finally the fax got through to Africa, impressing Jarreau with flashed greetings in three languages. Here is the body of Jarreau's letter to Ms. Hofmeyr:

I am an eleven-year-old student at the Applied Learning Academy in Ft. Worth, Texas. At our school we do projects instead of work from textbooks and my project for this semester in social studies is African oral history and literature. Last semester I did some reading on the subject and memorized part of an oral history.

Now I am writing a book on oral history for young people. Finding your address was not easy. Heather Smith from Heinemann Publishing Company recommended you because of your book you are writing. The reason I am writing this book is because I recently (last semester) tried to read a

book on the subject, but it was too advanced for an eleven-year-old to comprehend. So I am creating a book that young people can read and understand.

Can you send me some information on books or articles that I can read? I am an excellent reader but remember I am only eleven! If you could send me anything to use for my research, I would be very grateful. My teacher and I plan to order your new book as soon as we can. Perhaps you have some articles that could inspire me. Just knowing that you are working on a book on this subject has been inspiring! I hope I can correspond more with you during my work.

If I can be of assistance to you in any matter, please call on me. Thank you for your help in advance.

That day in class, as I went from group to group getting updates on projects, Jarreau breathed a sigh of relief and accomplishment as he related the ordeal of sending the simple fax and told me he had started work on a group project with a museum. He told the group that he could not abandon his research but would work on the new museum project during "down times."

During the four weeks that followed, Jarreau threw himself into the museum project and rarely discussed his research. He only betrayed his anxiousness by stopping by the secretary's office each day to ask if any mail had come addressed to him. Finally, the letter came. Dr. Isabel Hofmeyr of the University of Witwatersrand in Johannesburg had written to tell him that she would assist in his research and that she was sending him a book. She also gave him another lead: A professor in the United States had begun a network of people interested in oral history!

There were more letters to write, more books to read, and best of all, Jarreau was on his way to publishing a book for young readers on what had become his favorite subject. When John Posey, publisher of *The African American Literary Review* visited our school, Jarreau approached him to tell him about his book. Mr. Posey agreed to present the book at meetings with publishers as a sample of work by a young African American researcher/ writer.

School ended for the six-week summer break, but with the new term, we are back at work on projects. Jarreau began work on his

I fought to overcome the sinking feeling that Jarreau didn't need me at all. After all, weren't independence and self-direction the strategies for learning we were trying to foster?

book the first day of the new school year. Here is Jarreau's outline for his book:

Outline for Book On Oral History

African Oral History

1. How do oral historians present their work to the community? How are they chosen?

2. How is the tradition of oral history in Africa reflected in today's African American culture?
   - in religion
   - in music
   - in everyday life

3. Examples of oral history

African-Indian Oral History

1. How are the two types of oral history alike? different?

2. How are the histories related to everyday life? African-Indian-American life today?

3. How were the persons chosen to be oral historians? Who taught them?

4. Examples of oral history

Following the work on his outline, Jarreau drafted a proposal for funding his research and printing his book to Sally Hampton, Director of Writing and Reasoning Skills in Ft. Worth.

In his individual study, Jarreau learned to develop his proposals further and become more adept at addressing different audiences in letters. He organized and maintained his own files as his project developed. His old telephone scripts seem contrived now that he has experience interviewing and persuading adults over the phone. Still, the most exciting skill Jarreau acquired was networking. From the public relations woman at Heinemann, to the professor in South Africa, to the oral history network in the U.S., Jarreau learned how to gain access to information through people resources, a practice that will remain with him long after the project is completed. For example, last Sunday our local newspaper published a feature article about a Texas tribe of Seminole Indians and their oral historian. Jarreau has already spoken to the journalist who wrote the piece to get the address of the historian. This week he will meet with the journalist to compare research in hopes of finding some new material.

So, for those who still doubt that students learn from projects or that they can sustain interest over a long period of time, I urge you to contact Jarreau. He knows how to use a fax machine, and he'll get back to you.

From the public relations woman at Heinemann, to the professor in South Africa, to the oral history network in the U.S., Jarreau learned how to gain access to information through people resources.

Applied Literacy Learning Moves Out into the Community

In 1982, untrained but brave, I purchased my first computer to use as a word processor for court transcripts. I had to learn to use the cumbersome software quickly and accurately in order to maintain my client base. I had to conquer this new technology solo since there was no training available. Having made this discovery, I went to the Small Business Association, learned how to write a business plan, and soon was busy training rather than transcribing. Almost nothing is as motivating as this kind of applied literacy learning, yet it is almost absent from schooling.

But imagine what would happen if we asked students to become literacy detectives, posing questions and finding out how to find out. The resulting sense of ownership and the knowledge that real audiences will review and benefit from their work could mobilize students to want and then to use their literacy.

When Fort Worth Independent School District launched a new middle school, the Applied Learning Academy, our faculty wanted a curriculum that would move beyond simulated "real world" experiences; one that would allow our students to grapple with the genuine dilemmas faced each day in the world of work. Our goal was to develop students' thinking skills by insisting that they encounter authentic problems and then work towards a solution. We wanted to grapple with John Dewey's concept that:

The problem for progressive education is: What is the place and meaning of subject matter and of organization within experience? . . . The lesson for progressive education is that it requires in an urgent degree, a degree more pressing than was incumbent upon former innovators, a philosophy of education based upon a philosophy of experience. (Dewey, 1963, pp. 20, 29)

During the first year of the Applied Learning Academy's operation, students became active researchers. As teachers, we grew increasingly willing to engage in discovering, trying out possibilities, and enabling student research (Johnston, 1992). Also, the literacy we were after shifted away from textbooks. Instead, students used multiple sources: libraries, computers, government/community agencies, etc. We concurred with Nancy Martin's statement:

Writing assignments given to students have been—and are still, I would say—dominated by the idea of "practice"—for some future, unspecified use. Yet, language exists in a context of immediate use, exists to do something with now and is therefore rooted in a context of meaning. (Martin, 1983, p. 155)

But there are realities that mandate curriculum and content. For example, in Texas, middle school students are required to trace the role of natural and man-made resources in the economic development and growth of Texas. It was this hard fact of life that brought us to the steps of the Southwest Cattle Raisers' Association (SCRA) Cattleman's Museum.

Initially, the museum's director, Carol Williams, was tentative. Would sixth graders be able to sustain interest in research long enough to complete a project that would benefit the museum? Would they be able to turn out a product that met the high standards of the museum? Would students interfere with the museum staff's primary responsibilities during working hours? My colleague, Kay Shambaugh, and I stated firmly that we *could* meet their high expectations and asked to pilot a junior docents program, where our students would study exhibits and design ways to extend and enliven them for visitors of all ages. What emerged was a remarkable situation in which—suddenly—writing emanated from very clear and specif-

Paula C. Miller

Applied Learning Academy, Ft. Worth, Texas

ic needs directed at very particular audiences. Equally compelling was the students' realization of the varied powers of writing: It could focus their thinking, enable clearer planning, affect what people thought of their work, and help them evaluate their own progress.

As a first step, a team of nine students phoned Carol Williams and scheduled an appointment to meet with her. Students toured the museum and were impressed by the entertaining techniques used to relate information. Following the tour, we were escorted into the museum's conference room and Carol suggested several ways the student team could help the museum. One suggestion was to build a display cart that would show an artifact and explain its historical importance; another idea was to write an article for the museum's quarterly magazine. Gathered around the conference table, the nine students brainstormed more ideas. They began to discuss the display about famous Texas ranching families. Compared to other exhibits, it was boring. Why not become junior docents, they wondered, and modify the exhibits for younger audiences? Carol requested that the student team develop a written plan to present to the museum board who, in turn, would make the final decision.

At school, the Cattleman's team huddled in a corner with pencils, paper, and ideas. They went to work on the problem they had identified: the dead spot in the middle section of the museum's exhibits. They identified the topics they would have to research if they were going to make their tours informative as well as entertaining. Carol Williams offered her assistance and invited students to use the museum's archives. I taught the students how to make a timeline to establish deadlines for each phase of the project—and how to adjust it.

The students drafted a plan for presentation to the museum board. When we reviewed it, it was clear that they needed more details; the museum board needed to be convinced that the students had developed a feasible plan that could be realistically implemented. I explained that a proposal is similar to a contract: By spelling out exactly how plans would be executed and what resources would be needed, both the student team and the museum director would be able to refer back to it occasionally and confirm that the project was on target. With this in mind, the students divided up the labor. Working in pairs or triads, they chose the best phrases to state the problem, wrote a description of their target audience, made notes about the sequence for the interpreter scripts, and listed the resources needed by the team. Figure 1 shows a sample of what they prepared.

Junior Docents Project
Modifying the Docents Tour for Younger Audiences

INTRODUCTION
The junior docents who have been hired for your museum request to install an educational skit which brings the museum to life. This will complement your interesting exhibits and get younger audiences involved.

TARGET AUDIENCE
The target audience for our presentation is children in grades 1–5. The reason we do not wish to do any group younger than 1st grade is because we think they will not be able to make the complex connections needed to comprehend our guided tour/play. We plan to practice with a group of 3rd grade students from Alice Carson Applied Learning Center. The date we have set up for that rehearsal tour is January 4, 1994.

PLANS FOR CHANGE
We propose to weave a skit or play into our tour of the museum. The skit revolves around a rustler, his exploits, and his capture. Melissa goes first and is Kerry, a regular farm girl. She begins her performance as part of the diorama and moves the children to the movie theater. After the movie, Jarreau, a bad rustler, introduces himself to the children and talks to them about his exploits. (Jarreau's character is talked about briefly in the film. The rustler, Jarreau, must leave quickly because he spots the brand inspectors coming.) The inspectors (Chad and Blake) tell a bit about their jobs and also about the manhunt for Jarreau's rustler character. (There follows a very detailed account of the episodes that take place to explain each of the different exhibits.)
This presentation makes the whole museum interactive.

RESOURCES
We will need to use primary source materials from Memorial Hall and the museum's library as well as the computer software on cattle and the Texas Rangers or brand inspectors. We will provide our own costumes (with help from parents, friends, and teachers.) We are planning to ask Justin Boots to help us with authentic boots.

CONCLUSION
Our group is very impressed with your exhibits as they are now and hope we can add to them! Thank you for allowing us to plan our tour and be creative.

FIGURE 1. Sample project proposal draft

Clip and File

Reviews of Books for Middle Level Readers

Reviews for Kids by Kids

Shabanu, Daughter of the Wind
Suzanne Fischer Staples
Knopf, 1989, 256 pp., $18.99
ISBN 0-394-84815-2

The life of a Pakistani girl, Shabanu, and her family is what this book is about. Shabanu is nicknamed, "Daughter of the Wind" because she is wild, just like the wind. Shabanu and her sister, Phulan, are barely teenagers, and are about to get married to their cousins: Phulan to Hamir, and Shabanu to Murad. The two cousins live in the city, where the girls must travel to meet their cousins' extended families from the Cholistani Desert. On their journey, they meet the evil, but wealthy and powerful, Nazir Mohammed. Hamir gets killed by Nazir and his army in a fight to save their land. Phulan ends up marrying Murad, and Shabanu has to give up her dream. She is forced to marry the nasty Nazir's relative, Rahim-sahib, so he will leave her family alone.

Suzanne Fischer Staples uses lots of descriptive language, similes, and metaphors to enrich her writing. I loved this book. It will touch your heart and might even make you cry. If you like this one, you'll love the sequel: *Hazeli.*

Christopher V. Ruperto
Horace Mann Middle School, San Francisco, California

The Texas Tales Your Teacher Never Told You
C.F. Eckhardt
Wordware, 1991, 224 pp., $12.95
ISBN 1-55622-141-X

This collection of Texas history tales was gathered by the author who heard the stories from people "who done seed the elephant"—an expression to show that all his sources had actually been at the described events. In reviewing history textbooks, Eckhardt discovered that publishers had simply skipped Texas history following the Battle of San Jacinto when Texas was an independent nation. A fascinating period of Texas history was missing from schools' curriculum. Gathering some of his favorite tales from this era, Eckhardt mixes cold facts with an entertaining writing style, and the result is a blunt yet funny analysis of history.

My favorite story, "Wilbarger," involves a blend of truth and fiction. Wilbarger, a Texas tour guide, was attacked by Indians, scalped, and left for dead. His life was saved by a townswoman who was guided to Wilbarger by his sister. However, his sister had died the day *before* the Indian attack. Was it a ghost? We'll never know, but it sure was a good story—as are all of *The Texas Tales Your Teacher Never Told You.*

Blake Holt
The Applied Learning Academy, Ft. Worth, Texas

"—and He Built a Crooked House—"
in *Classic Science Fiction: The First Golden Age* (T. Carr, ed.)
Harper & Row, 1978, 445 pp., $14.95
ISBN 0-06-010634-4

This science fiction short story by R. A. Heinlein is about an architect who builds a house in a fourth-dimensional design. An earthquake sends the house into the hypercube stage, which appears to be something like a cube inside a cube connected at all the corners. When the happy new owners take a look at the interior, they find out it is more unique than they imagined.

This story helped me further understand tesseracts and the fourth dimension because when you go to the top of a house, you normally end up on the roof, but they ended up down in the garage. Everything was all mixed up because it was in the fourth dimension and we are trying to understand it in the third dimension. I think it would help the future of science and math if the author wrote a series of stories about the other dimensions because it would help everyone understand these topics better.

Jeff Rust
Frederick Douglass Middle School, Rochester, New York

Flatland: A Romance in Two Dimensions
Edwin A. Abbott
HarperCollins, 1983, 144 pp., $10.00
ISBN 0-06-463573-2

Flatland is about a two-dimensional world where the men are shapes — like triangles, hexagons, etc., but the women are just lines. It is very sexist and there are many unfair laws. Then you find out that these people have their brains in their front angle and the bigger their angles, the bigger the brains. So you know that they're saying women don't have any angles or brains either and that's wrong. Also, they kill off all the Irregulars (shapes that don't have all the same size angles and sides).

This book makes you want to find out what's going to happen to the people and you start learning a lot of math without even trying. Then, when the Sphere visits A. Square's house, you start to understand that the only thing they can see in Flatland are lines.

I recommend this book to anyone who wants to get really involved in a story even if it makes you mad. I think a woman author should rewrite this book for the 1990s and do it right. Not sexist and stupid.

Monique Sullivan
Frederick Douglass Middle School, Rochester, New York

Hatchet
Gary Paulsen

Macmillan, 1987, 208 pp., $14.95
ISBN 0-02-770130-1

Hatchet is a wonderful story for the adventurous reader. Gary Paulsen, the author, did a spectacular job writing this book. I believe it will be a great book for any sixth grader, or for somebody in any other grade.

Brian, a teenage boy, is confused and upset about his parents' divorce. He takes a plane ride up to his father's house in the Canadian Mountains. Suddenly, the pilot has a terrible heart attack and dies. Brian, the only living person on the plane, lands the plane in an unsafe manner. He is lucky he survives. He is left in the mountains all alone, with only a hatchet that his mother gave him. Brian must find food and he must build a shelter for himself.

Brian has many tragic incidents in the mountains. He starves for many days until he learns a method to find food. For being a young person, Brian did a superb job surviving. He was eventually rescued.

Ilana Miller
Muirlands Middle School, La Jolla, California

Lupita Mañana
Patricia Beatty

Morrow, 1992, 192 pp., $4.95
ISBN 0-688-11497-0

Lupita Mañana is a fictional story about a Mexican family. Even though *Lupita Mañana* is fictional, it is a story that happens all of the time in Southern California.

Whenever the news broadcasts a story about undocumented immigrants, you get the impression that they are inhuman. When you read *Lupita Mañana*, you realize that they are real people with personalities, problems, and families.

Lupita Mañana was written with feelings and a realistic style. It is filled with adventure and tragedy that keeps you reading. I highly recommend *Lupita Mañana* to anyone who enjoys reading novels that are exciting in some places and heartwarming in other places. The book is recommended for kids over 12, but I say if you are a good reader, you should read *Lupita Mañana*.

Erin Cutler
Muirlands Middle School, La Jolla, California

Walkabout
James Vance Marshall

Transaction, 1990, 174 pp., $14.95
ISBN 1-85089-969-X

Walkabout is an adventure story with a message about prejudice. Only a few decades ago, most white southerners were prejudiced against blacks just because of their skin color, and many still are. In the book, Mary was scared of the bush boy because he was black and unclothed, not understanding that this was just his culture. Instead, she should have been thankful. The bush boy had never seen any white people, but he never got scared of her or mistrusted her. She was also jealous because the bush boy took the lead and her brother started looking up to him. Nowadays, kids are used to being with children of many cultures and there's not so much prejudice.

Walkabout is also a great book about survival. It tells about how the kids learn to live off the land with the help of the bush boy. But will Mary change? Will the children survive? You'll find out, if you read this great adventure book with a message. I give it two thumbs up!

Corey Bengisu
Muirlands Middle School, La Jolla, California

Middle Ages
Louis Sabin

Troll, 1985, 32 pp., $2.95
ISBN 0-8167-0175-X

The time between the fall of the Roman Empire and the beginning of strong national governments is known as the Middle Ages (A.D. 500–A.D. 1500). Under the feudal system, the king owned all of the land and divided it among powerful lords who became his vassals. In return for the land, they swore loyalty to the King and agreed to provide him with soldiers. The lords worked the same bargain with wealthy knights. Barons and knights lived off the labor of their peasants.

The most interesting information was about the Crusades. The Crusades never accomplished their original goal, and most Crusaders died, settled in different parts of Europe, or simply gave up and went home. As time passed, people no longer felt that they should be ruled by the Pope. This was a time of new ideas. People were beginning to explore their world.

This book is short, but informational, and has both easy words and beautiful pictures. I would recommend this book to others interested in the Middle Ages.

Chintana Phetphanh
Thomas Jefferson Middle School, Rochester, New York

Knights and Castles
Judy Hindley

EDC, 1976, 32 pp., $6.95
ISBN 0-86020-068-X

I liked the book because it helped me visualize how people lived, their surroundings, and the things they used. In my project, my favorite part was when I had to act as if I was a citizen of a medieval community. I had to talk about a lot of different things like how I ate and lived, what I saw, and the things I did. *Knights and Castles* helped me to be more creative by giving me ideas about the details of that time period. The illustrations of the castle helped me to decide what my own castle was going to be like—then I used math to design and measure the angles of the rooms in my castle onto a blueprint.

This book would be good for people studying the Middle Ages and it makes writing a report fun. The most interesting thing about *Knights and Castles* is how it captures the day of a regular person long ago. Instead of trying to imagine what the Middle Ages were really like, this book gives examples to help. I also couldn't have done it without a good teacher!

Willie Sanders
Jefferson Middle School, Rochester, New York

"Christmas in the Big House, Christmas in the Quarters"
Patricia C. McKissack and Frederick L. McKissack

Scholastic, 1994, 68 pp., $15.95
ISBN 0-590-43027-0

"Think of yourself as a time traveler, a visitor who has just gone back to a Virginia plantation in 1859 at Christmas time." So begins a Christmas book about the events and traditions of the Big Times (Christmas). All the people and events in the book are historically accurate, although not everything happened on this one plantation. The book is organized in an unusual way. Main characters are not developed—just word snapshots compare the very different families. First you see a tradition in the Big House and then the same tradition in the Quarters.

I recommend this book for history teachers or anyone who wants to know about the period right before the Civil War that ended that way of life. The full-page pictures, traditions, and dialogue would give students an idea of how life looked in those days. It is important to know about the life slaves were forced to lead and the inequalities inside that way of life.

Jarreau James
The Applied Learning Academy, Ft. Worth, Texas

Life on a Medieval Barony
William Stearns Davis

Biblo & Tannen, 1990, 414 pp., $22.00
ISBN 0-8196-2061-0

Life on a Medieval Barony is a nonfiction book without many pictures. It describes people, castles, and daily living in the Middle Ages, like how people hunted, how they protected themselves, and how they punished people for their crimes. I thought it was very interesting to read about castle life, but I was very bored with the Church stuff (monks, bishops, ceremonies).

I had fun writing two stories using the facts that we got from our research. Also, we had to design a castle floor plan to scale, and measure and label the rooms in our castle. The book explained the details of castles and daily living very clearly to me. This part wasn't very exciting, but I think it was very educational.

I would recommend this book to people who like to read a lot and aren't very interested in pictures. This book is long, and can at times be confusing without pictures to help. I'd say the best combination would be this book combined with another book with lots of pictures to get a complete picture of medieval times.

Alexander Kozitsky
Thomas Jefferson Middle School, Rochester, New York

"The Hag" in *Talk That Talk*
Linda Goss and Marian E. Barnes

Simon & Schuster, 1989, 521 pp., $13.00
ISBN 0-671-67168-5

"The Hag" is basically about this lady—it can be any kind of lady—and she's a spirit, but she's alive. And at night she slips out of her skin and she goes out into the night. What she does is she gets on people's backs and she stays on them. And then she'll suck the voice out of you, so you can't speak. So, when you wake up, you cannot move. You can't get up until somebody touches you. You can't call anybody 'cause she has slipped your voice out. She does this for pleasure, like the thrill of you being scared and thinking of what happened.

It helped to learn that not all mythology is Roman and Greek. In this book, it shows you what people believed in and what they were afraid of back then. I would recommend this book for kids who are 10 or 11, but not for little kids because they would get scared. Most people just read it for the fiction or the fantasy, but some things are fiction and nonfiction at the same time. That's what this book is.

Martel Brown
Schiller Classical Academy, Pittsburgh, Pennsylvania

Clip and File

Reviews of Books for Middle Level Teachers

Reviews: Lanny van Allen, Texas Education Agency, Austin, Texas

---

Portfolio Assessment in the Reading-Writing Classroom Christopher Gordon, 1991, 216 pp., $21.95
Robert J. Tierney, Mark Carter, and Laura Desai ISBN 0-926842-08-0

The authors believe assessment should "empower teachers, students, and parents; that worthwhile classroom practices should be ignited and not extinguished by assessment; and that students should view assessment as *an opportunity to reflect upon and celebrate their effort, progress, and improvement, as well as their processes and products*. . . . Portfolios not only provide insight into individual student learning, they can also serve to provide aggregate information for schools, districts, and states. Already documented within a portfolio is evidence of the standards being met by children." Further, looking over the portfolios of an entire grade level will provide immediate information about a program's effectiveness.

Building on this point of view, the authors offer thorough groundwork for getting started with portfolios, sustaining them, analyzing them, and keeping records for them. Their description of a two-year study provides a concrete point of reference. Finally, the authors present bibliographies replete with articles about portfolios and assessment.

Portfolio Portraits Heinemann, 1992, 202 pp., $17.50
Donald Graves and Bonnie Sunstein, editors ISBN 0-685-63030-7

This rich collection of excellent articles takes us into classrooms where the value of portfolios is strikingly apparent. From first grade to graduate courses, these teachers discovered the impact portfolios had on students' abilities to reflect on who they are and what they think.

In Mark Milliken's fifth-grade class, a parent who was an interior decorator shared *her* portfolio, giving the class an idea of what a portfolio was and room to choose how to develop their own. Linda Rief feels she has come to know her students through their portfolios. One of them, Nahanni, writes, "Writing isn't just a school subject. . . . I write because I need to figure out what I'm thinking." Even at the college and graduate levels, these contributors ponder the evolution of their use of portfolios and the impact on their teaching and their students.

Donald Graves reflects on his early teaching: "They wrote for me, and I was proud of my standards. They feared my red pen; I called their fear respect. Worse, I called their fear learning." Graves discusses the value of students learning how to select and evaluate and revise their own work with only "nudges" from the guiding teacher. They learn about it—and care about it.

Reading Reconsidered College Entrance Exam Board, 1988, 75 pp., $6.95
Dennie Palmer Wolf ISBN 0-87447-326-8

Wolf's essay is about helping *all* students to go beyond the superficial to "deep literacy." And just what is "deep literacy"? For students, it means that the teacher is more concerned with understanding than coverage; that they should have *questions*, not just answers; that they have the opportunity to learn about the process of reading and about themselves as readers; that they draw on their own experiences to find meaning; and that they will learn to read "resonantly," seeing the way *this* story is linked to another. For Clarissa, it meant Mr. P. He was the "hard" teacher who bypassed worksheets. He made students read whole books—and write. Previous teachers assigned reading, "but this teacher, Mr. P., *teaches* reading." Clarissa worked her way from "registered detail to metaphoric reading."

Wolf urges us to create this classroom climate of "deep literacy" in our own classrooms. And what else can we do? We can get rid of tracking and other inequities. We can read with students, sometimes *to* them so that they can hear all of the intricacies of the language. And above all, create a climate in which no one says, "You should have learned to read in elementary school."

Portfolios: Process and Product Heinemann, 1991, 315 pp., $20.00
Pat Belanoff and Marcia Dickson, editors ISBN 0-86709-275-0

An excellent compilation of varied articles, this book effectively speaks to the appeal of portfolios to teachers. We know assessment tends to "drive" curriculum and instruction, so we are drawn to portfolios' many benefits: increased validity, student writing abilities; "a richer and more sophisticated understanding of writing"; assessment that "rewards rather than punishes" the things teachers try to focus on in their writing courses; a reduction of the "adversarial stance" between teachers and students. The authors have divided this book into four types of exploration: portfolio proficiency testing, portfolio program evaluation, portfolios in the classroom, and the politics of portfolio assessment.

One particularly appealing article, "A Portfolio Approach to Teaching a Biology-Linked Basic Writing Course" by Pam Gay, chronicles her lowest-level basic writing class on a trip. These science-oriented students did not see themselves as writers, but after reading together, observing outdoors and taking notes, and some modelling, Gay pulled it all together with portfolios; the students who started out as "invisible" writers began to see themselves as developing writers. This article truly represents what is involved in the finest teaching.

When all parts of the proposal were prepared, the entire team met again, read their proposal sections to each other, made recommendations for improvements or corrections, and merged their proposal parts into a whole. The final written proposal to the museum board outlined the students' plan of action and included a schedule or timeline to demonstrate how they would complete their work by the museum's deadline. Each student would create a ranch character and write individual skits about the characters, weaving in factual information from their research. Their plans included locating a drama coach to develop their acting abilities. They would also locate costumes, schedule a dress rehearsal, and design a brochure about the project to present to visitors at the end of each tour.

The museum needed the junior docents to conduct tours during the annual Ft. Worth Stock Show that attracts hundreds of additional visitors to the museum. Students wrote several drafts of their proposal and after all editing corrections were completed, the students faxed their work to Carol Williams. Carol reviewed the proposal, submitted the students' plan to the museum's board of directors for final approval, and when approval was granted, the students set to work implementing their plan of action. As junior docents for the Cattleman's Museum, the students performed an original first-person narrative. Each student's performance included both informative and imaginative strands. Figure 2 is one student's lively introduction to the exhibit on branding.

Students guided tours for more than twenty groups of elementary students, senior citizens, and international visitors. Following each performance, the team introduced themselves to their audience and presented each person with a brochure that described the Academy, the process students used to develop their presentation, and short biographies about each docent/actor.

The Cattleman's Museum staff acted as an evaluation team for the docent project, using clearly defined standards that were negotiated among students, myself, and the museum staff prior to the genesis of the pro-

ject. However, the most exciting evaluation was the fan mail they received. Here are three examples:

Dear Sixth Graders,
    I liked your play. It was cool. I liked Black Beard Billy. I liked the Brand Inspectors. I liked the talking cow, too. Your play was a good play. It could not be any better.
    Your friend, Patrick

Dear Sixth Graders,
    Thank you for coming to the museum to pretend you lived a long time ago. I enjoyed it. You did very well. I can't believe how you wrote all your lines and memorized them. Thank you, love, Chris

---

Script for Joe Turner (An introduction to the brand room)
by Tiffany Turner

Hello there, my name is Josephine. They call me Joe for short. You know my great great grandfather Turner owned a large ranch. Can you guess how large? (Reply) Pretty big, almost all of south Texas. Yup, his ranch was perfect. He and his family hadn't a care in the world, until the rustling started. Most of his friends had at least one or two cows stolen. One of his friends had over 40 cows stolen; it put him clean out of business. Then one morning Turner got out of bed and went on the front porch. Can you guess what he saw? He saw something that he sure didn't want to see. As he looked off into the sunrise he noticed the cows were gone. Every last one of 'em! He knew there was trouble 'cause the cows had not been branded. Since the cows weren't branded, he had no way of finding 'em.

You know most ranchers spend their whole life buying, selling, and raising cattle, and that is just what Turner had done. The main reason people started cattle rustlin' was for quick cash. Turner had never bothered to get a brand registered, which was very foolish.

He decided to go down to the county court house and register his brand, the Running W. Can you guess which one is the Running W? The county clerk wrote it down in the Brand Book. The next step was where on the cow should he put his brand? Where would you put your brand? (Reply) That's where Turner put his [pointing]. This was also registered in the Brand Book. You know that branding is like putting your name down on a piece of paper. For years man has marked his property. Branding actually came from Mexico. Why, men brand horses, saddles, and even guns. You know different ranchers can have the same brand, but it has to be placed in another location of the cow's hide.

If Turner had had his cattle branded the Brand Inspector could probably have found 'em, cause he would check other ranches and at local auctions. Do you know what a Brand Inspector does? (Reply)

Well, Turner did buy some more cattle but this time he branded 'em.

I've learned from my great great grandfather Turner that when you start a ranch, you first purchase your cattle, second and most important, *get 'em branded*, so that if your cattle are rustled, the Brand Inspector can go on an investigation and find 'em. Then you get your cattle back, the cattle rustler gets put in jail, and everyone is happy, except the cattle rustler.

History has taught me well, cause I'm startin' my own ranch and you can be sure I'm going to brand!

Thanks for lending an ear, and by the way if you see a fellow with dark skin, glasses, and about 5 feet tall, it's been reported that he's been rustlin' cattle in these parts.

FIGURE 2. Sample script written by a student to introduce an exhibit

Dear Sixth Graders,

I loved your performance! It wouldn't be fun without you! You made history come alive. I hope to see you again.

Sincerely, Rachel

In addition, Carol Williams was so pleased with the team's work that she invited them to continue and expand the project this year. Another marker of the team's success came when they were featured in the Southwest Cattle Raisers' Association quarterly magazine as well as a Public Broadcasting System (PBS) telecommunications feature. A final and vitally essential form of evaluation was each student's self-assessment. Students recorded their own evaluation of their efforts throughout the project and noted their own development as learners. Here are some self-assessment pieces from Blake and Geronimo. Each is testimony to the depth of their learning and integration and to the fact that this was so much more for these students than a chapter in a textbook or a trip to a museum.

In Cattleman's I learned to have confidence in myself, to have courage inside myself and in my character. I think courage was the most important thing because talking in front of little kids takes guts and talking in front of people from France and England who visit the museum takes nerve.

I learned that if you mess up, don't kick yourself in the behind. each time you mess up you learn one more thing that will help you next time.

— Geronimo Reyna

I learned a lot of valuable lessons with Cattleman's this year. Here are a few of those lessons: present an alternative to people in charge, develop a different way to present information, research information about the past from museum resources, form a script that intertwines reality and fiction using our research, to perform in front of an audience.

> *Because they initiated the project and were in charge of planning and implementing it, the students took responsibility and needed little if any external motivation.*

On a personal level, I learned to have courage (it takes guts to get out in front of a crowd), to keep persistent at improving my presentation, to adjust to the audience that I'm speaking to, to portray another person's view through acting, to get along with other performers/peers.

—Blake Holt

Throughout this project, students learned from necessity and experienced the same trial, error, inventiveness, and desperation that I did when I began learning about computers. They experienced failures along the way, but they also learned to look at failures as opportunities to try again. Because they initiated the project and were in charge of planning and implementing it, the students took responsibility and needed little if any external motivation. My task as their teacher was to guide the thinking process when they were stumped, to teach negotiation strategies when they could not agree, and to stand back in amazement, delighting in the emerging leaders and thinkers I saw before me.

References

Dewey, J. (1963). *Experience and education.* New York: Collier Books.

Johnston, P. (1992). Coming full circle: As teachers become researchers, so goes the curriculum. In N. A. Branscomb, D. Goswami, & J. Schwartz (Eds.), *Students teaching, teachers learning* (pp. 74–75). Portsmouth, NH: Heinemann.

Martin, N. (1983). *Mostly about writing: Selected essays.* Portsmouth, NH: Heinemann.

Standards: A New Language for Expectation and Equity

A good friend of ours is a leader in the standards movement. He recently quipped, ". . . our motto is Standards: We set 'em, you keep 'em." He was joking. But in a very real sense, this is what is happening in schools across the country. Spurred by the availability of state and now federal monies for standard setting, many schools and districts are working to set district and building-wide standards for teachers and students to "keep." But suppose we want schools where "keeping standards" means more than "keeping" copies in the files in the front office. What if we want standards that students can "keep" on using to inform their thinking and their work? That will take more than writing, printing, and mailing out.

Not long ago, we looked at videotape footage of writers' circles from two different classrooms. We noticed several things. Both teachers were committed to helping their students learn the process of peer review, work as an independent group, and maintain focus and a clear sense of purpose. Students in both video clips were intent upon helping the writer improve the work. But when we listened closely to students' language, the focus of the dialogue in the two groups was very different. In one group, students asked questions like:

"How long was the draft before this one?"

"Did you know you erased so hard that you made a hole in the paper?"

"Do you want two exclamation points here?"

"Is this the right way to spell this?"

In the other group, students split their attention between a piece of student writing and a rubric that was posted on the wall. The rubric spelled out the important features of various genres in which students might be writ-

ing (e.g., uses supporting detail, uses describing words, uses dialogue, uses suspense or humor to keep the reader's attention). This conversation was peppered with questions like:

"Where is your surprise?"

"What did you do to keep the reader's attention?"

"Where is the humor? How did you do it?"

"Do you think that you have enough detail so that the reader will understand?"

Often, in this clip, when there was a lull, the leader of the review circle would look up at the rubric on the wall, mentally checking off points that had been covered and raising points that were still in question. These young writers were clearly fluent in the language of the rubric and the young author consistently rose to the focused challenges of his peers. This is a very different view of "keeping" standards. Here, students keep forging a common language, working with shared definitions of quality, and using those standards to shape and revise their own work and the work of their peers.

There is an important equity issue here. Typically, standards are established by adults, articulated by adults, monitored and assessed by adults. But it is the student who suffers the consequences of failing to meet a standard. It is the student who does not graduate, the student who does not make it into a special program, the student who must, in the end, "fess up" (Linn, 1983). But if we don't want such punitive results as a side-effect of standard-setting, then one goal of the standards movement should be that students understand and help to shape the expectations they are to meet. After all, isn't it the student who must, in the end, apply them and, in a very real sense, "own" the standards? This seems the only way that standards can begin to realize their full

Eunice Ann Greer

Harvard Graduate School of Education, PACE

> *One crucial step in the struggle for equity is a single, common language for talking about work, a shared set of expectations.*

potential as tools for learning for *all* students, rather than simply as immutable exit seals of approval or disapproval. When we assume that students come to school with a common shared set of guidelines for making good work, we sustain and perhaps amplify differences in opportunity. We keep secret what lies between C and A, satisfactory and good. Therefore, we absolutely must involve students in crafting language that communicates standards in ways that will make them challenging, equitable tools for students and teachers.

Portfolio work can eliminate this differential access to standards *only* if we design it to do so. In many middle schools, we find as much variance in student portfolios *within*, as across, classrooms. If we look at struggling and successful students in the *same* classroom, we find that these individuals have quite different senses of their own agency, their teachers' expectations, and the standards for strong work (Bachofer, 1993). For instance, struggling students often refer to length, neatness, or the grade on a piece as the criteria for quality. By contrast, successful students may nominate novel ideas, the use of diverse sources, or the mastery of significant content. These two different groups of students have acquired two very different sets of ideas about what "matters" and what makes a piece "good." As long as competing definitions of quality exist within a single classroom, or a single building, equity is impossible. One crucial step in the struggle for equity is a single, common language for talking about work, a shared set of expectations.

In the following four articles, Angela Joseph, Tammy Swales-Metzler, Carol Barry, and Sharon Saez discuss how they have addressed the issues of common standards, review, and reflection. Angela Joseph presents a review process that involves the use of videotape. Her work poses two important

questions: If we make it easier for students to be reviewers by allowing them to speak, rather than write their comments, and if we record those spoken comments so that the writer has a record to revisit, do we get qualitatively different reviews? And does the quality of the resulting reviews have a positive influence on the quality of the writer's revisions? In the second piece, Tammy Swales-Metzler describes the year-long evolution of her students' critical reflective voices. She reminds us all that students' honest reflections are hard-won and that if we listen, they can teach us much about our own work in the classroom. In the third piece, Carol Barry describes how her students developed ownership of their classroom portfolio standards by "translating" outside standards into their own language and by illustrating those standards with examples from their own portfolios. These "kid-friendly" standards, accompanied by multiple models of excellence, then became resources for the next year's class. And finally, there are Sharon Saez's thoughts on standards. But that, as she says, "is another story."

These educators are, in their own right, "models of excellence." By opening up the discussion of standards, they each help to make the possibility of equity real.

References

Bachofer, K. (1993, April). *Looking at San Diego middle school students' reflections and reactions to work in their portfolios.* Presented at the annual meeting of the American Educational Research Association, New Orleans, LA.

Linn, R. L. (1983). Testing and instruction: Links and distinctions. *Journal of Educational Measurement, 20,* 179–189.

Taping Student Presentations: Promoting Oral Language and Shared Expectations

We talk all the time about the language arts, but the oral language component of those arts has been "inaudible" for far too long. Often we explain, "It's too slippery, it disappears, it is hard to grade." Nonsense. As human beings, we have enormous capacities to follow, interpret, and make sense of speech. Moreover, the technologies of audio- and videotaping provide remarkable ways of getting oral language to "stay still" long enough to be thought about. Just last year, I began videotaping students presenting their writing. It quickly became an integral part of our classroom system of writing, review, reflection, and self-assessment.

When school opened in September, along with my usual overview of the curriculum and request for parent involvement, I wrote to parents requesting that each child bring in a blank videotape. I explained how it would be used to keep a running record of their child's work and asked them to sign a permission release form for videotaping. I explained that students who could not supply their own tape would still be videotaped on my tapes, and that all children would have equal opportunity to see themselves on tape; this feedback would help students to chart their progress over time. I was delighted when 45 students out of 120 brought in tapes right away. The others trickled in throughout the year as the idea caught on.

At the end of September, we began by taping the students' first piece of writing, the "Interview with a Friend." I taped the students' final drafts of this first piece, as it was their first writing effort and first time in front of the camera. Reading a polished piece seemed to give them more self-confidence. We viewed the tapes the next day, and the students enjoyed watching themselves on tape and began to get comfortable with being viewed by their peers. Students were taped reading all of their subsequent major pieces of writing. Each time, we viewed them afterwards. As students gained confidence, I began to ask questions and to model feedback. Gradually, the students took over the role of giving feedback, in writing and on the tapes. A system began to emerge.

In this system, the discussion was crucial and came first. Whenever a writing assignment or project was introduced, we talked as a class about what it would take to produce an excellent piece. We generated a list of criteria on a piece of poster board and kept it on the wall so that students could refer to it during their writing. Discussions like this helped ensure that all of my students were working toward a common definition of excellence. The list of characteristics for the myth that the students wrote in March included originality/creativity, meaningful dialogue, character development, organization, and a lesson or moral at the end. Of course, we expect to edit for mechanics as part of the writing process.

Over time, students began to internalize these characteristics. I began to see these criteria used when students reviewed one another's work. It was not unusual to overhear one student say to another, "You need better dialogue for Zeus here" or "Your moral is hard to understand, what does it mean?" Gone were the loose, bland comments like "Okay" or "Fix your sloppy handwriting."

The next step was to videotape feedback that followed students' readings of their drafts. This way, student writers would have those comments on tape immediately, giving them the luxury of viewing reviewers' sug-

Angela Joseph

Schiller Classical Academy, Pittsburgh, Pennsylvania

gestions again in school or at home, alone or with parents. Comments on tape seemed to be more meaningful than written comments on a peer feedback form that may just be filed away in a writing folder. The opportunity to take a tape home to watch in private or to share with parents really appealed to my students. Oral presentations were a new challenge for many of the children, and even though most students love to share out loud, hearing a room full of your peers offer critical feedback can be touch and go at first. Many students preferred sharing their oral presentations with their parents before or instead of with the rest of the class. This strategy let students choose the audience for their work at various times throughout the process of a piece. I make a point to ask for permission from the reader/writer to use a video with other classes.

Self-assessment became another element in our system, and our classroom criteria for excellence showed up again here. As students discovered the usefulness of their peers' comments, they identified a desired area for improvement, such as writing or speaking. They noted this focus area on an index card, and shared it with their parents as they practiced at home. Then we listened for improvement in that area when they videotaped their next draft. Based on their new tape, students decided whether their focus area was improved or needed more work.

The tapes became a great method of giving feedback to (and getting it *from*) parents as well. It had been our custom for parents to read their student's drafts and respond to questions about content, organization, and structure using the Parent Feedback Forms I had provided. When parents began to view their child's presentations on tape, these forms took on new life. In addition to their comments about their student's writing, parents began to volunteer comments about the children's oral performances. For example, one parent wrote a note on his child's index card explaining that he had never really listened to his child read her writing aloud and that he was "surprised at what a good little writer" she was;

another noticed some poor speech habits and began to practice with her child at home before presentations. The extra attention was a great help.

With student permission, we began selecting some of the tapes as models of our classroom standards and criteria. We worked together to choose examples of what to do or not to do as writers and speakers. These discussions let my students refine their criteria and learn about how to give feedback. It became quite clear which students were strong presenters of their writing and which were in need of improvement, and why. As viewers, the students were very frank in their appraisals of the speakers. In fact, we had to have a few discussions on how to give positively worded, "friendly" feedback, and how to appreciate that their fellow students had put themselves "on the line" as models for the class. The majority of students handled this with great finesse. They recognized that their tapes might be the models for discussion next time around!

Discussions around videotapes helped my students realize that many students, not just themselves, struggle with the challenges of becoming a strong oral presenter. Students relish the opportunity to act as "critical friends" for one another. (One girl liked that role so much, she began speaking up after every student was taped. Eventually, other students told her to, "Cool it, and give somebody else a chance!") Most students noticed gradual improvements in classmates who were focusing on a specific area. These students had begun to learn from each other; I was often simply "the lady with the video camera."

As they gave feedback both on tape and in writing, students gained proficiency in using the language of our "home-made rubrics." Finished pieces were often evaluated using rubric rating forms that grew out of our conversations about the criteria for success on an assignment. Figure 1 shows a class-generated "Myth Rating Form"; Figure 2, the "Oral Presentation Form," was adapted from the Arts PROPEL Writing Rubric by Kathryn Howard's class at Reizenstein Middle School in Pittsburgh.

> *Oral presentations were a new challenge for many of the children, and even though most students love to share out loud, hearing a room full of your peers offer critical feedback can be touch and go at first.*

As the school year progressed and students began to internalize the language of the speaking and writing processes, their reflections included more and more language from rubrics and elements of criteria they had generated. For example:

I kind of struggled with the type of myth I was going to write. In my myth, I didn't want to put a god or goddess in my myth. I wanted just humans in my myth. But I had to add them and it was hard. . . .

—Milea

I think this piece of writing met the criteria because I did a lot of revision and reflection. I changed a lot of paragraphs. I made some shorter and some longer. I changed some of the dialogue in this piece of writing. . . . I changed things in each draft that I wrote. . . . I think i did especially well drawing my pictures, writing dialogue and coming up with a lesson for my myth.

—Anonymous

. . . before, I didn't have good dialogue and had a lot of run on sentences. . . . In this piece I use good dialogue and many paragraphs. Now I know how to give and take feedback and do revision. . . . I really learned how to work in a dialogue. I'm a better writer because I can write longer and better thoughts.

—James

In this piece, I spent a long time thinking of the myth. This piece has great dialogue. It shows a lot of growth in my writing ability and is different than most of my writing so far because it has Gods, Goddess, dialogue and chapters. I have many drafts of my myth. This is the best piece I ever wrote.

—Jennifer

I analyzed it. I did three different rough drafts. The first draft I simply wrote sentences that didn't have any structure to them. Then in my second draft, I used paragraphing. My third draft I changed the words around and in the final copy, I made them not so bunched up like run ons.

—Shelly

Suggestions from peers for revision also became more specific and discerning. For example, as my students listened and observed oral presentations, they identified errors or inconsistencies in story lines and characters that they (or I) might have missed in reading through a draft (or in my case, 120 drafts).

Myth Rating Form

1 - 5 points each

Does this myth have:

Creativity?

A universal theme or lesson?

Character development?

Meaningful (deep) dialogue?

Figurative language?

Audience appeal/appropriateness?

Organization?

Student Voice?

Other_____?

FIGURE 1. The Myth Rating Form was developed by students from class discussion.

Oral Presentation Rating Form

Contents of Presentation:

Meets a worthwhile challenge

Fulfills the task

Is appropriate for the audience

Establishes and maintains a purpose

Is aware of the needs of the audience (organization, development, use of detail)

Content Performance Rating (6 point scale from no evidence to outstanding performance)

Style of Presentation:

Engages and holds the attention of the audience

Demonstrates a smooth and flowing command of the language

Is aware of the needs of the audience

Fulfills the task

Presentation Performance Rating (6 point scale from no evidence to outstanding performance)

The Process of Public Speaking:

Projects the voice

Maintains eye contact with the audience

Speaks clearly

Public Speaking Performance Rating (6 point scale from no evidence to outstanding performance)

FIGURE 2. The Oral Presentation Rating Form, based on a previously published rubric, was adapted and used by students.

The opportunity to rewind or re-view made us all more astute "critical friends." Students could stop the tape, for instance, look on the wall chart listing criteria for that project, and relate a problem specifically to one or two of the standards that we had set for that task. It was so much easier to make the connection and see what was missing or inconsistent. Students could spot a haiku with way too many syllables, or a character in someone's myth whose age or place of origin just didn't make sense. This was also the case for the writers, the consumers of our feedback. Students tended to elaborate more on tape than they did when they were asked to write their responses to drafts on the Peer Response Feedback Forms. Hence, young writers got more elaborate and helpful feedback that focused on the shared criteria on our class wall charts. As a writer worked to revise a piece, having a tape of such focused peer responses was a welcome resource.

Our videotaped review system had an additional, unanticipated benefit. My students' work as writers and readers, and their experiences as self-assessors and critical friends prepared them well for another performance, their End-of-the-Year Exit Exhibitions. This was our school's first attempt at year-end portfolio exhibitions. Based on their taping experiences, my students were quite comfortable with the prospect of orally delivering a 5–10-minute presentation of their Portfolio Selections. They did not seem to mind being viewed by a panel and videotaped. Students had two weeks to prepare their Exit Presentations, but we had really been getting ready since that day in September when we sat down as a group and had our first discussion about standards and criteria.

Don't Just Sit There. Talk to Me! Helping Students Find Their Voices

I think this piece was a good piece. I liked it from all the other pieces.

—Chintana

On the first day of class, I tell my sixth-grade students, "This year is going to be a time for you to think and write about what you do in this classroom. I will ask you to reflect on what you have learned from doing a particular activity. Your reflections will help both of us decide what succeeds, and what is frustrating."

Reflecting or writing about themselves and their work critically was something my students had little or no experience doing. As a result, I wasn't getting the range and depth of response I wanted. Where was their insight? Where was each individual voice telling me truths I had not heard? I believed that by encouraging my students to think and write critically about themselves, their work, and their learning, I would open the door to self-reflection and introspection. I was surprised to learn that providing opportunities for student reflection forced important issues for me as a teacher as well. Looking back at what was successful is something everyone does—particularly teachers. As I began to look back at student responses, I discovered a powerful resource for professional growth—my students!

Every school day, my students and I share our self-contained classroom; they know what works and doesn't work, and what keeps them engaged. But I had to help them find the language they needed to reflect. Once they began to acquire that language, and as I began listening to their reflections, my own learning began. As my students learned not to be afraid of asking for what they wanted and needed in the classroom, I used their new-found voices to guide my efforts toward a more reflective and adaptive teaching environment.

It is hard and confusing when you learn something on the board and it goes by so quickly. This is an imperfect project. I learned that math is so hard when you don't get something, and sometimes confusing.

—Jamie

If we are going to ask our students hard questions, and we expect them to be honest, we have to be open enough to accept and act on their frank responses. Students can be insightful if given the proper encouragement. They have to know that it's okay to be truthful; that they can say what's on their minds in terms of education.

I hated this activity because I didn't understand what we had to do. . . .

—Jenny

Allowing students to become partners in the learning process has to include letting them ask why they have to learn about certain things, why they need to complete a project, etc.

I would like to change the language I take because it doesn't make sense to me. I wanted Spanish and instead I have to take Latin. Why?

—Elizabeth

As adults, we demand to know why we have to do certain things. Don't students have the same right? Sometimes, as human beings, we don't have the answers. Luckily, life is a learning process. That's the message I try to communicate to my students.

It is a struggle for students to find language for what they inherently know about the ways they learn and engage. Students are not comfortable looking inside themselves for answers. "No one ever asked us to write about that before," each class says predictably. Students have to start somewhere, and saying "I liked it because I worked hard

Tammy Swales-Metzler

Thomas Jefferson Middle School, Rochester, New York

on it" is all they know how to say at first. True introspection involves teaching them the vocabulary, providing them with models, and practicing the vocabulary, so that everyone begins to speak the same language. I work with my students on this through teacher-directed, whole-class discussions that are centered around a particular word or concept. Students examine and use their own language to define a word from their own experience. For example:

Quality: What does it mean?
    More value
    Worth something
    To take pride in something
What makes Quality schoolwork?
    Feeling satisfaction about it
    The product isn't boring
    Putting a lot of hard work into it
    Really try
    Not always your best work

I extend these class discussions over the course of the first two months of school so that students have a chance to practice the language of reflection and make it their own. Convincing these grumbling skeptics of the value of self-reflection, however, takes me almost the entire year.

Throughout the year, I keep insisting that students take an active role in their education. When they dig their heels in, I push and ask them more questions. "Why don't you like this? What would make it better? What have you learned?"

What would I change and why? I would change the math we do. You probably know why, because I stink at math. I never can do it. I would change it to my convenience—real easy math, not hard.

—Jamie

Discovery (a medieval study) was a fun project to do. When we had to write a character diary, I thought it was too structured. It is a good idea (writing a diary about the same event for two separate medieval characters), but would have been better in a story.

—Alex

The process is not easy and demands perseverance, modeling, and encouragement of my students to take greater risks. I regularly hold whole-class discussions around what

makes a "good" piece of work. I ask for examples of both good and not-so-good work. I keep pushing, asking "What's the difference?" "Show me!"

I think this piece is better than all of the other ones I wrote. I learned that it is not how many words you write, it's what you write.

—Jamie

I wage an ongoing battle against students' beliefs that education is a collection of correct answers, and that defining quality is my job. They are convinced that there is only one right answer for every question, particularly inside the four walls of the classroom.

If I could've practiced just a little harder for the chapter 5 math test I could have gotten over an 85%.

—Bobby

After a cooperative activity that first day, I ask students to take out paper and answer reflective questions. They look at me with such bewilderment, I have to resist the temptation to reach up and see if I've sprouted a second head. But because the educational system has taught them to obey the teacher, they get out their paper and begin to write.

"Why was it unsatisfying for you?"
"It was boring."
"It was sloppy."
"If the grade had been higher then I would have been satisfied."

As I have watched my students struggle to become reflective, I have learned that writing and thinking-while-writing are two different things. That first day, first week, first two months of school, my students *think* very little. They respond with the first idea that occurs to them. They spend more time second-guessing what they think I want to hear than they do thinking of themselves as experts on their own learning. For example, in his first reflection, Alex wrote:

I like this piece because it took me a long time to write it, and it turned out to be very nice and neat. I like this piece because it taught me about what I wrote and how it's supposed to be written. It's really nice making projects and learning how they work.

> As I have watched my students struggle to become reflective, I have learned that writing and thinking-while-writing are two different things.

Alex was giving me the answers he thought I wanted to hear. By the end of the year, Alex—the thoughtful, reflective person—came shining through:

If I had the chance to change anything about this past year, it would be that I wouldn't take it such for granted. I would try to think for my future and try to get as much education as I could. I would also care about my work more. I don't like it (my previous work) now, because the work doesn't (for me) show much effort. I wish I knew what I know now earlier.

Self-reflection is a learning process. It is not just having the language, it is about engaging in a process. Clearly, it is not mastered in one attempt—a hard lesson for students. To help them see this, I ask them to complete three introspective reflections over the course of the school year: one in late October, one in March, and one at the end of the school year. These reflections are not a graded assignment, but they are required and must be included in their final showcase portfolio. They supplement the curriculum-driven reflections they complete almost daily.

For each reflection, I ask students to respond, as specifically as possible, to variations of the same questions: "What did you learn?" "What were your successes?" "What were the challenges?" "What would you change and why?" "How have you grown as a student and an individual?" "What do you need to focus on?" and "What are your goals?" I guide students through each question, and we talk about what in-depth responses might look like. We examine the language. Students offer suggestions for each question, and as we record them, each idea leads to something deeper. It's very important that students have time to listen to one another and to think out loud about their experiences. I take the time to model and discuss the reflection process with them, to tell them of its importance, and to reassure them that they can express themselves honestly and concisely. This think-aloud time is an opportunity for them to practice the process, and for me to act as mentor and coach.

After we talk about the reflection as a whole group, I give students time to look through their portfolios, and to begin developing strategies for organizing their reflective writing. I treat each of these reflections as independent work. I am very definite about deadlines (usually two weeks), and students are expected to come to me for as

much or as little help as they need. The first two reflections require a lot of class discussion and individual help. The third is almost completely independent. Students have the tools they need by year's end to express their thoughts and ideas.

I think the most important thing I learned this year was learning about Chernobyl. I am really glad that I learned about Chernobyl, because when I first got the assignment I said, "I can never do this stupid report." When I was almost done with it I was very happy. I regret what I said about it in the beginning. (that I couldn't do this "stupid report")

—Jenny

These reflections give students a point of entry for talking about their school year and their learning process. More than anything else, they are extremely persuasive indi-

cators of individual student growth over time. When I lay the three reflections side by side, I see concrete evidence of critical thinking development; I see students struggling to express the evidence of their learning; I see students going beyond what is happening in the classroom to think about what learning means to them as individuals, as learners, and as interpreters of their own worlds. When students have the language, understand the process, and begin to reflect on their learning, they surprise themselves with what they know and what they are capable of. They discover that they really do know what they want to learn, and what they need to do to be successful. Math, Social Studies, Science, and English all come under student scrutiny.

In math group, we had to work together doing a tangram. I didn't like my group but I had no choice but to work with them. I realized that I am not an easy person to work with. I also realized that I tend to give up quickly. When I am in that situation my brain does not function. What made it difficult was that I didn't look at all the different ways I could do it.

—Chintana

About halfway through the school year, the conversations and practice begin to pay off. Reflections show signs of students thinking for themselves about what is valuable and necessary. Their reflections become more introspective. Instead of focusing on external

causes for success or failure, my students begin to look at the process they went through that was unique to themselves.

The most important thing I learned is not about learning, but to think about my future. I used to just come to school and learn, go home and wait until the next school day. In the meantime I was hearing people tell me to think about my future. I thought it would come to me. I have changed now. I think if I think about my future, I will be much stronger when I'll have a chance to bring it alive.

—Alex

I didn't have to tell students what was good or not so good about an experience. Eleven- and twelve-year-olds are in a critical period and can see for themselves with far-reaching clarity.

The most serious thing I did was to make my castle floor plan. I had to create a scale and measure to find the exact area of each room and building in the blue print. Studying about the Dark and Middle Ages was challenging. It was hard to understand some of the things and to find information about the people and how they lived back then.

—Charley

At the end of a year of reflecting, students could diagnose what caused success or failure, what "turned them on" to learning, and what techniques they used to solve problems. This skill grew out of whole-group discussions, shared examinations and debates about work, and modeling and practice.

I'm a very creative person, and I like to show what I can do with a piece of paper and a pen. My work was done carefully and I was very committed to it. I created a cartoony character for my book. I consider it my best piece—the text was great. I modeled the book after some kids on my street. At first I thought the book was plain and boring, so I added humor to break it up. I've become a lot better writer and editor. I've become successful because I try to be more serious (about my work), and to not make a big deal out of it.

—Willie

Using language and writing as a tool to promote reflection and literacy across disciplines in my classroom has been extraordinarily powerful. I use students' reflections to show my students that they have power, that they have indeed been successful, and can and will go on being successful as they continue on their quest for knowledge.

If we don't ask the questions, and give students the language and the chance to give us their own individual answers, then we deny ourselves the opportunity to grow as professionals. We also stop short of giving students the voice and the vision they need to look at themselves as individuals and learners. Tiffany's year-end reflection is its own vision of what is possible:

I learned how to make blue prints of a castle. I know how to do math better. I learned to keep calm and not yell. I now know a little bit of Latin, science, and cooking with groups. I learned a lot about the Medieval Ages and about the Egyptians. I learned how to use a Macintosh and an Apple computer and printer. I learned how to make games out of wood. I learned how to make a book, and a nice report. I learned how to use a mouse and a Powerbook. I learned how to swim in the deep end. I also learned that it takes time to do something hard. I learned how to write about myself and my family. I learned it takes time to be a good student.

Swales-Metzler / Don't Just Sit There. Talk to Me! Helping Students Find Their Voices

37

Putting Standards in Their Own Words

Carol Barry

Muirlands Middle
School, La Jolla,
California

Imagine my state when, after a half year of portfolio work, Natalie, a student in my sixth-grade classroom, told an interviewer that she frankly didn't understand how to choose what went into her portfolio. I felt exhausted, and a little surprised. For three years, I had struggled, along with my team members at Muirlands Middle School, to develop a strong portfolio system. Students had copies of the criteria attached to their portfolios at the beginning of the year, and we were constantly working in the work folders and the portfolios. I had reviewed our criteria with parents at open-house and had ongoing conversations with parents and students about the criteria for selections for this very reason. Natalie and her classmates had made at least two selections for their portfolios. So how could Natalie fail to get it?

What Natalie taught me is that students need to use their own language to set standards, select work, and reflect on the portfolio process. This is, after all, part of what portfolios are about—providing students with the opportunity, the language, and the literacy to reflect and think critically about their own work. Natalie helped me to see that we have to take students beyond looking at their work with other people's yardsticks. Students need to use their own literacy as a means to explore, clarify, and deepen their understanding of the environmental elements that shape their work, their use of the portfolio process, and the curriculum. This article traces my discovery of the importance of students' use of language as a tool to look critically at the elements of a portfolio culture and a curriculum.

Our latest portfolio model is the result of three years of discussion in a challenging setting. Our school is located in La Jolla, a coastal community north of San Diego,

California. Sixty percent of the students are Anglo and thirty-two percent are Hispanic. The remaining eight percent are African American, Asian, and Native American. Resident students are from predominately white, upper-middle-class families. The Hispanic students are bused from a barrio south of downtown San Diego. Twenty-six percent of the students qualify for federally supported breakfast and lunch programs. Four years ago, our school district moved from a junior high to a middle school system. It was decided to adopt the GATE (Gifted and Talented Education) system, in which groups of 12–14 gifted students were placed into heterogeneous classes. All sixth-grade teachers were required to have training in gifted education, and all students would be taught using strategies for gifted programs; portfolios were the natural tool to assess individual progress.

My first attempt at portfolios was a folder where I asked students to keep their four or five best pieces. The following year, after reading and looking at some of the models being developed in other parts of the country, I adopted a system similar to the "Arts PROPEL" model from Pittsburgh. I asked my students to select pieces that fit into the following categories: favorite piece, least favorite piece, most difficult piece, and most persuasive piece. In addition to these student selections, parents made a selection, and I interviewed each child and made a selection. Finally, students wrote "Dear Reader" letters to introduce outside readers to their portfolios. I felt great about this model. I had successfully added the element of guided student selection to my portfolio system.

When I allowed one of my student's portfolios to be duplicated and distributed to English Language Arts participants at

Harvard's "Systems of Coherent Assessment" Institute in July of 1993, I took a more critical look at my system. As I listened and watched my colleagues look through the portfolio, I realized that it did not represent what had happened in my classroom over the course of the year. The portfolio was a representation of that child's strengths, likes, and dislikes. My guidelines for selection weren't working. I wanted a portfolio that would illustrate the breadth and depth of classroom experiences and curricula. On the last day of the Institute, Joan Baron, an educational consultant from Connecticut, introduced us to Alverno College's *Ability-Based Learning Program.* Alverno College outlines eight "Abilities and Developmental Levels." The "abilities" were much closer to what I was looking for, and they helped me to generate the guidelines I took into my 1993–1994 classrooms. Last year, our classroom portfolios contained representations of the following abilities:

Muirlands Middle School
Sixth-Grade Portfolios

1. Demonstrates growth in learning
    a. sets learning goals consistent with stated objectives
    b. locates and uses a variety of sources of information
    c. takes effective and efficient notes
    d. refines, reshapes or refocuses existing work
2. Demonstrates communication ability
    a. engages critically and constructively in an oral exchange of ideas
    b. asks and answers questions correctly and concisely
    c. delivers oral presentations using coherent sequence of thought, clarity of presentation, and appropriate nonverbal communication for the purpose of the audience
    d. identifies strengths and weaknesses as a communicator
3. Demonstrates analytical capabilities
    a. develops observational skills
    b. makes reasonable inferences
    c. analyzes structure and organization
    d. perceives and makes relationships
4. Demonstrates problem-solving skills
    a. defines problem
    b. designs strategy to solve problem
    c. evaluates and articulates problem-solving process
    d. collects and analyzes data
5. Demonstrates collaboration
    a. identifies personal interaction behaviors in group process
    b. analyzes behavior of others
    c. assesses group project
6. Applications and Extensions
    a. assesses and analyzes local and global issues
    b. articulates understanding of interconnected local and global issues
    c. formulates a response to a local or global issue
    d. responds artistically to contextual information
    e. expresses response to selected artistic expressions
    f. appreciates the importance of art in expressing human experiences

I knew the language was too difficult for eleven- and twelve-year-olds. But I was not sure how to simplify it without sacrificing meaning. I thought that if I talked with my students about the different abilities, and if I showed examples to illustrate these expectations, they would begin to understand my

My guidelines for selection weren't working. I wanted a portfolio that would illustrate the breadth and depth of classroom experiences and curricula.

model. I began by sharing the new and improved model with parents at the beginning of the school year. They were interested and eager to help me pilot the new guidelines. Before introducing them to my students, I developed reflective sheets for each of the six abilities. I was still reluctant to simplify the language, but I knew that if the students were to get experience in using the language, it would have to be accessible to them. These sheets asked students to write a definition of the ability in their own words. As we worked on an assignment, we discussed which ability it might represent in their portfolios. I was working with my students toward a common understanding of the categories.

The first time students actually selected a piece and wrote the reflection was hectic for me and confusing for my students. Not all of the students had a clear idea of the purpose of their selections. We continued to talk as a class about portfolio selections and definitions of abilities. By the time they made their second selections, the process went much more smoothly. I can remember walking over to my teaching partner, Paul Daras, and saying, "I think they get it." Finally, I had found a model that could represent the classroom experience, provide an alternative form of monitoring individual student progress, and provide me with feedback about my instruction. So why didn't Natalie get it?

We continued selecting pieces, writing "Dear Reader" letters, and preparing to present portfolios to parents. We had not simplified the language, but my original resolve had begun to crumble, and I began to make radical revisions for the coming year.

By the end of the year, I saw my "great" system as "good but in need of polishing." In the last few weeks of school, I asked students to help me rewrite the abilities so that the new sixth graders would have an easier time getting started in the portfolio process. Reluctantly, my students agreed to help. I divided the class into groups. Each group of four or five students was asked to rewrite one ability in "kid-friendly" language. They were given the original ability on a small slip of paper. They scattered to all corners of the

> **Finally, I had found a model that could represent the classroom experience, provide an alternative form of monitoring individual student progress, and provide me with feedback about my instruction. So why didn't Natalie get it?**

room, taking up residence in small clusters on the floor, assigned a scribe, and began dictating. They talked, read, reflected, reconsidered, and revised. Then they began again. They were remarkably attentive to the nuances of language. Comments flowed from all corners: "You can't just say 'good.' Good doesn't mean the same thing as interesting." "Does efficient mean the same thing as well-written?" "This says 'defines' but it really means 'figure out.'" When a group believed they had reworded their ability accurately, they wrote it on a transparency and shared it with the rest of the class. The larger group questioned their interpretations, made suggestions, and either registered approval, or sent the group back to work with a new set of ideas for revision. This was critical reading, review, and reflection at its best!

Finally, we had the Muirlands sixth-grade portfolio guidelines. It had been difficult, but most of the groups had worked hard to understand and redefine the ability. They had used their own language and literacy to explore the limitations of different words and phrases. They had negotiated a shared understanding of a standard with their peers. There was no mistaking what they meant. They agreed, or they revised until they could agree. These were *their* abilities, *their* standards. As they worked, I realized that there had been areas that I could not articulate, elements that I had no language for. I began to struggle alongside of them to find the words.

The redefined guidelines did not look very different to me, but the students assured me that they were easier to understand. They are:

Muirlands Middle School
Sixth-Grade Portfolio (Student Definitions)

1. Demonstrates growth in learning
   a. sets positive goals for future learning
   b. uses a variety of sources of information
   c. takes clear, well-written notes
   d. analyzes and changes existing work
   e. compares and contrasts new and old work

2. Demonstrates communication ability
   a. exchanges ideas through discussion in the group
   b. asks and answers questions briefly
   c. presents information orally for a specific audience
   d. determines your strengths and weaknesses as a communicator
3. Demonstrates analytical capabilities
   a. makes clear and careful observations
   b. makes acceptable conclusions
   c. analyzes organization
   d. compares and contrasts relationships
4. Demonstrates problem-solving skills
   a. figures out what the problem is
   b. finds a way to solve the problem
   c. describes how you solve the problem
   d. organizes information (What does your information mean?)
5. Demonstrates collaboration
   a. works with a group of students to accomplish a common goal
   b. looks for the different actions that occur during the group process
   c. observes how group members behave during the work process
   d. demonstrates the ability to judge the final product
6. Applications and extensions
   a. analyzes local and global issues
   b. explains how local or global issues affect your life
   c. formulates a response to a local or global issue
   d. responds to information in an artistic manner
   e. demonstrates an appreciation of artistic expression

After the process of negotiating the new definitions, I asked students to go back through their work folders and find good examples to represent the ability that they had redefined. This was an amazingly easy task for all of the students. Now that they had the language, it was easy to use it to guide their selection process. Students tagged the pieces they had chosen and wrote a few sentences as to why they thought it was a good example of a particular ability. Tagging exemplars helped make the ability much less

of an abstract concept, and their comments justifying the selection were definitions of the criteria. Now they were terrifically fluent with the system!

So, back to Natalie. Why didn't she get it? I believe that she really did understand the portfolio criteria on some levels. She could not articulate the meaning, but she had a partial working sense of how they played out in her assignments. She selected her Primitive Culture Group Project because it was a great example of collaboration. She enjoyed working in a group and said that the project was a success because she had drawn on the ideas of each member of the group. It was also successful because her group divided the tasks to complete the project. Natalie could recognize collaboration but she was not comfortable with the word. As I thought about this, I realized that I had been struggling with portfolios for the last three years, but I had just begun to articulate successfully what I wanted one of the abilities to represent.

I am glad that I took the time to ask my students to help me define the abilities. They helped me remember that we are engaged in a process. They were working with portfolios for the first time in their school careers and I was working to fine-tune a model. My goal now is to get these students to explain portfolios to my new students. I want them to use their work to demonstrate the different abilities. I plan to use the pieces my students tagged as a library of exemplars to illustrate specific abilities. This next group of students will be engaged in a year-long conversation that allows them to explore and further refine the list of abilities. They will learn from the examples of their predecessors and they will add their own models to the library of exemplars. In this way, the system will continue to improve and expand.

As Muirlands moves toward a school-wide portfolio system, we will all learn and become familiar with a common language across classrooms and grades. What I have come to realize is that we don't just need to make the language easier to understand, we need to use our own literacy and language to reach an agreement on a common portfolio language.

I am glad that I took the time to ask my students to help me define the abilities. They helped me remember that we are engaged in a process.

Remembering His Shoes and Hat:
The Standard of Memory

**Sharon
Saez**

Delaware
Department of
Public Instruction

When we speak of meeting standards, we often picture externals—high jump bars or yardsticks set up or applied from without by others. But there are also the standards that we keep—ones that we remember like the sound of voices from a room beyond the one where we slept. Surprisingly often, it is these ancient standards that inform even adult thought and choice. They are like what dancers have once they have performed a piece night after night with all the body's weight and force: Martha Graham called it "blood memory." Runners and point guards must have it, too.

When we think of the metrics for excellence we want students to carry with them, we would be wise to ask how these "habits of the heart" first ignited and continue to fuel what we count as brave, wise, hard-working, lovely, or just.

My grandfather, Papi—they all called him Don Tato—what I remember about Papi is that he was the one who taught me how to read and write in Spanish. I never heard him speak English. But he taught me what it means not to be able to communicate. He had been an apprentice in old San Juan. It was a family-owned pharmacy and his adopted father, his mentor, passed away and his real daughter sold it. He was too old to begin all over again. He had heard all these wonderful things about New York City and he still had six kids to raise. So there was no sitting back and saying, "It's too bad what happened." He packed his kids up and moved to New York at 109th Street. That was Spanish Harlem then—well, now, too.

But all he could get was odd jobs. That's all the whole family could get, even my grandmother. It was all odd jobs. He got one at Ideal Toy Company and he stayed until 1968. I remember this vividly because I was only a toddler and he would bring home very beautiful Shirley Temple doll clothes and dress me in them. They were my nicest dresses. Maybe because he never learned English, he just kept working for Ideal part-time and, I think it was, for a funeral home. But he always said that wasn't for me. And I always believed him because he always had this dream to return to the island. To Puerto Rico. Because of the way it was in his heart; it was for him *la isla del encanto.*

He kept a nice suit that was always pressed and hanging in his closet. He always had it ready because he was always waiting to go back. And his wingtips, his Sunday shoes, always polished, sitting right under the suit. And a brand-new hat he never wore, a little felt hat with a brim, just waiting for that special day. But he never earned enough money to go back. Not for good. This one time when we lived in Jacksonville, North Carolina, we drove all the way up to the city to see him because everybody knew he was really sick.

We were all standing around his bed cracking jokes and laughing when a fire broke out in the building. There was all this smoke coming out. And everybody was yelling to get out. And my uncle, he went to carry my grandfather out of the bedroom. We were all out, safely standing at the corner looking at the fire, and suddenly my uncle looks for my grandfather and he isn't there. We were all scared to death. And so, we can't find him and we look through the crowd and one of the neighbors says, "Oh, Don Tato, him, we saw him go back in the building." My uncle leaps to go back to get him and then we see my grandfather on the stoop. There he was carrying his Sunday hat and his shoes and his suit in his hand. I mean there he was, standing in the smoke holding his shined shoes. With his white

white hair and a little mustache that he tried to put a little dye on.

That's when I realized how much he really desired to return, all dressed right for going home. Shortly after that, we buried him in those clothes back on the island of his dreams. Next to his mother, that's the grandmother who buried five husbands, five different husbands, and who lived to be 105. The one who could make remedies. But she's another story.

So what place do we make in schools for keeping alive the kinds of standards that Don Tato passed on? This conversation between a sixth-grade student (N) and an interviewer (I) as they pour over his portfolio offers possibilities.

I: Could you find me a favorite piece of work in here, in your portfolio?

N: Yeah. (pages through) Here, it's an interview with my grandpa.

I: Why is it the best?

N: (pause) I learned things that I never knew before.

I: Like what?

N: About lots of things, mostly the Mexican Revolution, and about how America is the land of opportunity, only it's hard work to find it, and how families have to move around a lot and take chances.

I: Was that news for you?

N: Well, my dad, he's a history teacher, had to show me his books for me to learn about it. Because it isn't a revolution that happened here. Like I also learned things I never knew about my family . . . about how my great-grandfather was *in* Pancho Villa's army. He was one of his men. But they forced him to come to here afterwards.

I: Why?

N: A lot of them had to leave the country because the government didn't want them to make trouble. And he had to come here and he moved to Texas. And then to Michigan. Where there was more work. And he was working on a farm. And when he came to get his money, the man who owed it to him had gone. And he had done all the work and didn't get anything for it. And then they went to Denver. So I still have a lot of family there. My mom's sister is there.

I: So what does that make you think about the revolution?

N: It was hard on families. Even if it looked good, exciting . . . Pancho Villa had a real gold suit. Really. A real one.

I: Another question, maybe a hard one. Not everybody has a dad who has all those books, or a grandpa who they can interview to tell them the kinds of personal things about the revolution. So what if you were a history teacher . . . .

N: Good. My dad's a history teacher. He has all these books that we looked in.

I: Great. So maybe this won't be so hard. Imagine you are a history teacher and you want kids to understand about the Mexican revolution. What would you do?

N: Well, I would teach it wasn't just all Pancho Villa and like in the movies. And . . . see, my dad told me how Pancho Villa made movies of the revolution . . . even afterwards. Like "Pancho Villa Returns" and "Pancho Villa Rides Again." With him leading everybody and winning. He made millions of dollars that way. My dad used to go just to watch the movies. But it was really about how it was just families having to make decisions and how people had to leave the country afterwards. So . . . it wasn't just the fighting. And about what happened to their lives afterwards. About how my grandpa had to go to Texas and then up north, then back. And how he didn't get paid.

I: How could you do that? What would you use to do it? To make kids understand?

N: (puzzled)

I: I mean, how would you get the kids to understand that?

N: Okay, well, first I would ask them to do a project. . . . So it lasts a while. 'Cause if you just read it, you forget it.

I: Okay. But what kinds of things would be in that project?

So what place do we make in schools for keeping alive the kinds of standards that Don Tato passed on?

N: Different kinds of things. Stories. Like in fourth grade, we read this book about an Indian girl, I forget what it was called, but it was really good. It let you see how she lived. About an island. So, fiction about the time of the revolution and what ordinary people did. And I . . . could I show those old movies to the kids?

I: What would they get from them?

N: What Pancho Villa and his men wanted people to think. And I would show them what it says in the history book, and then give them things like what I wrote about my grandpa.

I: How come? What does your grandpa's stuff add?

N: What really happened. That's not in the movies. 'Cause they could see how many different stories there are of the revolution. . . . See I am part Indian. And you know how people say that Columbus discovered America when it was really here? And how he was all nice and kind and gave the Indians—they weren't even Indians—gave the Indians stuff? He mostly gave them diseases and cheap stuff. Like that, there are two sides. Maybe three, the history book, my grandpa, and Pancho Villa's.

Between themselves, as they talk, this eleven-year-old and adult hammer out quite a challenging vision of middle school literacy. It is one where both sides of conversation—speaking and listening—play a role. When the interviewer wants to understand, asking "What does your grandpa's stuff add?", Nathan pulls together the threads of what he has only implied earlier about history as the interplay of "many different stories." The questions, answers, elaborations, and revisions that fly back and forth draw more out of the assignment than was originally there. Possibly through this talk, Nathan finds himself in the role of a teacher, considering how and what *he* would hand on, what he understands about the Mexican Revolution, immigration, and the reasons for telling a history that is more than easy mythology.

Perhaps if we make portfolios more than storehouses, if we make them the occasion for talk that is more than managerial, if that talk touches on memory, origins, and connections, perhaps portfolios can help us out. If we could manage that, Don Tato would be proud.

Selected Readings

Atwell, N. (1987). *In the middle: Writing, reading, and learning with adolescents.* Portsmouth, NH: Heinemann.

*Belanoff, P., & Dickson, M. (Eds.). (1991). *Portfolios: Process and product.* Portsmouth, NH: Heinemann.

Carnegie Council on Adolescent Development. (1989). *Turning points: Preparing American youth for the 21st century* (Report of the Task Force on Education of Young Adolescents). New York: Author.

Englert, C. S., & Palincsar, A. S. (1991). Reconsidering instructional research in literacy from a sociocultural perspective. *Learning Disabilities Research and Practice, 6,* 225–229.

Estes, T. H. (Ed.). (1991). Thinking and learning across the curriculum. *Journal of Reading, 34*(7).

*Graves, D. H., & Sunstein, B. S. (Eds.). (1992). *Portfolio portraits.* Portsmouth, NH: Heinemann.

Herman, J. L., Aschbacher, P. R., & Winters, L. (1992). *A practical guide to alternative assessment.* Alexandria, VA: Association for Supervision and Curriculum Development.

Langer, J. A. (1986). *Children reading and writing: Structures and strategies.* Norwood, NJ: Ablex.

Marshall, R., & Tucker, M. (1992). *Thinking for a living: Education and the wealth of nations.* New York: BasicBooks.

Morrow, L. M., Smith, J. K., & Wilkinson, L. C. (Eds.). (1994). *Integrated language arts: Controversy to consensus.* Needham Heights, MA: Allyn and Bacon.

Monson, P. M., & Monson, R. J. (Eds.). (1994). Literacy in the content areas: New definitions and decisions for the 21st century. *The Reading Teacher, 47*(7).

Pearson, P. D. (1994). Integrated language arts: Sources of controversy and seeds of consensus. In L. M. Morrow, J. K. Smith, & L. C. Wilkinson (Eds.), *Integrated language arts* (pp. 11–31). Needham Heights: Allyn and Bacon.

Petrie, H. (1992). Interdisciplinary education: Are we faced with insurmountable opportunities? *Review of research in education, 18,* 299–333.

Resnick, L. B. (1990). Literacy in school and out. *Daedalus, 119*(2), 169–185.

Rief, L. (1992). *Seeking diversity: Language arts with adolescents.* Portsmouth, NH: Heinemann.

Santa, C. M., & Alvermann, D. E. (Eds.). (1990). *Science learning: Processes and applications.* Newark, DE: The International Reading Association.

Scholes, R. (1985). *Textual power.* New Haven, CT: Yale University Press.

Thiessen, D., & Matthias, M. (Eds.). (1993). *The wonderful world of mathematics: A critically annotated list of childrens books in mathematics.* Reston, VA: The National Council of Teachers of Mathematics.

*Tierney, R. J., Carter, M. A., & Desai, L. E. (1991). *Portfolio assessment in the reading-writing classroom.* Norwood, MA: Christopher Gordon Publishers.

Valencia, S. W., McGinley, W., & Pearson, P. D. (1990). Assessing literacy in the middle school. In G. G. Duffy (Ed.), *Reading in the middle school* (2nd ed.) (pp. 124–153). Newark, DE: International Reading Association.

Valencia, S.W., Hiebert, E. H., Afflerbach, P. P. (Eds.). (1994). *Authentic reading assessment: Practices and possibilities.* Newark, DE: The International Reading Association.

Venezky, R. L., Wagner, D. A., & Ciliberti, B. S. (Eds.). (1990). *Toward defining literacy.* Newark, DE: The International Reading Association.

*Wolf, D. P. (1988). *Reading reconsidered.* New York: College Entrance Examination Board.

Wolf, D. P., LeMahieu, P., & Eresh, J. (1992). Assessment as a tool for educational reform. *Educational Leadership, 49*(8), 8–13.

Zarnowski, M., & Gallagher, A. F. (Eds.). (1993). *Children's literature and social studies: Selecting and using notable books in the classroom.* Washington, D.C.: The National Council of Social Studies.

*Books reviewed in journal

Voices from the Middle

Volume 2 • Number 2 • April 1995

... *blue river cuts its way through the hilly contour of my backyard. The vast open field has been violated, over time, by this moving mass of water. Trees, that should be reaching towards mother sun, now lean over the water, admiring their own reflection.... Fallen trees stripe the banks of the twisting river. A few daring ones reach for eternity. What seems like an impossible feat to you or me is a mere stretch for a tree....*

Reading Processes

A Publication of the National Council of Teachers of English

Contents

Cover photos and text by
Cody Clare, Oyster River
Middle School, Durham,
New Hampshire

Design: Doug Burnett

Editing and Production:
Carol E. Schanche

 Printed on recycled paper

Message from the Editors

Perhaps Scout says it best in *To Kill a Mockingbird* when she insists, "For me reading is like breathing." We who teach middle school know what she means. We read all day long—students' work, memos and notes from colleagues, professional articles and books, essays in *The New Yorker*, newspaper columns, young adult literature, and Jane Smiley novels. We read for information and we read for pure pleasure. We cannot imagine our lives without books, without breathing, without reading. As we share our own passion every day in classrooms, our strongest wish for our students is that they too will find the joy, the provocation, and the insight that we find when we read.

By the time children come to us in grade six, we expect them to be fluent readers. We recognize the occasional boy or girl who claims, "I hate to read," or "Reading is so boring," and we accept these comments as our own personal challenges. For such students, our job is to find the one book that will change everything. Indeed, there are few experiences more gratifying than hearing a young person exclaim, "This is the first book I've read all the way through. I just couldn't put it down." We keep up with the latest YA literature, so we will know which authors will appeal to individual readers. Gary Paulsen for Clay or S.E. Hinton for Jessica; Katherine Paterson for Marie and Robert Lipsyte for Jonathan. We know that, ultimately, these are the folks who will turn our kids into readers. Connecting authors to students is one of our biggest responsibilities, and when these connections are made, we are delighted.

Sadly, sometimes we miss the mark. We all recognize students like Judith Wright's Olivia who "pretends to read" in class, or Calen who erects his own seemingly impene-

trable walls. What of these lonely students who show little or no desire to come into what Frank Smith terms "the literacy club"? Sometimes, in our frustration, we send those students who do not or cannot read out of the room to specialists. Sometimes, busy as we are fostering extensive response to literature, sustaining productive writing workshops, and moving into more diverse ways to examine oral language, we abdicate our roles as teachers of reading. The sad lament of middle school teachers, "Why didn't they learn to read in elementary school?" is often on our minds if not on our lips.

Paul Crowley reminds us that "the rules don't change in middle school." Our students need much of the same support elementary children need when they open their books. They need to know that reading is not about decoding words but about making sense of what's happening on the page. Some readers do this with great vigor and enthusiasm, and others are more tentative. Paul Crowley, Judith Wright, Linda Morrow, and Carol Treu understand this.

As we look into their classrooms and eavesdrop on their conversations with students, we see that these teachers have not abdicated their roles as teachers of reading. They do not offer drills and skills to their kids; instead, they make every effort to know and understand their students' attitudes about reading and perceptions of themselves as readers. They share not only their passion for books but also their own approaches to texts that are difficult for them. They turn to parents in order to gain new insights and to build healthy partnerships that will nurture confidence and joy in reading.

Stressing the social nature of reading, Frank Smith writes, "All that children need is competent people to help them make sense

Linda Rief

Middle School Teacher, Durham, New Hampshire

Maureen Barbieri

Middle School Teacher, Greenville, South Carolina

Sometimes our students need to be tantalized by the possibilities of entering a whole new world of books.

and make use of written language." Sometimes our students need more reassurance, the kind of reassurance Paul Crowley is able to offer Gregg as the two sit side by side and talk about the ways each one copes with unfamiliar texts. Sometimes students need help understanding new words or new uses of words, as happens in Linda Morrow's class, setting off a compelling discussion of the organic nature of language. And sometimes our students need to be tantalized by the possibilities of entering a whole new world of books, a world they had believed closed to them for good. Carol Evans Treu tantalizes her kids by enlisting the help of local bookstore owners and organizing an early morning field trip. These students want to read because they have come to believe that reading is worthwhile. We learn by the company we keep.

Putting this issue together has been a bit unsettling. We have had to reexamine our own assumptions and take a closer look at methodology unfamiliar to us, and we have learned a great deal. We are reminded of Mem Fox's words, "Learning to read and learning to love reading owe a great deal (much more than we ever dreamed) to *the nature of the human relationships* that occur around and through books." Whether we are advocates of miscue analysis, reading aloud to students, or setting up partnerships between our kids and other readers, or whether we implement a wide and varied range of approaches to teaching reading in our classrooms, the essential mandate remains: Reading is too good to miss. We don't want to leave a single person—not breathing—on the sidelines.

References

Fox, M. (1993). *Radical reflections: Passionate opinions on teaching, learning, and living.* New York: Harcourt Brace.

Lee, H. (1960). *To kill a mockingbird.* New York: Warner.

Smith, F. (1983). *Essays into literacy.* Portsmouth, NH: Heinemann.

Smith, F. (1988). *Joining the literacy club.* Portsmouth, NH: Heinemann.

Listening to What Readers Tell Us

The other day, I received a call from the mother of a first grader who expressed concern that her son wasn't progressing well in reading. Her fear was that he would reach sixth grade and be lagging behind his classmates. She said she was desperate and would do anything possible to "catch him up."

I urged her to return the commercial reading kit she had purchased; I wanted her to know that the only thing first graders need to be "hooked on" is books, as Daniel Fader told us in 1966. We talked about how naturally he learned to talk and how we expect children to develop oral language at different rates; parents don't ponder sending their infants to "remedial talking" classes if they haven't begun speaking by a certain date. Children learn to talk because they are social beings and language serves both personal and interpersonal functions. Talking always takes place in a sensible, meaningful context. I wanted her to understand that in a literate society, learning written language is just as natural as learning to talk.

We agreed on the importance of taking the pressure off this young reader, supporting his efforts with meaningful and familiar print, identifying for ourselves how much he knows about written language (even though he could not, as yet, read unfamiliar print), and helping him appreciate all he knows.

The rules don't change for middle-school readers. We cannot expect all thirteen-year-old readers to look the same, any more than we can expect it of six-year-olds or sixteen-year-olds. However, as readers approach the middle grades and are struggling with reading, concern mounts on the part of the parents, teachers, and students.

We don't hide our heads in the sand. There *are* students in middle school (and beyond) who are struggling with the reading demands of school. Ken Goodman uses the term "readers in trouble" (in press; 1982a) to describe these students. The value of this term is that it doesn't place blame on students, teachers, or parents. What really matters is that these students become readers who can meet the reading demands in the curriculum and come to enjoy books. Teachers of English/language arts, though, can do much to help readers in trouble by changing their views of themselves as readers and their notions about reading process. Goodman (in press) points out that, in order to help readers in trouble, we must:

> help them revalue themselves as language users and learners, and revalue the reading process as a trans-active, constructive language process. They must set aside the pathological view of themselves, cast off the labels, and operate to construct meaning through written language using the strengths they have built and used in making sense of oral language or sign. To do that they need support and help.

Helping readers revalue the reading process and themselves as readers requires us to have an understanding of this process. As we assist readers in developing reading strategies for handling different texts and for responding to literature, readers must engage with texts. We learn to read by reading.

Gregg

Books were enemies to Gregg, a severely labeled reader in my seventh-grade class several years ago. He had been in special education classes since early in his elementary school career, and he now found himself in my classroom for students designated "learning disabled." The ill-defined label given to Gregg did not do justice to his strengths as a reader. I interviewed Gregg about his views

Paul Crowley

Assistant Professor, Sonoma State University, Rohnert Park, California of reading and had him read aloud for me so that I could analyze his miscue behaviors to determine the reading strategies he used.

Goodman (1982b) defines a miscue as "an actual observed response in oral reading which does not match the expected response" (p. 94). Reading is not an exact process; readers do not replicate the text. Readers sample from the text and make predictions as we construct meaning. As we formulate a personal text, we make miscues including substitutions, insertions, omissions, and regressions to correct.

Goodman favors the use of the term "miscue" in order to avoid the negative connotations of "error." All miscues are neutral until they are analyzed linguistically and pragmatically. Goodman, Watson, and Burke (1987) point out that the most important aspect of miscue analysis is that it assists teacher-researchers in developing a personal model of the reading process. They offer a list of questions teacher-researchers ask in order to determine miscue quality.

- Does the miscue make sense? (semantic acceptability)

- Does it sound like language? (syntactic acceptability)

- Does it change the meaning of the text?

- Was it corrected?

- Does it look like the text item? (graphic similarity)

As we listen to our students read, we begin to internalize these questions, allowing us to become informed observers of readers, which, in turn, provides us with insight into the reading process. Gathering information about Gregg's control of the reading process through miscue analysis was the starting point for developing a curricular plan.

Before beginning, I asked Gregg what he did when he came to something unfamiliar in his reading. Gregg reported that he "sounded out" words or asked for help. He said that he would suggest the same strategies to someone else who was having difficulty reading. As I listened to Gregg's reading, I kept these reported strategies in mind to compare with his actual reading behaviors.

Using standard miscue analysis procedures, I chose a text of substantial length that would be unfamiliar to Gregg; this gave him the opportunity to get into the text in some depth, while enabling me to determine how he handled new information. I audio-taped his reading so that later I could compare the tape with a copy of the story, and mark and analyze his miscues.

My instructions to Gregg were, "I want you to read this aloud and if you come to something that gives you trouble, just do whatever you would do if you were by yourself. Be sure to read to remember because after you read, I'm going to ask you to tell me about what you read."

Gregg read a story about an elephant named Sudana who lived in the zoo and was suffering from a fever. The zoo doctor and his helper tried to give Sudana a dose of sulfa in her water, which she spit out at them. The same happened when they put the sulfa in ice cream. Then they gave Sudana an injection of penicillin and all was well. (The story doesn't have to be compelling to be suitable for miscue analysis!)

At the beginning of the story, a number of Gregg's miscues were of low quality (syntactically and semantically unacceptable). For example:

TEXT	GREGG
The big African elephant was leaning against the steel bars of her cage in the Elephant House.	A big African elephant was leaning against the still bars for her change in the Elephant House.

Menosky's (1971) research shows that readers' miscues are often of lower quality at the beginning of the text because the reader has not built up enough background from the text. As the reading progresses, though, the text becomes more predictable because the reader is constructing meaning.

After reading only one paragraph, Gregg produced the following miscues:

TEXT	GREGG
He reached through the bars to lay a hand on the elephant's trunk.	He reached through the bars and laid his hand on the elephant's tusk.

In altering the verb in the phrase "to lay a hand," so that it read "and laid his hand," Gregg shifted the verb from the infinitive to the past tense, thereby maintaining tense agreement with the rest of the story. Also, *tusk* is highly predictable when the topic is elephants. Gregg drew upon all of the cueing systems of language—graphophonic, syntactic, and semantic information—as he constructed his text. This was a pattern in his miscue behaviors throughout the story.

However, when Gregg encountered difficulty with individual words, he reverted to the most abstract cueing system, graphophonics. He did what he said he would do when he came to something that gave him trouble: He "sounded it out."

TEXT	GREGG
Maybe if she's thirsty enough, she'll take some sulfa in her drinking water.	Maybe if she's thirty, thirty en- thirty enough, she'll take some s-, sss, shovel in, in her water dish.

Gregg hammers away at *thirty* because he knows it doesn't make sense. Although this indicates that he was monitoring his comprehension, it was clear that Gregg was frustrated and uncomfortable with his attempts. He was probably unaware of his substitution of "water dish" for "drinking water," a high quality miscue (syntactically and semantically acceptable; no loss of meaning). Gregg could not have made this miscue unless he was in control of the process, making predictions and confirming them as he made meaning.

We make predictions based on the meaning we have built up in our particular world, our knowledge of language, and the social context in which the language occurs. This explains why a friend's Jewish mother looked at the sign in the store window that said "Boxes and Labels" and read "Lox and Bagels." Our brains tell our eyes what to see.

Gregg overused graphophonic cues in a number of places throughout the text, as evidenced by his multiple attempts at individual words. For example, when he got to the word *patient*, he read *pat* (14-second pause);

pat (9-second pause); he regressed to the prior word, *heavy*, paused for 11 seconds, and then read *patnight,* and mumbled "or something." Clearly, Gregg had little confidence in his attempt. His editorial comment indicated that he knew the word wasn't *patnight.*

TEXT	GREGG
As he stepped back over the guardrail, the doctor spoke to Bob, her keeper. "Did you give her anything to drink today?"	As, as he stepped down over the guardrail, guardrail, the doctor spoke to Bob. Her, Her keeper didn't (5-second pause) Her keeper didn't (5-second pause) Her keeper did you give her anything to drink today.

Gregg substituted a period for the comma after Bob. (It is clear through intonation.) This caused him to change the dialogue to a declarative sentence with "Her keeper" being the subject. Gregg substituted *didn't* for *did*, but when the structure of the sentence broke down, he was unable to work it out for himself, even after multiple attempts. Although Gregg's miscues rendered the sentence syntactically and, therefore, semantically unacceptable, his multiple attempts and grammatical transformations indicate his facility with the structure of the language. As Gregg read further into the text, though, his regressions to correct were successful more often than not. As he constructed a meaningful text, it became more predictable and Gregg's miscues were fewer in number and higher in quality.

The word *sulfa* gave Gregg problems throughout most of the reading. He made multiple attempts to "sound it out" (s-/sss/shovel [perhaps looking for the /sh/ as in *sure*]; suchful/shmmm; shiffa; shome; snufn), and grew visibly frustrated. At one point, he growled at the book as he held it up and shook it when he came to the ubiquitous *sulfa* yet one more time. Gregg finally pronounced the word /surum/ (the first *u* as in *surf*) and stuck with it. I can't help but think he was trying to say *serum*. Interestingly, toward the end of the story, Gregg read "injection of penicillin" without hesitation.

> *We make predictions based on the meaning we have built up in our particular world, our knowledge of language, and the social context in which the language occurs.*

No miscue analysis is over until the reader retells what was read. Frequently readers are able to retell a great deal more than we may expect from the observed miscue behaviors because they have silently self-corrected as they read, rather than regressing to correct. Gregg was able to retell the main points of the entire story and many details. He talked about the elephant without referring to her name and described the way the doctor and his helper tried to get the medicine into the elephant. Gregg knew that *sulfa* was a medicine because the text taught him. His frustration with the word throughout the reading was unnecessary; his "sounding out" strategy got him nowhere.

Gregg was an effective reader; he understood the text. However, he was also an inefficient reader because of the high degree of effort he put forth to get through the reading. At one point, Gregg tapped the table vigorously and grunted in frustration as he attempted to force his reading to make sense.

Gregg's tenacity with the story was context-specific. That is, in his first week of seventh grade at a new school, he found himself across from an attentive adult, clipboard and pencil in hand, who was audiotaping his reading. Gregg was willing to stick with the task because he was a captive audience. Otherwise, he would use his most common reading strategy—abandoning the text (which, by the way, is a strategy proficient readers use as appropriate).

There is much to value in Gregg's reading. His greatest strength is that he understood what he read; he was able to retell all the main points of the story. To the untrained ear, Gregg's reading can be almost painful to listen to. He made many partial attempts, regressions, and pauses up to 17 seconds. However, an analysis of his miscues indicates that many of his miscues fit the structure of the text and made sense. He made sensible predictions (e.g., "her water dish" for "her drinking water") and his regressions were made in an attempt to correct. As the reading progressed, Gregg's miscues decreased in number and were of a higher quality. He developed strategies to handle the words that

gave him problems early in the text. For example, after making multiple attempts at the elephant's name, *Sudana* (e.g., S-/Sha/Shado-/Shadan/Shadan; Sh-/Shu-/Sh-/Shuden), he said *Shana* and used it, almost exclusively, from then on without making multiple attempts at sounding it out; similarly, *sulfa* became *surum*.

Gregg saw himself as a failed reader. The first step in creating a reading program for him was to help him revalue his reading strengths, and to gain an accurate view of reading so that he could gradually unlearn the strategies that were tripping him up.

From Miscue Analysis to Reading Instruction: A Program for Gregg

The reading strategies Gregg employed at the beginning of seventh grade, while successful in helping him gain meaning, frustrated him to the point of seeing books as enemies. Gregg's miscues show us that he isn't just making haphazard random errors, but that he, based on the cues available to him, is predicting, confirming, disconfirming, and re-predicting when necessary, and constructing meaning. This information is essential for building a reading program for him.

Gregg also needs to know his strengths as a reader, and to unlearn the view that he is a poor reader because he messes up on words. Gregg's reading program must provide him with strategies that will assist him in moving more efficiently through the text. It isn't enough that Gregg has these strategies; he must also *use* them. He must be willing to put in the effort to engage with texts in order to grow as a reader—to learn to read by reading.

Revaluing Gregg's Reading

Following the reading and the retelling of a miscue analysis story, I ask readers how they feel about their reading. Gregg, like many readers both successful and less successful, was critical of his reading. He talked about "messing up" a lot. I used this opportunity to give my side of the story, to tell Gregg that he

> Gregg was an effective reader; he understood the text.

was already successful in the most important aspect of reading—making meaning. I also pointed out places in the text where he regressed and corrected.

Over the next few weeks, I would sit next to Gregg and ask him to read aloud from whatever he was reading at the time (or *should* be reading, such as his science book). We would stop once in a while to reflect on what he was doing; we talked about the miscues he made and evaluated their quality. I wanted Gregg to know that *he* is responsible for getting his reading to make sense and, if it doesn't sound like language, it can't make sense. The revaluing process requires readers to realize that *they* are in control of the process of meaning making.

Retrospective Miscue Analysis

A number of teachers and researchers have investigated the power of teaching students miscue analysis (Goodman & Marek, in press). A set of procedures called "Retrospective Miscue Analysis" has been developed in which readers, as young as elementary age, tape their reading, listen for miscues, and ask themselves: Did the miscue make sense? Did it sound like language? Did it look like the text? Did you correct?/Should you have? Readers' examinations of their own and their classmates' miscues provide them with specific data for discussions of the reading process. Knowledge of the reading process provides students with an explanation for their reading behaviors, and helps to establish what they are doing well and what they need to change.

Reader-Selected Miscues

As they read independently, readers are invited to jot down those places in the text that give them problems. Readers' selected miscues (Watson & Hoge, in press) also help them move through the text because they know that following the reading, they will have the opportunity to discuss these problems. Readers often find that when they finish the selection, they have figured out the miscues they selected earlier. They may also find that the difficulties they experienced did not interfere with their understanding.

I shared my confusion about Wilson Rawls's reference to the "coon hounds barking treed" in *Where the Red Fern Grows* (1961). When I reported this to the class, Randy (who took two weeks off each year during deer-hunting season) was incredulous. Hooking his thumbs into his jeans and crossing his cowboy boots, he told me, "the dogs barked treed." (Maybe I hadn't been listening the first time.) "What does that mean?" "You know, they barked TREED." (Maybe he's hard of hearing.) "I still don't get it." (Who's on first?) Rusty finally explained that coon dogs bark as they're chasing a coon, but that their bark changes when they get the coon trapped in a tree.

It is important that students see their teachers as readers and know that, as readers, we employ the same strategies we encourage them to use. We can share how we handle tax forms (I phone my accountant), requests for grant proposals (I study the proposal to learn the language of the funding organization so that I can use it in the writing of my proposal; then they can know how smart I am and how worthy of their money), and James Joyce novels (I don't worry about understanding everything; when I'm confused, I just enjoy the language). These open discussions demonstrate how proficient readers' strategies always focus on meaning, the social demands of the situation, and the purpose for reading.

Reading Aloud

Hearing good literature read aloud gave Gregg access to books that he would have avoided because he found them too difficult or, as most middle school teachers have heard many times, too boring. This pressure-free activity allows readers to hear the flow of written language, as well as their own teachers making miscues. Reading aloud demonstrates to students that written language does not sound like oral language. This is why the stories of six-year-olds often start with "once upon a time." They are learning the conventions of written language that will make independent reading more predictable. Similarly, hearing books read aloud helps

> *It is important that students see their teachers as readers.*

older readers gain a tacit understanding of their structure and conventions, which will assist them as independent readers. Reading aloud to Gregg also helped him know that there are compelling books out there about kids like him and the people he knows.

Reading Extensively

Gregg was given numerous opportunities for uninterrupted silent reading time. He was invited to read texts that offered the potential for engaging him, that is, books about things that interested him and that spoke to his experiences. He was *able* to read a great deal more than he was *willing* to read, but he avoided many appropriate books because of the pressure he put on himself to "get all the words right." Therefore, the challenge was to maintain a ready supply of materials that would be interesting and effortless enough for Gregg to buy into. He read magazines about fishing (one of his passions), paged through *Rolling Stone* and *National Geographic* magazines (looking at the pictures and reading captions, as I usually do), and read poetry by Shel Silverstein, Nikki Giovanni, and Eloise Greenfield.

As Gregg felt more comfortable with reading and himself as a reader, I wanted to engage him with texts that were challenging for him. I had picked up Robert Cormier's *I Am the Cheese* (1977) a year before and, after reading a few pages, put it on my guilt shelf (the place where unread and unfinished books stay and haunt me to the grave . . . or until they're read). I had recently resurrected the book and read it with a vengeance in an afternoon. I knew the book was for Gregg. It was strange and troubling (highly appealing qualities to many middle school kids, including Gregg; Robert Cormier knows his stuff). I told Gregg that I had put this book down for a long time because of its strange beginning; it hadn't hooked me at all. When I finally read it, though, I loved it and thought of Gregg a number of times during the reading. I said it was a "weird book" (I knew this would carry weight) and I thought he would like it. Gregg picked up the book and began reading, only looking up to say,

"This really is weird!" He finished it in a week. Gregg learned that not all books are immediately accessible, but that if you give them a chance, they might be worth the effort.

Reading Intensively

All of the readers in our classes—successful readers and readers in trouble—deserve access to the ideas that come from books. Gregg joined in intensive reading with a community of readers in literature study groups. If students have difficulty reading the literature study book, we can support them in a number of ways. If they are having trouble keeping up with the other readers, we can invite them to read as much as they can with understanding and then fill them in on the rest. We can read the book to them or put it on tape. The important thing is that they are members of the community of readers and have the opportunity to share their perspectives and to hear those of others.

Readers negotiate meanings in literature study groups, but then can also discuss *how* they make meaning. The students or teacher might ask: How did you handle that part of the story? What did you do when you came to that word? Why does the author use this kind of language? As we explore answers to questions like these, we add to our repertoire of reading strategies.

Reading beyond Words

Gregg thought reading was about words. In response to the question on the Reading Interview (Goodman, Watson & Burke, 1987), "When you are reading and you come to something you don't know, what do you do?" he said he would "sound it out" or ask someone to tell him the word. I wanted Gregg to learn that individual words are rarely problems for proficient readers.

Glossaries, dictionaries, and asking someone for help—going outside ourselves—are *confirming* strategies, and, even then, rarely does a single word make much difference in a text. I've had graduate students who swear they always stop reading when they come to a word they don't know

> *Readers negotiate meanings in literature study groups, but then can also discuss* **how** *they make meaning.*

and look it up in the dictionary. If they really do that, I tell them, they must not read very much. And if they do, they must not be reading many challenging books.

As teachers, we need to define for ourselves what we mean when we say a reader "doesn't know a word." Do we mean: The reader is unfamiliar with the concept? The reader is unfamiliar with the label? The reader can't pronounce the word? The reader is unfamiliar with the label in English, but understands the concept and knows the label in a primary language?

In order to engage with larger units of text, Gregg needed to "keep going" in his reading and not become hung up on individual words and confusing syntax. If he understands the story, he should keep reading.

Naming Strategy

As Gregg progressed through the miscue analysis text, he developed a successful strategy for dealing with *sulfa* and *Sudana.* Although Gregg didn't believe he was successful with these words, he eventually began using a "naming strategy" that helped him move through the text. At the beginning of the story, Gregg made multiple attempts at a number of words, including the name of the elephant, the medicine, *patient,* and *thirsty.*

It was important for Gregg to understand that his naming strategy was good, he just needed to use it earlier in his reading and with more consistency. Once you know that *Sudana* (however you pronounce it) refers to the elephant's name, call her *Shana* (or *Sinbad* or *Sherry*) and move on, sticking with that name throughout the story. Removing this self-imposed pressure makes reading much easier.

The next time I scooted my chair up to Gregg and listened to him read, he began again to sound out words. I told him to skip them or say "blank" and go on. This simple suggestion met with incredulity; Gregg's view of successful reading was reading all the words correctly, and here he was being told to skip words. As Gregg began to abandon the misguided notion that reading is an exact, word-by-word process, though, he was

much more apt to spend time reading. A burden had been lifted. He stopped asking himself to attempt an impossible task.

Selected Deletions

At times, no matter how we cajole them not to get stopped by individual words, some readers continue to make multiple and futile attempts at reading every word. "Selected Deletions" (Watson & Crowley, 1987) is a strategy lesson to help these readers keep going.

Selected Deletions involves removing potentially troublesome words from the text. The first two or three sentences of the text are left intact to help the reader get a handle on the story, and then only highly predictable words are removed. If readers have difficulty putting in a word that makes sense, the purpose is defeated; coming up with a sensible word must be effortless in order to demonstrate to readers that they bring something to the reading process and that the text helps them to make meaning.

A single unfamiliar word that occurs repeatedly in the text can also be deleted. It would be interesting if Gregg had read this story with the word *sulfa* deleted. It probably wouldn't have taken him long to begin putting the word *medicine* in the blank.

Writing to Support Reading

Although this discussion highlights Gregg as a reader, he was also engaged in oral language and writing activities each day. Nothing is more predictable than our own language, and Gregg, as the first reader of his own writing, regularly connected with texts he could handle well. Through writing, Gregg had many opportunities to engage with his own texts as well as with his classmates' and mine.

It was important that Gregg be involved in varied writing experiences with real audiences, including written conversation (legal note passing), dialogue journals (if I neglected to write back, I was quickly told), pen pals with Education majors at a local university, story writing, book publishing for elementary school partners, and literature response logs. Gregg learned that writing, like reading, serves multiple functions.

It was important that Gregg be involved in varied writing experiences with real audiences.

Reading and Writing with Younger Students

Gregg and his classmates met regularly with primary-age students at a nearby elementary school to read and write with them. I used this opportunity to discuss the reading process with my middle-school students. We talked about how young readers have varied interests and facility with oral language. They are involved with written language every day on cereal boxes, T-shirts, books, TV. They need to use the language cues that they have the most control over, syntax (grammar) and meaning, in order to gain command of the abstract (symbolic) cueing system, graphophonics. Providing young readers with good stories that have supportive structures helps them to use these strengths and enjoy the reading experience.

In preparation for writing their own predictable books, our class read (aloud and silently) many predictable books for young readers. Approaching these books with an eye to studying technique and elements of story prevented these readers from being insulted by their easy reading level. Each student then began to write a book—one line of text and one illustration per page. Figure 1 is the text of Gregg's book.

Gregg was funny and smart and contributed a lot to our class. He was also surly, distracting, and moody in that unique teenage way. So one morning, when I received a call from the teacher in the first-grade classroom where Gregg had been reading and writing with a little boy, a multitude of potential horrors flashed through my mind. What had he done? The teacher, however, was delighted. "He was listening to Ty reading and when Ty asked Gregg, 'What is this word?' Gregg told him not to worry about it—to put in something that makes sense or go on. He said it's more important to get the meaning of the story and to enjoy it. When Ty asked Gregg to spell a word for him while writing in his journal, Gregg told him that his ideas were more important than spelling and besides, it only interrupts your ideas when you stop to get help." She was pleased to see this first grader gaining confidence using Gregg's advice.

No Excuses

by Gregg

One day my teacher asked where my homework was. I told her my dog ate it!

The next day my teacher asked me where my homework was. I told her a bird used it to wallpaper his nest.

The next day my teacher asked me where my homework was. I told her a giant fly took it!

The next day my teacher asked me where my homework was. I told her it got caught in a big spider web.

The next day my teacher asked me where my homework was. I told her a flying saucer stole it!

Then all of a sudden a dog, a bird, a fly, a Martian, and a big spider said, "Sorry" then gave her the papers and left.

FIGURE 1. *Gregg's book*

Gregg had recommended strategies that he was not yet using consistently, but this was a good start. He was able to articulate what we had talked about and must have thought it had some validity. In the context of working with a younger reader, he had had a chance to look at the reading and writing processes from a teacher's perspective.

Organizing Our Classrooms for Reading Instruction

It is unnecessary for teachers to conduct a formal miscue analysis with each student. The teachers in this issue describe ways in which they gather the information about their students, and how they use this information—in concert with their knowledge of the reading process, readers, and learning—to build curriculum with their students.

Linda Morrow describes how natural curricular contexts enable her to listen to her students read aloud. She then incorporates the information she has gleaned into her instructional planning. Judith Wright paints a portrait of her students' varied experiences with literature, and explains how, in this context, she brings the reading process to a conscious level with her students and their parents in order to help them appreciate readers' strengths. Carol Evans Treu uses her understandings to "lure readers from hiding" by demonstrating to them how much they know and can do with reading. These teachers know that middle-school students are still growing as readers, and that teachers can make a difference in helping them see themselves as readers in control of their reading process.

Middle school is not too late to help readers in trouble. Students come to us with a wealth of language, experiences, and curiosity that form a solid basis for a meaning-centered reading program. The challenge for us is to strip away the sense of failure, to overcome the defensive attitude, and to involve them as members of a community of readers. This is not an easy task, but helping readers revalue themselves and what they know about reading is the starting point.

A powerful aspect of involving all of our students, including successful readers, in discussions and analysis of the reading process and their own reading is that they can begin to see the reading strengths of their classmates. With an understanding of the reading process, our students no longer hear only mistakes when they listen to their colleagues read. They hear readers.

Ken and Yetta Goodman (1994) remind us:

> Everything people do, they do imperfectly. This is not a flaw but an asset. If we always performed perfectly, we could not maintain the tentativeness and flexibility that characterize human learning and the ways we interact with our environment and with one another. This model of imperfection causes us as researchers not to worry about why people fall short of perfection; rather, we are concerned with why people do what they do and with what we can learn about language processes from observing such phenomenon. (p. 104)

Middle-school kids are trying to figure out who they are and who they want to be. They need to feel comfortable with their successes *and* their errors, to know what they know and use it. They need to know that taking risks is essential to learning, including learning language, both written and oral. It's liberating for students to acknowledge that errors are natural and can demonstrate complex problem-solving. These are things I tried to teach Gregg and his classmates.

Gregg is still teaching me.

References

Cormier, R. (1977). *I am the cheese.* New York: Dell.

Fader, D. N., & Shaevitz, M. H. (1966). *Hooked on books.* New York: Berkley.

Giovanni, N. (1973). *Ego-tripping.* New York: Lawrence Hill.

Goodman, K. S. (1982a). Revaluing readers and reading. *Topics in Learning & Learning Disabilities, 1*(4), 87–93.

Goodman, K. S. (1982b). Miscues: Windows on the reading process. In F. V. Gollasch (Ed.), *Language and literacy: The selected writings of Kenneth S. Goodman: Vol. 1. Process, theory, research.* Boston: Routledge & Kegan Paul.

Goodman, K. S. (in press). Principles of revaluing. In Y. M. Goodman, & A. M. Marek (Eds.), *Revaluing readers and reading: Retrospective miscue analysis.* Katonah, NY: Richard C. Owen.

Goodman, Y. M., & Goodman, K. S. (1994). To err is human: Learning about language processes by analyzing miscues. In R. B. Ruddell, M. R. Ruddell, & H. Singer (Eds.), *Theoretical models and processes of reading* (4th ed.) (pp.104–123). Newark, DE: International Reading Association.

Goodman, Y. M., & Marek, A. M. (in press). *Revaluing readers and reading: Retrospective miscue analysis.* Katonah, NY: Richard C. Owen.

Goodman, Y. M., Watson, D. J., & Burke, C. L. (1987). *Reading miscue inventory: Alternative procedures.* Katonah, NY: Richard C. Owen.

Greenfield, E. (1972). *Honey, I love and other love poems.* New York: Thomas Y. Crowell.

Menosky, D. M. (1971). *A psycholinguistic description of oral reading miscues generated during the reading of varying positions of text by selected readers from grades two, four, six, and eight.* Unpublished doctoral dissertation. Wayne State University, Detroit, Michigan.

Rawls, W. (1961). *Where the red fern grows.* Garden City, NY: Doubleday.

Silverstein, S. (1974). *Where the sidewalk ends.* New York: Harper & Row.

Watson, D., & Crowley, P. (1987). How can we implement a whole-language approach? In C. Weaver (Ed.), *Reading process and practice: From socio-psycholinguistics to whole language* (pp. 232–279). Portsmouth, NH: Heinemann.

Watson, D., & Hoge, S. (in press). Reader selected miscues. In Y. M. Goodman, & A. M. Marek (Eds.), *Revaluing readers and reading: Retrospective miscue analysis.* Katonah, NY: Richard C. Owen.

Readers "Fresh" from the Middle

Our students come to school with rich and varied experiences. Before we begin reading, my first question is, "What do you already know about this topic?" By asking them to share their expertise, I am not only validating them as learners, but I am also demonstrating how efficient readers use their prior knowledge to help make sense of new information.

I am alert to readers' strategies, such as rereading to correct what doesn't make sense, making meaningful miscues (for example, substituting an acceptable synonym for the word in the text), overrelying on graphophonic relationships (excessive "sounding out"), or skipping words they don't know. I make mental notes of their particular reading strategies and sometimes write my observations in my planbook or journal.

Goodman, Watson, and Burke (1987) remind us that an understanding of reading miscue analysis enables teachers to discover patterns of students' oral reading behaviors, thus providing more information about an individual reader than any other instrument available. Knowledge of the reading process gained through miscue analysis is essential for middle-school English/language arts teachers, allowing them to develop a greater understanding of students' reading strategies and, if needed, to help them develop more effective and efficient ones.

When students read plays aloud, I have the opportunity for an informal miscue analysis. My instructions to them as readers are to try to make sense as they read, and reread if necessary; I remind listeners to be patient and not to correct the reader. Being patient in this situation is difficult for some listeners, but it encourages readers to use their own strategies to construct meaning.

This wait time also illustrates my confidence in student strategy use.

The overarching question for me and my students in any language context is, "Does this make sense?" I ask myself this question when considering the experiences I will offer my students in reading, writing, listening, and speaking. I want them to have authentic reasons for using the language arts; I also want them to make choices about those purposes. Throughout the school day and week, our program is organized around opportunities for varied language experiences; embedded in these experiences are opportunities for assessment of readers' strategy use, which provides me with information for instructional planning.

Organizing Our Program

I have the following goals in my seventh-grade language arts classroom:

1. read aloud to my students

2. give students choices in reading and writing

3. read a common text (students and teacher)

4. write every day (students and teacher)

5. share poetry with students

6. make connections with core (science, math, and social studies) through literature

7. demonstrate reading and writing strategies for my students.

Right! you say. All of this in one fifty-minute class period.

Although our school is organized as a junior high, there is a very strong sense of

Linda R. Morrow

Oakland Junior High School, Columbia, Missouri

middle-school philosophy among administrators and faculty, especially in seventh grade. Teachers are in close contact with parents regarding academic and behavioral issues. There is a strong sense of community in which the child feels safe, an atmosphere of collaboration where all are expected to be successful.

Our core classes (math, science, English, and social studies) are taught by interdisciplinary teams with flexible scheduling in order to emphasize the interconnectedness of concepts. Exploration is encouraged through electives, such as industrial technology, keyboarding, human environmental sciences, health, art, music, and foreign languages. This school-within-a-school is an attempt to provide a balance between teacher-subject specialization in the high school and the supportive interpersonal structure of the elementary school.

I teach English on a seventh-grade core team in a school containing grades seven, eight, and nine. Our core team from English, math, social studies, and science works with 100 heterogeneously grouped students. One of the goals of our team is to create an interdisciplinary experience for our students, where all subjects are closely integrated.

In order to conserve time in the fifty-minute period, we meet as a whole class for announcements, mini-lessons, reading strategy lesson instruction, and planning for the remainder of the period. Students then move to other areas of the classroom or into the hallways to pursue their day's plan. Dorothy Watson reminds us that we should never do for students what they can do for themselves. My students check the roll, put out the absentee slip, and record absences in the class attendance book. They also distribute and collect writing portfolios and other materials.

The reading experiences I offer my students are based on the understanding that reading is a meaning construction process that is embedded in the situational context; it requires readers to draw upon their prior experiences and their language strengths. These reading experiences include the following elements:

1. prior knowledge and context of situation
2. shared personal reading
3. book conferences
4. reader selected miscues
5. content connections
6. teacher read-alouds
7. newspapers as classroom texts.

Prior Knowledge and Context of Situation

I frequently use cartoons to demonstrate the importance of prior knowledge and how meaning is embedded within particular situational contexts. In order to "get the joke," we have to understand the cartoon's context and the author's reference to some idea in our commonly held experiences. At times, we have to work at making meaning from cartoons, but the sharing of ideas builds that meaning, becomes part of our knowledge base, provides an opportunity for identifying and labeling literary techniques, and sparks ideas for writing.

One of the first cartoons I use has no text, but features a police lineup of four little blonde-haired girls suspected of a crime. Accompanied by a police officer, the victims, the Three Bears, are viewing the lineup. I ask my students to study the cartoon, decide what makes it funny, and what we have to know in order to understand the cartoon.

Because this is a parody of a familiar story, most of the students are able to make the connections almost immediately. For example, as Frankie began to explain the story and our knowledge of the criminal justice system, I heard another "I got it!" from a student who struggles with reading and writing. Other responses ranged from, "You have to know the story of 'Goldilocks and the Three Bears'" to "The author was trying to make a new, funny twist on an old fairy tale."

It is valuable to do this activity first with a familiar text and always as a community of readers so that we can learn from each other in a nonthreatening situation. Because of our shared experience with "Goldilocks and the Three Bears," this strategy reaffirms the importance of using prior knowledge and emphasizes that we are all learners using similar meaning-making strategies although readers' abilities vary. The fact that a few students stated in their written responses that they didn't understand the cartoon at first underscores the need to demonstrate this strategy of drawing upon prior knowledge and making connections to other texts, and to encourage students to use this reading strategy in the future.

Shared Personal Reading

At Linda Rief's (1992) suggestion, I decided that the personal reading component of my curriculum would become homework. The standing homework assignment for my students is to read at least thirty minutes each evening from a book of their choosing. For the first two quarters of the school year, the students keep a log of dates and pages read in order to establish a reading habit.

In addition, we have sustained silent reading (SSR) each Friday for 20–30 minutes. Twice each quarter, students share their books through a conference with me, our librarian, another adult, or through a book review or a book talk. These book conferences give me information about readers that is available only in a one-to-one situation. In these conversations, students make theme statements, make comparisons with other books and movies, connect personal experiences, and describe personal reading strategies.

Book Conferences

In a recent conference, Christina and I were able to touch on several literary elements, and noticed how clues in the text affected our ability to make meaning. For example, we found we had differing opinions on the identity of the main character in *Daphney's Book* (Hahn, 1983) and we both had good arguments to support our views. As the discussion progressed, we focused on the setting, noting that it was raining in Maryland

and that the protagonist kept hoping it would change to snow as the storm in New England grew. There was also a reference to another character's father's being killed in the Vietnam War, allowing me to point out that clues given by the author help to establish the historical time period.

Another student, Tri, speaks English at school and Vietnamese at home. He had read a collection of ghost stories, and I discovered that he couldn't retell much of his favorite story. We read the story aloud together to demonstrate the value of rereading in order to remember a good story.

Julie, Laura, and Stephanie recently read *A Taste of Blackberries* (Smith, 1973). Julie compared the character Jamie, who dies of an allergic reaction to a bee sting, to the boy who cried wolf and wasn't taken seriously when he was really in trouble. Laura connected the narrator's depression over his best friend's death with the study of depression in her health class. Stephanie, a new student, told me that she had difficulty remembering what happened from one chapter to the next.

Book conferences provide me with valuable information about my students' personal connections and difficulties with texts that I can't access in a whole-class setting. I learn a great deal about how readers are handling texts and this information helps me plan activities and reading strategies. I also benefit from the sheer enjoyment of discussing books with the kids.

Reader Selected Miscues

Reader Selected Miscues (RSM) (Watson, 1978) is a strategy lesson that gives me the opportunity to discuss my own reading strategies as well as those of my students. Hoge (1983) and Watson suggest giving students 2″ x 8″ bookmarks to record three miscues (and their page numbers) that caused them to lose meaning or to be distracted from their reading. Reader selected miscues may include new or unusual words or confusing syntactic patterns. After sustained silent reading, these examples are shared in class. The miscues are discussed that day or

Book conferences provide me with valuable information about my students' personal connections and difficulties with texts that I can't access in a whole-class setting.

are collected and used for a mini-lesson the following day. This enables me to demonstrate reading strategies for handling difficult text and to verbalize my thinking as I learn from text.

Following sustained silent reading, students share any unfamiliar, interesting, or confusing words or language patterns they have found and we talk about the strategies proficient readers use when they encounter such words or structures in text. For example, we ask: What information does the author give that explains the word or phrase? What do we already know about the topic?

Recently, Jessica greeted me with "Hey, Mrs. Morrow, look what I found." She showed me a passage in her book which read, "Your salad days are over." "Salad days" was clearly an unusual term for this seventh grader. We read the passage together and Jessica decided that the rich young man in the novel was being forced to go to work. Jessica was using a reading strategy demonstrated in class, indicating her awareness of its usefulness.

I share my own reader selected miscues with my students. One example comes from an historical novel set in Germany during World War II. I showed my students the name of a political party discussed in the book: National Sozialistsche Deutsche Arbeiterpartei. Because I don't speak or read German, there was no way I could pronounce this term, but I knew from the other information the author provided that this was the name of the Nazi party. I told my students that, as I continued reading, I called it Nazi and did not worry about the pronunciation. In this naming strategy, the reader predicts that the word is a name; omits that name and substitutes another name, nickname, or initial; determines some characteristic of the name (person or place); and determines the importance of the name in the story (Hoge, 1983; Watson, 1978).

Joel provided an example of going back to the text for more information and using prior knowledge. He was reading a mystery and one of the clues was to be found on the moor. He read the piece of text aloud, and the rest of the class speculated on the mean-

ing. From the context, we decided that it was a land form. Claire remembered reading about the moor in *The Secret Garden* (Burnett, 1987). At this point, Alan reminded us that *moor* can also mean to secure a boat or a native of Morocco. This exchange is a clear example of why it would be pointless to plan a vocabulary lesson prior to reading: I don't know what my students already know or what they might learn as they read. Reader Selected Miscues empowers students to use their background knowledge and to question the text for needed information.

Jackson was reading *Mississippi Bridge* (Taylor, 1990) and asked about *onliest*. He knew immediately what the word was after reading it aloud. This provided the perfect opportunity to discuss the author's use of dialect to create authentic characters. During this same discussion, Claire asked about the word *taffeta*. She read a description of a girl dressed for her senior prom. As we discussed the text, Claire explained that she knew about the situation, the fancy prom dress, and the fact that the fabric made a swishing noise as the girl walked. Claire knew that taffeta was a fabric, but she had not actually seen or worn it before. Claire needs to be aware that she has a clear understanding of the text, and knowing more specific information about such things as taffeta can satisfy her curiosity, but is not required to understand the story.

At the beginning of the year, I demonstrate the RSM strategy through shared reading of a short story. Our discussions have produced some clear examples of changes in word meanings over time, definitions determined by use or context, and etymologies.

Several students asked about the word *fresh* in Shirley Jackson's (1968) "Charles." When we discussed the term, I heard a ripple of giggles across the room because their first assumption was that it was a sexual innuendo. When I asked them to reinvestigate the text, they decided that the word, used by a kindergartner, was describing an example of back-talking or being a smart aleck. They came to this conclusion because they had already established the period as the 1950s and the character as being disrespectful to his parents.

> *What information does the author give that explains the word or phrase? What do we already know about the topic?*

This led to a discussion of how the meanings of words change over time. A similar situation occurred when the students read "Practically Everyone Knows" (Blume, 1978). From the clues given by the author, they figured that a seventh-grade "mixer" was a party for seventh graders featuring a band because one of the characters was going to play drums.

In this same story by Blume, several students asked about the word *lectern*. We talked through the passage noting that it was something used in place of a desk when one was standing. Another clue in this particular story was that the lectern was in the auditorium. At this point, I heard a number of students say *podium*. This gave me one more opportunity to say, "See how much you already know." Switching the context from school to church, the students easily produced *pulpit*.

Content Connections

I encourage my students to continue the use of reader selected miscues as they respond in their reading journals. They often read non-English words or phrases in the novels and folktales we read as we follow their social studies class around the world. For instance, as some students read *Waiting for the Rain* (Gordon, 1987), set in South Africa, they encountered Afrikaans words. This gave me the opportunity to become a learner with them. We used several strategies: What do I think it means based upon its use in the particular scene? What additional information does the author give me? Do we have any information from social studies materials? Is there a glossary? Can we use the glossaries in the other novel set in South Africa? For most of the Afrikaans words, one of the above strategies worked and we were able to confirm our predictions and construct meaning from the text. For those few where we just had to make our best guess, we were able to move on with the story rather than being overwhelmed and giving up. This is a very powerful demonstration for struggling readers because they can see that adults have to work at making meaning and that there are many strategies on which to rely.

Because my students do most of their individual reading as homework, I rarely give them additional outside assignments. Class time is used for writing and for reading texts that provide opportunities for making content connections with particular world cultures as the students explore them in the social studies segment of our interdisciplinary team. As Brozo & Tomlinson (1986), Du Bois & MacIntosh (1986), Levstik (1985), Sanacore (1990) and Spiegel (1987) remind us, the rationale for using literature in content areas includes broadening one's knowledge of the world, adding depth and meaning to concepts studied in a specific content area, encouraging comparisons of multiple texts, connecting prior knowledge with new information, generalization and application of concepts, affecting students' social attitudes, and presenting content in a dramatic and personalized manner.

The students' exploration of India and Pakistan in social studies was complemented by reading a collection of folktales and nonfiction about this region. As we read *Shabanu: Daughter of the Wind* (Staples, 1989) together, my students were aghast that the protagonist was, at their age, betrothed to one of her cousins, enticed by the idea that she didn't have to go to school, and intrigued by the fact that she had the same worries as they did. Reading *Shabanu* enabled the students to acquire a feel for a young Muslim girl's way of life in present-day Pakistan. Because the book is written in familiar narrative style, they could easily add to their background information about this culture and relate to the concepts being presented in their social studies class. Students could not help but compare their own way of life with Shabanu's. They often asked questions and wondered why life-changing decisions were completely out of Shabanu's hands. As they wrestled with the fact that Shabanu was being forced into an arranged marriage, they began to think of possible alternatives, and realized that all adolescents must make tough decisions.

When my students studied Africa, the books *Journey to Jo'burg* and *Chain of Fire* (Naidoo, 1986, 1990) provided personal views of apartheid in South Africa, a policy that the students were exploring in social studies. Apartheid came to life as students made the more than 300-kilometer journey with thirteen-year-old Naledi and her nine-year-old brother Tiro from their village to Johannesburg to find their mother who was working for a wealthy white family. Through these novels, plus *Waiting for the Rain: A Novel of South Africa* (Gordon, 1987) and *In the Middle of Somewhere: A Story of South Africa* (Gordon, 1990), my seventh graders grappled with the realities of a political system that did not value its citizens as equals. Social attitudes were affected as my students expressed their anger over the inequities suffered by the black South Africans.

My goal is to provide literature study groups with enough titles for each culture that our students explore. Those involved in this search for sets of multicultural selections include my colleagues on the core team, our language arts department chair, our colleagues on the other seventh-grade team, our media specialist, and colleagues outside my school (such as local Teachers Applying Whole Language [TAWL] members). Margaret Mooney (1987) provides the following criteria for identifying high-quality literature:

1. Does the piece have charm, magic, impact, and appeal?

2. Does the piece say something worthwhile?

3. Is the shape and structure appropriate?

4. Is the language effective? Does the language suit the subject and the characters?

5. Is the piece authentic? Does it avoid the sham, the misleading, the prejudiced, the stereotyped, and the superficial?

I search for literature from the various world cultures that my students are exploring. We read fairy tales, folktales, poetry, novels, and nonfiction pieces. I use dialectical response journals, partner reading, and teacher read-aloud to support readers who are still word bound, overrelying on sounding out words, and those who would prefer walking on hot coals to reading. Students

> *I search for literature from the various world cultures that my students are exploring.*

participate in literature study groups, reading novels set in various cultures of the world. As they read, they respond in dialectical journals, which become their agendas for group discussion. As students discuss the connections they have made, raise questions, and acknowledge strategies they have used for constructing meaning, they model effective strategies for students who are struggling with the reading process.

For example, Ryan, who was in a literature study group with three other boys and one girl, compared the friendship dilemma in *Waiting for the Rain* (Gordon, 1987) with the similar conflict between the animal characters in the movie *The Fox and the Hound*. As these group members shared their notebook entries, Ryan read, "The part where Frikkie has captured Tengo in an apartheid protest is like the movie *Fox and the Hound* when the animals realize that when they are grown up one will be chasing the other."

Other entries focus on new or unusual words such as *pannier* (camel saddle) in *Shabanu* and *veld* (open, rolling grassland) in *In the Middle of Somewhere*. In *Waiting for the Rain*, the main character, Frikkie, calls his little sister a domkop. Since there was no glossary of Afrikaans words, the students used their knowledge of syntax and their own experiences with siblings to surmise that the word meant dummy or stupid. In this same novel, the students discovered that often the writer will define unusual words such as kraal (a group of round mud huts with thatched roofs where the farmworkers lived, Gordon, 1987, p. 7) as a part of the text. These situations present opportunities for modeling independent reading strategies.

Students needing support in reading often engage in partner reading (reading aloud with another student) or, in the case of my class-within-a-class, another teacher reads aloud with small groups, using the hallway as an extension of the classroom.

Teacher Read-Alouds

I often introduce *Middle School Blues* (Kassem, 1986) at the beginning of the school year because the protagonist, like my students, is experiencing a new school setting:

seven different teachers, classes with all new faces, lockers, hall passes, and choices in the cafeteria. I read this novel aloud because I want to demonstrate my own love of reading using a piece of literature that parallels my students' current experiences. While we enjoy a good story together, I also have the chance to demonstrate reading strategies such as prediction, using prior knowledge, using the context of situation in the story, graphophonic relationships, grammatical knowledge, and, most of all, meaning. As I read about Cindy's experiences in seventh grade, I ask my students to predict what will happen next or what they would do in the same situation based on their experiences and what has happened so far in the novel. I also ask them what specific events in the plot bring to mind. For example, at the beginning of the book, Cindy's grandmother passes away and the funeral is a fiasco. At this point, we talk about our own experiences at funerals. I often begin by relating a similar incident that involved my own children at their grandfather's funeral.

Newspapers as Classroom Texts

Current news provides another source for reading strategy lessons. I write a daily message on the chalkboard that deals with current events, often tying into the culture being explored in social studies. This gives the students a chance to use their knowledge from that discipline to make meaning of new information. Current events also give me a chance to think out loud or model how an adult deals with new and difficult information. For example, we followed the dismantling of apartheid and the elections in South Africa. As we read newspaper accounts, I struggled with the names of the tribal townships and the Afrikaans words, some of which we had not encountered in the novels we read or in the social studies textbook. I made the point that we knew what the words meant and quite possibly we would hear them pronounced by newscasters. Students need to know that at times we must look outside ourselves for more information.

Conclusions and Dilemmas

I want to provide two days of writing and two days of reading for my students each week. Friday is reserved for sustained silent reading and sharing personal reading. Unfortunately, this schedule is difficult to keep because we always seem to need more time for one or the other. I feel it is crucial to allow my students ample time for free writing in response to their reading. Their writing may take the form of jokes, poetry to share in class, or personal reflections on current events, family life, and extra curricular activities. These reading and writing processes spill over into each other. Most of this writing is done in class because I want to model the writing process as my students write, and I want them to avail themselves of help from their peers. The challenge is to make the time for these important activities.

Before starting any new reading activity, I ask myself the following questions:

1. What do my students already know about a particular topic?

2. Does this experience mirror life in the real world? Is it authentic?

3. How can I learn about my students' reading and learning strategies as they engage in this activity?

An understanding of the transactional, social, psychological, and linguistic aspects of the reading process (K. Goodman, 1979) is essential to us as English teachers in order to help students who are struggling readers. The expectation that in elementary school one learns to read and, consequently, will read to learn in middle and secondary schools is not always realistic, as middle-school teachers know. We need to present to our students the reading strategies that we use effortlessly and unconsciously, and help them become aware of and use the strengths they bring to their reading.

Knowledge of the reading process gained through reading miscue analysis enables us to examine a student's oral reading, thereby gaining specific information about his or her reading ability. This con-

I feel it is crucial to allow my students ample time for free writing in response to their reading.

scious knowledge of the reading process helps us plan reading experiences that will enhance that student's reading strengths rather than add to the struggle.

References

Brozo, W., & Tomlinson, C. (1986). Literature: The key to lively content courses. *The Reading Teacher, 40*(3), 288–293.

Du Bois, B., & McIntosh, M. (1986, September/October). Reading aloud to students in secondary history classes. *The Social Studies,* 210–213.

Goodman, K. S. (1979). The know-more and the know-nothing movements in reading: A personal response. *Language Arts, 56,* 657–663.

Goodman, Y., Watson, D., & Burke, C. (1987). *Reading miscue inventory: Alternative procedures.* New York: Richard C. Owen.

Hoge, S. (1983). A comprehension-centered reading program using reader selected miscues. *Journal of Reading, 27,* 52–55.

Levstik, L. (1985). Literary geography and mapping. *Social Education, 1,* 38–43.

Rief, L. (1992). *Seeking diversity: Language arts with adolescents.* Portsmouth, NH: Heinemann.

Sanacore, J. (1990). Creating the lifetime reading habit in social studies. *Journal of Reading, 33*(6), 414–418.

Spiegel, D. (1987, Summer). Using adolescent literature in social studies and science. *Educational Horizons,* 162–164.

Watson, D. J. (1978). Reader selected miscues: Getting more from sustained silent reading. *English Education, 10,* 75–85.

Adolescent Literature Cited

Blume, J. (1978). Practically everyone knows. In T. Clymer & L. Ruth (Eds.), *To make a difference* (pp. 56–62). Lexington, MA: Ginn.

Burnett, F. H. (1987). *The secret garden.* New York: Henry Holt.

Gordon, S. (1987). *Waiting for the rain: A novel of South Africa.* New York: Bantam Books.

Gordon S. (1990). *In the middle of somewhere: A story of South Africa.* New York: Orchard Books.

Hahn, M. D. (1983). *Daphney's book.* New York: Clarion Books.

Jackson, S. (1968). Charles. In *The best of both worlds: An anthology of stories for all ages* (pp. 123–128). Garden City, NY: Doubleday.

Kassem, L. (1986). *Middle school blues.* New York: Avon Books.

Naidoo, B. (1986). *Journey to Jo'burg: A South African story.* New York: HarperCollins.

Naidoo, B. (1990). *Chain of fire.* Philadelphia: Lippincott Crowell.

Smith, D. B. (1973). *A taste of blackberries.* New York: Thomas Y. Crowell.

Staples, S. (1989). *Shabanu: Daughter of the wind.* New York: Alfred A. Knopf.

Taylor, M. (1990). *Mississippi bridge.* New York: Bantam Skylark.

Lingering Questions

1. How do I stick to a schedule that provides for a reading and writing workshop?

2. How can I have more frequent reading and writing conferences with individual students?

3. How do I balance the experiences of shared reading of novels and short stories with literature study groups and personal reading choices?

4. How can knowledge of the reading process and use of strategy lessons be shared with high school English/language arts teachers?

Not Just Words on a Page: Kids, Parents, and Teachers Learning about Reading Together

Olivia picks up a book, brushes her hair from her face with a sweep of her hand, looks around the room to see if anyone is watching her, looks at her friend across the room, giggles, tosses her hair out of her face again, stares blankly at the page of print, then, with a contorted expression, begins to read. During thirty minutes of silent reading, Olivia is repeatedly distracted. Her eyes wander away from the page to objects on her desk, to other people in the class, to passersby outside the window.

This "pretending-to-read" behavior is the rule rather than the exception for Olivia, a sixth grader in a self-contained classroom of 30 fifth and sixth graders. I believe this slightly-built, blond, vibrant eleven-year-old was trying to mask her discomfort with reading. I wanted to know if Olivia's beliefs about herself as a reader led to her distraction. I needed to gather information about Olivia's reading and her views of her reading in order to assist her in seeing her strengths, and to help her use these strengths to grow as a reader.

Students' Views of Themselves as Readers

For some time, I have been hooked on the notion that students must evaluate their own learning in order to grow. Understanding how students see themselves as learners helps teachers plan curriculum. Similarly, students' views of their own reading behaviors help us gain insight leading to successful reading instruction. This school year, I wanted to know if a student self-study in reading would assist them in becoming better readers.

During the first two weeks of the school year, I sent students off, one-by-one with tape recorder in hand, to record themselves reading a passage from *The Trouble with Tuck* by Theodore Taylor, a middle-grade book from the district shared literature list. I asked the students to read a selection from the beginning of the book and then to meet with me for a retelling of the passage and a discussion. Figure 1 shows excerpts from Olivia's reading.

Through these and other passages, I saw patterns in Olivia's miscues. Although she produced nonwords (*undoubtfully*) and syntactically unacceptable (and, therefore, semantically unacceptable) structures (*beginning a dog*), more often Olivia demonstrated proficient reader strategies, including regressing to correct (*he had* corrected to *he couldn't*), making sensible substitutions (*veteran* for *veterinarian*—there is no reason *veteran* would not fit at this point in the story) and using a naming strategy (*Frerer Tuck* for *Friar Tuck*).

Judith A. Wright

Cherry Valley School, Petaluma, California

Text	Olivia's Reading
No one can definitely say when Friar Tuck began to go blind, not even Dr. Douglas Tobin, who was undoubtedly one of the best veterinarians in California.	No one can definitely say when Frerer Tuck began to go blind, not even Dr. Douglas Tobian, Tobin, who was undoubtfully one of the best veterans in California.
But the light probably began to fail for big Tuck long before any of us suspected it, and of course, being a dog, he couldn't very well talk about it.	But the light probably began to fail for big Tuck long before any of us suspected it, it, and of course, beginning a dog, he couldn't, he had, "wait" he couldn't very well talk about it.

[The Trouble with Tuck, p.1]

FIGURE 1.

Following her taping, Olivia was invited to retell the story and to reflect on her reading:

"I didn't know how or why he got blind and I didn't get what the cat fight was all about. When they star-. . . started to describe things, I shut down. I wasn't having fun. I was really slow. I usually go on, but not really. I stop, pause, five seconds or so. I don't know a lot of big words. I put words in that aren't there. Little writing [font size] makes me tired. I don't get into a book easily; the action must be right in the beginning to get me going. I sound like a computer when I read. It makes me feel really bad, like . . . I can't do it again." Olivia

Hearing Olivia reflect on her reading and the reading process reveals quite a bit about her views of herself as a reader. She has *nothing* positive to say about her reading. Olivia admitted that she was more concerned with identifying the words than with understanding what was going on in the passage. Olivia is in trouble with reading, not because of her reading strategies, but because of her views of the reading process and herself as a reader. Olivia's reflection indicates that she believes:

- it's important to have fun while reading

- reading shouldn't have to be work

- reading slowly is bad

- not knowing big words is a problem

- insertions are dishonest

- small print size creates drowsiness

- there must be action in the beginning or you can't get into a book

- oral reading should be expressive

- skipping words is deceitful.

Many of Olivia's beliefs, as Dorothy Watson would say, stop her in her linguistic tracks. Olivia maintains that being slow is bad when she states, "I was really slow. I stop, pause, five seconds or so." Olivia believes good readers read quickly. Since she doesn't do this (at least not all the time), she feels she must not be a good reader and loses confidence. Olivia indicates that reading should be expressive but that she sounds "like a com-

puter." Her lack of variation in tone when she reads aloud causes her concern because she has observed that good oral readers use expression. She even explains, "It makes me feel really bad, like . . . I can't do it again."

Olivia concludes that knowing large words makes someone a good reader. She explains, "I don't know a lot of big words. I put words in that are not there." By substituting one word for another, Olivia feels that she must be cheating. Even though her substituted word fits the context of the sentence and the larger text, she views the substitution as a weakness. Her miscues indicate *to her* that she is not a proficient reader.

How will knowing about Olivia's beliefs about her reading and her actual reading behaviors help me assist her in becoming a better reader? Using a set of procedures based on retrospective miscue analysis (Goodman & Marek, in press), I help my students gain an accurate perspective on the reading process and on themselves as readers. The following pictures from our classroom show how this unfolds.

Readers' and Writers' Workshop

In our classroom, we explore reading through self-selected books, whole class involvement with a shared piece of literature, or partner/small group reading. I also read to my students daily from a potpourri of literature. Our readers'/writers' workshop, which takes place three mornings one week and two mornings the following week, allows for large blocks of silent reading time. There are some students who choose to read with a partner or in a small group. On some occasions, if we are reading a shared book, I ask the students to gather in groups of four to six and read aloud. This affords me time to do a quick observation with a large number of students in an authentic context. I begin to compose a mosaic of the total class in terms of reading strengths and boundaries. Moreover, I become aware of the particular reading strategies individuals use.

After this time for book exploration, we will sometimes do a silent dialogue with a partner in which one person will write about

How will knowing about Olivia's beliefs about her reading and her actual reading behaviors help me assist her in becoming a better reader?

a part of a book that touched them in some way. Partners will respond and may also write about a different passage from their book. This continues back and forth until the conversation is exhausted.

Students also use their literature journals to cite places where they had difficulty in their reading. They might mention disagreements with the author's language usage or sections they found confusing. On the other hand, they may choose to write about exciting parts, or make connections to other books, movies, and events in their lives.

We also meet in small groups to discuss the literature, referred to as "book talks." Often the group decides what they wish to talk about, such as characters, changes that have occurred, the plot, themes, symbols, conflicts, and so on. Occasionally, I or another class member will suggest a topic for discussion before reading. These book talks take place once or twice a week.

Recently, the class read *Maniac Magee* by Jerry Spinelli (1990). Students gathered in self-selected groups of four or five; they decided what they wanted to discuss, how far they wanted to read before meeting again, and what type of project they wanted to do to extend their connections with the book. I visited one group that was discussing symbolism from the book and how it added meaning to the story:

"I think Cobble's knot symbolized power because before [the untying of the knot] everyone thought Maniac was an out of place white boy. Afterwards, he was popular and that gave him power." Danny, Grade 6

"I saw Grayson as a symbol. He couldn't read and he symbolizes that even grown-ups have barriers." Calen, Grade 6

I moved on to another group that was talking about which character changed from the beginning of the book to the end:

"I think that Mars Bar changed through the book from being really mean, powerful, and competitive to being a good friend to Maniac." Morgan, Grade 6

"I think Mars Bar changed too. He was kind of cold and hard and didn't like any white kids at all. But after he had known Maniac for a while he knew that not all white kids were the same. In the end, he was friends with Magee, a white kid." Alyssa, Grade 5

We share many literature moments with the entire class, discussing ideas, characters, plot, themes, and anything connected to books. Someone will share a newspaper article they read, another might contribute a poem or essay, and someone else might tell the class about the differences between a book they read and the movie interpretation of that book. I find myself immersed in the discussions, the readings, and the writings. I often sit in on group book talks, either as a participant or as an observer, depending on my needs. At times I feel particularly attracted to ideas from a book, and I offer my insights and solicit student responses. I feel I must "sit inside my research" and become part of the research context (Watson, Burke, Harste, 1989). Yet, there are other moments when I wish to remain the mouse in the corner, observing the students' constructs.

Multiple Perspectives on Students' Reading

Readers'/Writers' Workshop offers me, my students, and their parents the opportunity to find evidence of literacy connections. In the past, we all contributed to student literacy portfolios for assessment purposes, documenting student learning and growth. Portfolios included:

- literature reflections

- written extensions of books read in class

- graphic and video extensions of the literature.

These artifacts provided a good snapshot of students' reading, but, in order to get a more complete picture, I sought multiple perspectives on their reading.

I decided to probe deeper into this area through parent interviews about their child's literacy, audiotapes of students' reading, student interviews following the reading, and students' self-reflection on their reading through retrospective miscue analysis. I wanted to know if students were able to identify and reflect on their strengths and areas of concern. Could they also use this information toward future learning, partic-

I decided to probe deeper.

ularly revaluing themselves as readers? I was wrestling with how the students and I would use the data once we became aware of it. Would it help the Olivias in my class? What about the successful readers? What was their place in this picture? What about parents' perspectives? How about my own understandings of reading? Where did these fit in?

Older students can learn to appreciate the successful reading strategies they use, learn techniques of proficient readers, and unlearn approaches that interrupt the reading process. I see a number of students who are not aware of the range of reading strategies available to them and who, therefore, have not derived much meaning nor pleasure from books. Many of them have been so concerned with attempting to accurately replicate the text that they do not engage with the text in personal and meaningful ways.

Goodman and Marek (in press) tell us that readers-in-trouble often see themselves as cheaters in the system rather than as literate human beings. These readers need to revalue themselves as readers and to develop a realistic view of the reading process.

Views on Reading and Readers: Calen, Alexanne, Olivia, and Their Parents

Calen, another student from our fifth/sixth grade read the selection from *The Trouble with Tuck* at the beginning of the year (see Figure 2 for excerpts). Calen's reading behaviors include getting distracted easily, exhibiting frustration through long sighs while reading, leaving out sections of sentences and paragraphs, substituting nonsense words for real words, running sentences and paragraphs together. With so many miscues, I wondered whether Calen was able to understand what he was reading. I questioned Calen about the passage. He could tell me in detail what was going on in the story:

"The story was about a dog named Tuck going blind. They couldn't figure out when the dog went blind. It took them a while to put it together. There was a cat fight in the backyard and Tuck got upset and went through the wire door. Tuck is Helen's best friend. Her mom is from the South and she seems nice. It would be weird if your dog went blind. The beginning intrigues me so much that I want to read on." Calen, Grade 6

The miscues did not interfere with the meaning for Calen. Did this mean that Calen thought he made no miscues on the reading?

"I stumbled a lot. I was conscious of being recorded. It was noisy in our cluster, too. I slowed down and wanted to have every word be exact. When I messed up, I would say, 'oh, no!', kind of apologize, and go back and try to get the word or sentence."

What was going on in Calen's head as he read? How was he actually making sense out of the print? How did he know so much about the story?

"I imagine what I'm reading after I read. I take time to imagine what I read. In my mind I change voices of people so I can get a feel for the story. Different characters have different voices."

Olivia and Calen struggled with reading. I wanted to investigate the views of a successful reader so I looked to Alexanne.

Text	Calen's Reading
No one can definitely say when Friar Tuck began to go blind, not even Dr. Douglas Tobin, who was undoubtedly one of the best veterinarians in California.	No one can difficult to say someone Trek ah began to get go blind, but not even Dr. Douglas Tobin, who (pause) Tobin, who was undoubtedly one of was (pause) undoubtedly one of the best veterinarians in California.
But the light probably began to fail for big Tuck long before any of us suspected it, and of course, being a dog, he couldn't very well talk about it.	But it was the light probably began to fail for big Truck long before any one was so suspected it, "I don't know" of course, being a dog, he couldn't couldn't very well talk about it.
[The Trouble with Tuck, p.1]	

FIGURE 2.

Clip and File

Reviews of Books for Middle-Level Readers

Reviews for Kids by Kids

Dragonwings
Lawrence Yep

Trophy, 1977, 256 pp., $4.95
ISBN 0-06-440085-9

Dragonwings is an ideal book for any sixth grader to read. It teaches valuable lessons and is a great story. This book is about a young boy who journeys to the United States to join his father. The boy's father is in the process of making a flying machine. They both face racial discrimination and other problems. But together, as father and son, they fight through an exciting adventure that can be learned from.

Some lessons to be learned from *Dragonwings* are that racial discrimination does not occur just between black and white races, but it also happens with Asians. Another lesson to be learned is if you keep trying to be friends, usually there is everything to gain and nothing to lose. In conclusion, all sixth graders should read *Dragonwings* because lessons can be learned and it is good practice for a sixth grader to be "dragged" into absorption in a book.

Tienmu Ma, Grade 7
Muirlands Middle School, La Jolla, California

Who Killed My Daughter?
Lois Duncan

Dell, 1992, 350pp., $5.99
ISBN 0-440-21342-8

Kaitlyn Clare Arquette, Lois Duncan's daughter, was murdered on July 17, 1989. *Who Killed My Daughter?* is a moving expression of how much a mother loves her daughter or son. Although it must have been painful for her, Lois Duncan did a sensational job of telling about her daughter's death and giving every detail of every fact. Lois Duncan is determined to find her daughter's killer or killers. The very thought of having a loved one murdered is devastating.

Lois Duncan puts facts in order and puts the events in a personal narrative that comes from a broken heart. Her book told me how a mother will never give up and how she will go to any cost to help her child. I now know a different side of Lois Duncan, not the horror, mystery novel writer, but the caring figure of a mother.

Victoria Peinado, Grade 7
Hayes Middle School, Albuquerque, New Mexico

The Once and Future King
T. H. White

Ace, 1987, 640pp., $6.99
ISBN 0-441-62740-4

The Dark Ages . . . Just the name inspires ideas about the type of period it was. Knights knocking each other off horses, blind massacres, and cruel living conditions are just a small part of this time in history. Yet, in the middle of all this confusion, one man becomes King and resurrects Justice. As a boy, he was unaware of his heritage and lived as a typical person. His teacher, Merlin, shows him the world through the eyes of many different animals. This helps him, Wart, to become King Arthur in his quest of establishing Justice. As the years pass on, he becomes torn between his duty of justice and his personal life. This tormented King wove the peace in England and was forced to watch it unravel.

This is the canvas on which T. H. White paints the dramatic history of Medieval England. From it, we can discover if true Justice exists, what it is, and whether Might is Right, or not. I highly recommend this book to anyone who enjoys a good story with humor, philosophy, and excellent description.

Paul Nicholas, Grade 7
Hayes Middle School, Albuquerque, New Mexico

The True Confessions of Charlotte Doyle
Avi

Avon Flare, 1992, 240pp., $3.99
ISBN 0-380-71475-2

The True Confessions of Charlotte Doyle, written by the award-winning author Avi, is a breathtaking and exciting novel about a thirteen-year-old girl and her adventures during her voyage across the Atlantic Ocean to America to reunite with her beloved family. At first, she enjoys the atmosphere and equanimity of the sea, but she is soon shocked to learn of the conditions of the ship and to realize that the other families, expected to act as her guardians, have not shown up. Through fear and pain, Charlotte learns about friendship and the need to fight—two intrinsic characteristics to survive the harsh times on the high seas. She witnesses murder, mutiny, near-death experiences, and bravery. She has to make critical decisions, choosing where and to whom to give her loyalty and trust, as well as whose trust she should accept.

I admired this book because of its adventure, action, and the sensation that you never want to put it down. This was an extraordinary book, worth reading, and I highly recommend it for all young adults.

Catalina Garreton, Grade 7
Spartanburg Day School, Spartanburg, South Carolina

Rascal
Sterling North
Puffin, 1990, 192pp., $3.99
ISBN 0-14-034445-4

Rascal tells the story of an unforgettable friendship between a boy and a raccoon, and all their adventures together. I really enjoyed this book. Some parts that I thought were really good were the times when they went camping, fishing, and riding bikes. They had many experiences doing all these things. Once when the boy and the baby raccoon went fishing, the baby raccoon got interested in a crab. But he got too close. Ow! When they went riding bikes, the raccoon sat in the front basket, while the boy pedaled and steered. On one of the trips, the boy and the baby raccoon went through the country. They saw a flock of magnificent birds.

There are some things that I would tell the author. For instance, the dog, Wowser, was brought in quite a lot in the beginning of the story but toward the end he was hardly mentioned. The author also seems to show cruelty to animals when he snatched the baby raccoon from his home. Despite these parts, this story was one of my favorites.

Claire Schlemme, Grade 5
Cherry Valley Elementary School, Petaluma, California

Eye of the World
Robert Jordan
Tor Books, 1990, 814pp., $5.99
ISBN 0-8125-1181-6

Eye of the World is the first book in a quintet. It is a fantasy novel where Jordan makes up his own creatures and types of characters, not just the typical elves, dwarfs, fairies, and wizards. Jordan is an incredible writer. Stephen King, watch out! You have a rival!

There is powerful action throughout the book. One scene finds the reader in the ruins of a city thousands of years old. There is an evil mist inside the city that if it touches you, you die. The city has been invaded by Trollocs (7-foot tall, two-legged, evil, dumb, part animal, part human, troops). There is a chase and the six "good guys" barely get out of the city with their lives. They must hide out, waiting to escape the city. As they depart the city, two of the "good guys" are forced to jump off a cliff with their horses into a river. They are separated from the party for a long time.

Jordan includes adventure, wit, action, and an awesome plot. I definitely recommend this book.

Elvin Meadows, Grade 6
Cherry Valley Elementary School, Petaluma, California

Here's to You, Rachel Robinson
Judy Blume
Bantam Doubleday Dell, 1993, 196pp., $4.50
ISBN 0-440-40946-2

Rachel Robinson is a gifted seventh-grade girl with a lot of problems. One, her brother Charles has just been expelled from his boarding school in Vermont. He's mean, rude, and worst of all, Rachel's two closest friends, Alison and Stephanie, think he's great. Another of Rachel's problems is her sister Jessica, who is suffering from awful cystic acne. Yet another of Rachel's problems is Stephanie, her best friend for years, who Rachel is slowly losing to Alison. Through all these problems, Rachel keeps her head up, keeps smiling, and keeps playing her flute.

I think that Judy Blume deserves a standing ovation for this book. It was very realistic, funny, and it made me wonder if Judy has, or has had, a seventh-grade child. She was totally correct in her displays of the seventh-grade mind, attitude, and dislikes. Readers who like *Just As Long As We're Together* will love and should definitely read *Here's to You, Rachel Robinson*. I did!

Claire Winkels, Grade 7
Oakland Junior High School, Columbia, Missouri

Jim Ugly
Sid Fleischman
Dale Publishing, 1992, 130pp., $3.99
ISBN 0-440-90010-7

Jake, the twelve-year-old main character in *Jim Ugly*, has a wolf his father left him in his will. Jake thinks his dad is really not dead, so he and his wolf, named Jim Ugly, set off to find his dad and the stolen jewels that his dad hid from a yellowleg man who is after them. Jake is surprised when Jim Ugly picks up the scent of Jake's dad. The sniffing led right into a yellowleg man who recognized who Jake was. Thinking Jake might have the lost jewels, he follows everywhere they go. Will Jake ever get past the yellowleg man and find his dad before the yellowleg man steals the jewels and gets away? If you're a *Whipping Boy* fan, you will enjoy this book also.

Russell S. Burnett, Grade 7
Oakland Junior High School, Columbia, Missouri

The Road to Memphis
Mildred D. Taylor

Puffin, 1992, 290pp., $3.99
ISBN 0-14-036077-8

The Road to Memphis is an excellent, detailed story about how blacks were mistreated at the beginning of World War II. When Moe, a kindhearted friend of Cassie's, lashes out at his white tormentors, Cassie, her brother, and his friends must take Moe to safety. Once they get to Memphis, they must get Moe on a train to Chicago to live with Cassie's Uncle Hammer. On the way up to Memphis, they are faced with many troubles.

I think this book is an exciting and action-packed book. I recommend it to anyone who likes challenging text. If you've read the first two stories in the Logan saga, then don't miss out on this one.

Daniel Lange, Grade 7
Oakland Junior High School, Columbia, Missouri

Sing Down the Moon
Scott O'Dell

Dell, 1970, 124pp., $3.50
ISBN 0-440-97975-7

Sing Down the Moon is a story about a fourteen-year-old Navajo girl named Bright Morning who lives in Canyon de' Chelly in the mid-1860s. Follow Bright Morning as she is captured by Spanish slavers and is taken from Canyon de' Chelly. Go with her as she escapes and finds danger, excitement, and love. She and her people fight for their land but fail, and must go with several other tribes on The Long Walk. Feel the depression as they are put on a reservation and have very little food and supplies.

She and Tall Boy escape from the reservation. Feel the joy and emotion as Bright Morning has their first child and makes their new home back in Canyon de' Chelly where the rain that falls is Navajo rain.

I really enjoyed this gripping story of life, love, and destiny. A timeless classic, I would recommend this book to young adults and up. I wish you happy readings!

Melissa Presley, Grade 7
Oakland Junior High School, Columbia, Missouri

Bridie of the Wild Rose Inn
Jennifer Armstrong

Bantam, 1994, 180pp., $3.99
ISBN 0-553-29866-6

Bridie has been waiting for ten years for her parents to send for her. They moved away from Scotland to start a better life when she was six and she stayed with her grandfather. After he dies, she decides to go to Massachusetts to live with her parents. She finds them and a few new problems once she gets there: Mrs. Goody Handy thought she was a witch and then Bridie falls in love with Mrs. Handy's son!

I have never cried while reading a book, but this one made me weep. I have never been interested enough in a book to want to read it at home. I constantly wanted to know what was going to happen next. I wondered if Bridie was going to marry Will or if she would be hung for being a witch. At the end, I could have cried my heart out when I found out what happened. I recommend this book to anyone who likes a mix of romance and problems.

Natalie Barnett, Grade 7
Kenilworth Junior High School, Petaluma, California

Go Ask Alice
Anonymous

Avon, 1976, 192pp., $3.99
ISBN 0-380-00523-9

Alice gets involved with drugs and runs away two times. She tries to stop using drugs but she can't. Her job is getting all messed up and her grandfather is dying (she spent the summer with her grandparents last year and their relationship deepened). She feels badly for what she did that summer because that's when she got introduced to drugs and her new boyfriend. She keeps on trying to stop but now she is an addict. When she gets help and stops, people at school still harass her for drugs. She tells them she broke up with her boyfriend and doesn't have any more drugs. But one day they get back at her.

I like this book because it got to the point. It didn't treat me like I was a first grader when it mentioned drugs. I especially like that it was nonfiction. I know I'm never going to get near drugs after reading this book. It scared me when she got high. She could never remember what happened or what other people did to her when she was high. I'm never using drugs.

Jessica McCormick, Grade 7
Kenilworth Junior High School, Petaluma, California

Clip and File

Reviews of Books for Middle-Level Teachers

Reviews: Lanny van Allen, Texas Education Agency, Austin, Texas; Thomas Mandeville, Southwest Texas State University, San Marcos, Texas; Anne Shaughnessy, Fort Clark Middle School, Gainesville, Florida

---

Crossing the Tracks: How "Untracking" Can Save America's Schools
Anne Wheelock
New Press, 1992, 311 pp., $12.95
ISBN 1-56584-038-0

For seventy-five years, most American schools have offered adolescents a tracked curriculum that groups according to abilities and probable futures. From the beginning, it carried racial, ethnic, and class overtones, but only a few questioned the inequity of providing an enriched curriculum to the "haves" in our society and an impoverished one to the "have nots." Today, however, there is not only a broad-based concern about the practice of tracking, but also a school reform movement that challenges schools to educate all students at higher levels.

How would such schools look? Anne Wheelock shows us. The process of untracking is young and fragile, she openly admits, but there are schools where the process of untracking has begun and where the genius of all students is being tapped. Essential ingredients of the process are identified: high expectations for students, professional development, phased-in change, parent and community involvement. Wheelock's book helps to fill the gap between what schools are and what they can be. *Crossing the Tracks* is a must-read for teachers, parents, and administrators who believe we must develop every mind.

Reading Miscue Inventory: Alternative Procedures
Yetta M. Goodman, Dorothy J. Watson, and Carolyn L. Burke
Richard C. Owen, 1987, 240 pp., $19.95
ISBN 0-913461-80-6

Though written nearly a decade ago, the Reading Miscue Inventory (RMI) still serves as a valuable tool for middle-school teachers concerned with students' literacy. The RMI, while similar to informal reading inventories (IRI), is different in that it doesn't provide a series of passages nor result in a grade level score. As a student reads, the teacher listens for variations from the text, that is, to miscues. The teacher then analyzes the miscues with six basic questions: 1. Is the miscue syntactically acceptable? 2. Is it semantically acceptable? 3. Was there meaning change? 4. Did the student correct the miscue? 5. Does the miscue have graphic similarity? 6. Does it have sound similarity? This reviewer has found it helpful to ask two additional questions: Is the miscued word phonetically spelled or is it a sight word? Is the miscued word one syllable, two syllables, or polysyllabic?

Two values are inherent in RMI use: teachers have a window into students' reading processes, and teachers hone their own understanding of the reading process. Understanding on this global level gives teachers welcome support in their efforts to provide whole language instruction.

Changing Middle Schools: How to Make Schools Work for Young Adolescents
Nancy L. Ames and Edward Miller
Jossey-Bass, 1994, 250 pp., $27.95
ISBN 0-7879-0006-0

This book is the story of four middle schools in Indiana. Why would we, in the other 49 states, even be interested? Because they have worked and won. "Won" means they decided to go for Change. They were observed and written about because they've made tremendous progress on a very difficult road, and because they illustrate that there are many different paths to restructuring a school.

We visit Sarah Scott, a little school in the poorest part of the city, where "Everybody is Somebody." We move on to Harshman Middle School, an inner-city school that serves what may be the highest-risk population in the state. A pioneer in interdisciplinary teaming, Decatur Middle School now serves as a model for others. And Portage Middle School has made significant progress in just two years by eliminating tracking, mainstreaming students with disabilities, and creating preventive guidance programs.

This must-read story is rich, exciting, and inspiring. The style is easy and jargon-free. I recommend this powerful book to anyone who cares about kids, public schools, and our futures.

Becoming Political: Readings and Writings in the Politics of Literacy Education
Patrick Shannon, editor
Heinemann, 1992, 304 pp., $20.00
ISBN 0-435-08701-0

Shannon has gathered a fascinating and diverse collection of articles originally used as readings for a summer institute on the political nature of literacy. Shirley Brice Heath, Linda Brodkey, Henry Giroux, James Paul Gee, and others join parents, practicing classroom teachers, and authors in exploring the roles played by race, social class, gender, and marginalization on literacy education. Of particular value are Gee's distinction between acquisition of literacy and learning of literacy, and Shannon's examples of overt and covert censorship. Some articles are very challenging, like Brodkey's discussion of the ways discourse constructs our teaching. Others are poignantly moving, like Paterson's experience with the censorship of *Bridge to Terabithia*. Bigelow's description of his high school course in which students explored the powerlessness of their own victim role experiences causes the reader to rethink her or his own teaching.

Also included are institute participants' reports, exploring areas such as advocacy for whole language, testing in special education programs, and AIDS education. All together, this book lends itself well to a group-study project.

Alexanne read the same passage and made two miscues which were syntactically acceptable. I asked Alexanne what she noticed about her reading:

"I did pretty well. I got a lot of the words and my voice was loud. I notice that when there are hyphenated words, I read the word as though there is no hyphen and then I have to go back and correct. I try to get something out of my reading, not just words on a page. I started reading *The Three Musketeers* this past summer, and was reading it very fast. I couldn't understand what was happening. So I slowed down, went back a little, and could understand the plot more." Alexanne, Grade 6

It became apparent to me that each of the students was quite aware of what he or she was doing while reading. But it is one thing to know what you do, and another to use this information to grow in your reading. I explored the parents' views of their children's literacy to get a fuller picture:

"Olivia doesn't enjoy reading. Unless she has to read, she doesn't. She has a tough time picking out books. She is a word-by-word reader and has always had problems in reading. I hear her getting frustrated. I don't think she feels good about her reading here. She has had tutors and a reading specialist. I have to say, I read to her very little because I don't like to read myself." Olivia's parents

"That's all we need to hear. It's painful. Calen was 'littered with literature.' He spent his life in bookstores. But he didn't come to reading naturally. We had to force the issue. He is not an initiator. We have him read for thirty minutes each night. He likes nonfiction and a variety of other books, especially if it is read to him. He was unsure of his reading until fourth or fifth grade." Calen's parents

"Alexanne is a maniacal reader. She knew words and letters at four months. She watched a lot of [a television program emphasizing phonics]. She reads everything: Time magazines, the personals columns, poetry, mysteries, anything. I think she did pretty well on the tape. There is a lot of inflection in her reading and she knows what she reads. This tells me that I don't need to worry about her reading." Alexanne's parents

I found all these parents to be honest and usually on target in their assessment of their child's reading. I wanted to know what they would do, if anything, with the information they received from our literacy conference:

"I guess I need to take Olivia to the library to try and find books that might interest her. I can set aside time to either read with her or read myself. Then we could talk about it afterward."

Calen's parents offered to continue to support Calen in his reading and to keep the thirty minutes of reading each night before bed. Alexanne's mother was not worried about Alexanne's reading since she did read such a great deal on a daily basis.

I went through this process with all students, be they lovers or haters of reading, and with their parents. I also asked Olivia, Calen, and Alexanne what they would do in the future, knowing what they know about their own reading.

"I haven't a clue as to what to do with this information. I guess I can stop a book when it doesn't feel right and go get a different one." Olivia

"When I read aloud, this will help me. It sounds weird, but if I correct myself in my head when I read aloud, it will help." Calen

"I have to understand the story; think about what's going on. I have to get pictures in my head and feel like I'm in the story." Alexanne

My understanding of the students' reading was augmented by both the students' and parents' perspectives. I was able to take their perceptions and add it to my understandings about the reading process. This process led me to recognize several aspects about Olivia's, Calen's, and Alexanne's reading.

I know that Olivia lacks the confidence necessary to find the seed of meaning in her reading. She needs to know that proficient readers don't read every word; they may substitute a familiar word for one they don't know, or keep going in the text to try and make sense from reading. Many of the miscues Olivia made did not detract from the meaning of the story. For example, she substituted *explained* for *exclaimed*, and she repeated words. She often employed predicting techniques and frequently self-corrected further on in the passage.

Olivia uses good reading strategies but she doesn't perceive them as strengths. For example, Olivia reads on when she can't

> *I found all these parents to be honest and usually on target in their assessment of their child's reading.*

make sense of a passage; she isn't hung up on word identification, thereby losing the flow of the story. Her substitutions are usually syntactically compatible; she substitutes verbs for verbs, adjectives for adjectives, and so on. If she learns to use pluses to offset areas of concern, she will grow in her reading. Olivia also needs to become aware of other strategies that will enhance her reading, such as creating pictures in her mind about what is going on; associating scenes and characters with experiences or people from her life; talking about, writing, acting out, and drawing parts of a book to help her make meaning. I also know that Olivia needs to hear the sounds of good literature read aloud to allow her to connect with books. In short, Olivia needs to know that reading can be personally rewarding.

When I shared with Olivia my perceptions of her reading behaviors, she said, "That's me!" She was quizzical about her strengths as a reader and my comments about proficient readers making some of the same miscues she made. I showed her some examples.

Calen knows what strategies have worked for him as a reader. However, through discussions about his reading, Calen will recognize the type(s) of low quality miscues he is making (such as inconsistent use of context clues to gain meaning of the sentence, and insertions that don't fit meaningfully in the text) and work out ways to diminish these. Discussion of the syntactic and semantic acceptability of his miscues would assist Calen in developing awareness of the types of miscues he is making. It would be advantageous for Calen to hear his peers share some of their reading strategies. This would validate some of his own reading strategies and acquaint him with others.

Readers' Awareness of Reading Strategies

After pondering the idea of shared reading strategies, I turned to my class for reflections on how they approached reading material, what they did during the process of reading, what they did when they had difficulty han-

dling unfamiliar text (words, structures, and meanings), and how they dealt with boring text. Many students reported that "big words" stopped them, but they either substituted words that made sense or they kept going with the reading. Several students said they went back and corrected after they read ahead to gain contextual meaning. Some of the students' suggestions for connecting with a text included:

- picture yourself as one of the characters
- try to figure out what a word means from the rest of the sentence
- get pictures in your head about what is happening
- place yourself in the book
- compare characters to someone you might know
- make up voices for characters
- draw, act out, write about what is going on or what is confusing
- talk to someone about what you read
- connect the ideas to something you might have read or seen
- expect the reading to make sense
- make predictions about what is going to happen
- check yourself as you read for meaning
- ask questions (even of yourself) as you read
- if the book is boring, give it a few chapters
- move ahead a couple of chapters and read a little to see if there is something of interest
- read the back cover of the book.

Conclusion

My understanding of my students' reading has led me to realize several things. I can use the knowledge I have gained from miscue analysis and retrospective miscue analysis to make curricular decisions. I see students discovering for themselves that reading is a

My understanding of my students' reading has led me to realize several things.

process of predicting, sampling, confirming, and correcting, as demonstrated through the classroom discussions of personal reading strategies. By reflecting on their reading through retrospective miscue analysis, students learn to value their proficient reading strategies and the reading process. They learn to control the process of making meaning. RMA helps them focus on their strengths rather than their troublesome areas. Students learn to trust the knowledge they bring to the reading process, which builds their confidence.

I recognize that students need a safe environment to take risks. They need time to practice free voluntary reading without threat of censorship. I need to continue to provide many opportunities for literacy engagement and to continue to read to my students daily from all genres of literature. Successful readers and readers-in-trouble need time to continue to share their strategies with one another so as to monitor their reading behaviors. Finally, I recognize that my students need to celebrate their efforts.

Much of what I have learned has come from my students' ability to look at their own reading behaviors and to share these with me and the class. Parents' perceptions on their child's reading, and my experience with looking at children's reading over the last two decades has added to my understandings.

My students and I continue to make our classroom a place that allows for choice, reflection, and an opportunity to spend meaningful time with print. We have begun the talk of learning more about reading strategies and making sense of texts; we are learning to analyze reading behaviors and to use this information to make curricular decisions. And we are working toward the goal of reading as meaning, or, as Alexanne tells us, "not just words on a page."

References

Goodman, Y., & Marek, A. (in press). *Revaluing readers and reading: Retrospective miscue analysis.* Katonah, NY: Richard C. Owen.

Watson, D., Burke, C., & Harste, J. (1989). *Whole language: Inquiring voices.* Ontario, Canada: Scholastic Canada.

Adolescent Literature

Spinelli, J. (1990). *Maniac Magee.* New York: Little Brown.

Taylor, T. (1981). *The trouble with Tuck.* New York: Avon.

Lingering Questions

1. Will self-study in reading reduce the number of low-quality miscues readers-in-trouble exhibit?

2. How will the strategies offered by the class be integrated into students' reading?

3. How will I know if the strategies are being used by students?

4. What will we as a class do with this information? How will the information change over the course of the year(s)?

How to Make It Work

- I use the students' silent reading time to audio-tape readings or hold interviews. Two to four students can be taped or interviewed in a thirty-minute reading session.

- I use the California Learning Record (CLR), an assessment tool fashioned after the Primary Language Record from England, to document students' reading, writing, listening, and speaking development. The CLR involves the student, parents, and teachers in compiling a full picture of the learner's progress in language. Teachers identify learners' strengths, note growth points, regard errors as information, and analyze patterns of errors in a constructive way. The CLR can be used with English and non-English speaking students. I complete the student interview portion during silent reading time.

- My school holds mini-conferences the first two weeks of the school year to allow parents to share information about their children. I use this time to hold CLR literacy conferences with the parents, gleaning information about their child's reading, writing, speaking, and listening.

- I set up a tape recorder in a corner of the classroom away from the other students; each child goes to this area individually and reads from books I have selected or the student has chosen (depending on the purpose of the evaluation). At times I want to see the reading strategies students will use with a book they have not seen before. I also want students to select familiar books to ensure their comfort level.

- I send students to the tape recorder and headsets to listen to their reading, after which we have a conference about their discoveries.

- I conduct a reading miscue analysis from the audiotape to see the kinds of miscues students are making. I also interview them about what they read to check for understanding. This is done twice during the year.

Luring Readers Out of Hiding

"What is the wall that keeps you from reading?" I posed this question to my new students early in September to get a sense of what they were bringing to the world of reading as they would experience it in my class. "Boring . . . No pictures . . . Dyslexia . . . Long . . . Can't sit still that long . . . Distracted . . . I'd rather watch TV . . . Doesn't interest me . . . Poor eyesight." My students gave me clear signals that reading was not their thing. An earlier survey (Atwell, 1987) had produced a total of three admitted readers, that is, people who read for pleasure in their spare time. The task I set for myself before these students even crossed the classroom threshold was to develop among them a community of readers. Given these students' lack of experience as readers and consequent negative attitudes about reading, my idea of community began to fade—a fuzzy dream threatened on all sides by harsh reality.

Building a Community of Readers: Starting from Scratch

This was my first year to teach ninth-grade English class after a dozen years with eighth graders. I was in a new district and knew little about my students' previous experiences with English/language arts instruction. I had their core reading lists (a district-adopted list from which teachers select the texts they will require for their classes), and eighth-grade writing portfolios for some, but the information was sketchy. This was a one-grade jump with a population and school system I didn't know well. Would I be able to achieve the same level of success with these students that I had with my eighth graders? What difference would a year of maturity make in their reading habits and tastes? Would they be

more skillful writers? Would a chronological year of growth make these students less receptive to the kinds of strategies that were effective with eighth graders? Would they be beyond the age of learning to appreciate reading?

My concerns evaporated when the first students came to class. They were close kin to the eighth graders I had taught and enjoyed for so many years. A summer had not changed them dramatically. Here were the restless, the impatient, the cool, and the rebellious. Here, too, the shy, the insecure, the immature, and the helpless. This was familiar territory. They came to me identified as predominately, but not exclusively, Chapter I students. They were a mix of socioeconomic and ethnic backgrounds, races, and languages. They came with poor grades in English; many would still have been in seventh or eighth grade in a district with a grade retention policy. These students knew what they didn't like about reading.

My challenge was twofold: to convince them that books hold secrets, adventures, and revelations worthy of their time and attention; and that they have what it takes to unlock the secrets, participate in the adventure, and learn from the revelations. We began by analyzing their list of reading walls. Students identified all the items on this list except bad eyes and dyslexia as things they could control themselves. We gave ourselves advice on scaling each of the walls. Boring book? Put it down and find one that is interesting. No pictures? Find a book with pictures. Can't sit still? Get up and move around for a while. Squeeze a Nerf ball, put on some music. Book is too long? Put it aside. Find a short book. Read as many short books as you like. Some day you may want to read a long one. Bad eyes? Have your eyes checked, keep

Carol Evans Treu

Sonoma Valley High School, Sonoma, California

your prescription up-to-date. Dyslexia we could not define satisfactorily, and no one claimed to have it. What a revelation—our reading walls were scaleable. My students put up the barriers and took them right down again. We were ready to look at ourselves as readers.

From the reading survey, I learned that during the previous year, most students had read two or three books, all assigned by English teachers. When I asked students if they included history, science, or other subject-specific books on their "How many books I read last year" response, they were adamant: "That's not reading!" Why the energy around this question? Granted, I had asked them as an English teacher representing an established expectation about reading, but when elementary students were asked what they considered reading, they identified workbook time rather than story time. Perhaps this kind of bias follows students into middle school. "We read in English class. In our other classes, we work in our books." I filed this information away and resolved to ask my question again after students had had more discussions about what it means to be a reader and what readers do with different kinds of texts.

Next, I asked students to answer questions about the following story from *Language and Thinking in School: A Whole Language Curriculum* (Goodman, Smith, Meredith, and Goodman, 1987):

Gloopy and Blit*

Gloopy is a borp.
Blit is a lof.
Gloopy klums like Blit.
Gloopy and Blit are Floms.

Ril had poved Blit to a jonfy.
But he had not poved Gloopy.
"The jonfy is for lofs,"
Blit bofd to Gloopy.
"You are a borp."

Gloopy was not klorpy.
Then Blit was not klorpy. (p. 244)

From K. Goodman, E. B. Smith, R. Meredith, and Y. Goodman, *Language and Thinking in School: A Whole-Language Curriculum*, Richard C. Owen, 1987. Reprinted with permission.

My "comprehension" questions included, "What are Gloopy and Blit?" "Who does Gloopy klum like?" "What did Blit bof to Gloopy?"

I asked them to do this before we began reading our first core (required) book for two reasons: first, it is a quick and easy way to share with them what I believe about reading, and second, it helps relieve students of some of the beliefs they hold that keep them from being confident readers. All students score well on this "test." When I ask them what the text means, none, of course, can tell me. This launches us into a discussion of how they were able to get right answers without understanding the text. Students are always able to provide logical reasons for their right answer: "It sounds the same." "It's the same kind of a sentence." "There are quotation marks." "Because the words in the question look like the words in story." They reveal to me and to each other how much they know about language structure, and how useless that structure is if it doesn't carry a significant message or meaning. I, in turn, let them know that I will not be playing "Guess the right answer" games with them from their reading. Instead, we will read and discuss and explore all kinds of literature together and see what we can learn from each other.

The next logical step to "Gloopy and Blit" is an authentic literature experience. This year I read aloud Gary Soto's poem "Black Hair" (1992). I did not give students the text. Instead, I read it three times, then asked them to draw an image or picture (graphic) in response to a strong mental image created by the poem or any part of the poem. Students responded happily to this task and predictably, many chose the same lines but had different visual interpretations. Some chose lines that had not elicited responses from others. During the next class meeting, I gave students a copy of the poem to read before we shared their graphic responses. Danny, who rarely volunteered in class, wrinkled his brow and asked, "Wasn't there a part in the poem about the bleachers?" There was, indeed, but Danny had received a faulty copy and those lines were missing. His question became a useful referent for future discussions with him about reading. Danny came in with low test scores, low grades, and a resistance to reading. This early clue showed me that despite his dismal "official" record, Danny had the ability to make powerful connections with a text, and could, indeed, get meaning from his reading. Graphics (drawings, collages, torn paper images, etc.) created in response to a text help readers clarify their reactions to their reading in a medium other than print. Sharing graphic responses extends the possibilities of the text beyond one reader's experience. It offers reluctant readers a comfortable structure for sharing ideas about reading without the fear of judgment that often attends more formal discussions of meaning.

A fact worth mentioning here: The students in this class were among the first to experience a block schedule recently instituted by our school. It consists of three 95-minute periods a day, with courses scheduled on alternate days, and a daily 40-minute tutorial period. The day Danny noticed the lines were missing from his copy of the poem was a Tuesday, five days since the Thursday I had read the poem. Alternating course days and a Monday holiday had created a five-day break between class sessions, and still he remembered. I wonder if his memory would have been so keen on a standard reading comprehension test that was interrupted by five days. His response to the words moved him enough to create an image for them, and that image cemented the words in his memory.

Expanding the Reading Community

I used the reading survey, "Gloopy and Blit," and our first literature response activity to gain my students' trust and to build their confidence as potential readers who have much to bring to a text and much that is worthy to share. In this particular class, however, I learned I was also dealing with the powerful social and economic circumstances of my students' lives that profoundly influenced their view of themselves as learners and severely limited their ability to respond to the literacy demands of our school system.

Our community is a lively and largely harmonious mix of rural and suburban people including professionals, dairy and grape farmers, merchants, service providers, and laborers. Our population also includes migrants, immigrants, the unemployed, and the homeless. I have students from all of the latter four groups, many of whom feel they have no voice. They do not see themselves as having anything worthy to add to the discourse in their school or community. Many are in survival mode physically, and just getting to school is a heroic act. They do not have print available in their homes. Lively, friendly talk at home about their lives, their school, or their reading is missing. For some, being a "nerd" (i.e., committed student) is the kiss of death. They need to be wary of looking smart or reading in front of their friends.

The oral language of these students' lives is significantly different from the language of school and of many books. When asked to discuss or to write their responses to an idea or a reading, they often say, "I don't know. . . . I don't have any ideas." To some teachers, this may look like deliberate resistance, even defiance. Instead, it is often a valid reflection of their own experiences. If such questions are not asked of them at home and the detailed kinds of responses expected from adolescent students are not part of their language experience, "I don't know" is not an evasion, it is the truth. I have designed my instruction around the belief that these students can move with confidence into the community of readers by slow, friendly, persistent immersion in the world of language. One of the ways to bring students to an awareness of their ideas is to provide them with experiences in and out of class that capture their interest and give them much to think and talk about. To that end, I planned a field trip early in the year.

Our community is small and safe enough to allow a walking expedition to the local bookstore. The proprietors generously offered to open an hour early for us and to have doughnuts waiting. I arranged for each student to have a $5.00 credit toward a book that he or she could use for recreational

> *The oral language of these students' lives is significantly different from the language of school and of many books.*

(homework) reading for class. Since much young adult fiction is $4.95, I hoped this would give students the chance to buy a book for a few cents of tax, allowing them the dignity of contributing something to their purchase. The results of this expedition far exceeded my hopes.

With hands and mouths full of doughnuts, students fanned out through the three small rooms of the bookstore taking in the look and feel of the place. Most hovered around shelves or circled tables cautiously for a while, too shy to take a book in hand. Others, familiar with bookstores, set off for a particular section.

Ken brought a list of authors dictated by his mother. It included Norm Chouomsey [*sic*], Kalil Gibrawn [*sic*], and Albear Kamoo [*sic*]. It took some deciphering to realize that this was mom's reading list. Eventually, Ken bought Gibran's *Broken Wing* to read himself and then give to his mother.

Shane, a conscientious student struggling with reading, came to me with a collection of mysteries by British writers (Dorothy Sayers, Agatha Christie). Since he had been plodding through a Hardy Boys mystery for a month and had managed to complete only fifty pages, I recommended he sit in one of the chairs provided and read several pages to see if this was the kind of a book he wanted to buy. Some time later, he came back with a contemporary mystery that was much shorter, and written in language more accessible to him. Instead of depending on an adult's recommendation, he made a choice based on what he liked and was comfortable reading.

Charles, who had not yet read a book for homework, came to me when no one else was around and whispered, "Do you know where the angels are?" Time ticked and he watched anxiously as I tried to figure out what angels had to do with book selection, wishing one would sit on my shoulder and tell me what this boy wanted. Determined to keep Charles' attention, I scanned the shelf titles, and there, just over his head, was the label "New Age." Voilà! I realized this reader was interested in the recent angels phenomenon. We were in the right place. Charles eventually found exactly what he wanted and

even had some company looking at books in the New Age section, which greatly relieved his anxiety about selecting such an unusual subject.

For the next hour, students scampered from room to room sampling books, looking for friends to share a "cool book" discovery, curled up in rocking chairs to enjoy books they couldn't buy on their budget, sat on the rug and read books to each other, and came to me to show off their selections. Some used their credit to order books not in stock. Others put more expensive books on reserve, planning to come back with their parents to complete the purchase. This was a benefit I had not anticipated. Several students would be making a second trip to the store. Maybe it would become a habit! At the end of our visit, students were offered a last round of doughnuts and a discount card—buy ten books and get a $5.00 credit toward their next purchase. We set off happily for school, all of us satisfied with the morning, but none so completely happy as I.

My delight continued the next week when students planned what they might write in a thank-you note to the store owners. Students first volunteered the predictable thank-yous for opening early and for providing doughnuts, then launched into a lengthy list of all the physical features that made the store so enjoyable. Sammy has earned a permanent place in my memory with his excellent description of the store's interior. Since the store was run by its owners, he said it was more like their home than a Hallmark store or, trying to be more precise, a Taco Bell. His observation led to a discussion of the differences between franchise bookstores and privately owned establishments. Students' thank-you notes were honest and touching—their best writing to that point (see samples in Classroom Connections, p. 40). They had good reason to write and lots of good things to say, which translated into a clearly identifiable voice from each writer. "I really enjoyed your store and I hope it will be open for many generations ahead."

Shortly after our visit came the coup de grâce—a thank-you note from our hosts for being such fine guests, and a request to have

> *They had good reason to write and lots of good things to say, which translated into a clearly identifiable voice from each writer.*

excerpts from our thank-you notes printed in the store newsletter. One short trip produced a lively and much appreciated introduction to the world of the bookstore, an important purpose for writing to a known audience, and best of all, publication!

Applying Lessons Learned with Eighth Graders

In 1986, I introduced an integrated, literature-based program to my eighth graders; the results were startling. That year, special education eligibility had just been changed. Many students who had been in special education their entire school lives were in regular classes. Teachers were warned that their classes would be more difficult as a result. Yes and no. Special education students mainstreamed for the first time were the first to accept my approach to literature. They understood from the beginning that this was no longer a competition against a standard they had not been able to achieve in the past. There were no right answers hiding in a teacher's answer book or a teacher's head. Their own ideas were honored and were given many means of expression. They understood that individual growth was possible and would be celebrated.

In order to capture my students' trust and interest, I begin each year by demystifying the reading and writing processes. (See an instruction sheet and journal form for our first formal response activity, double entry journals, in Classroom Connections, p. 39). The special education students took to the task immediately and wrote honestly and conscientiously in their journals. The students who were accustomed to getting easy A's were not so taken with the assignment. They resisted and complained and pronounced the work stupid and boring. It took a full nine weeks to win them over. They could do the work, it was just a shock that they couldn't zip out an English homework ditto sheet the hour before it was due, or copy answers to end-of-the-chapter questions from each other. In short, they could no longer coast in the system. They had to think, to express their own thoughts, and to support and justify them to others.

It took me a couple more years to figure out how to win over these A students earlier in the year. I did it by treating them as adults. I told them how each of the activities they participated in helped them learn. Double-entry journals, reflective writing, and writing letters and journals from the point of view of various characters all expanded our classroom discussion about our reading. Creating a graphic response to reading made them share their individual responses and come up with some important ideas they could agree on and transform into symbol. This required them to go back and reread the book for details, for more subtle implications, for justification for their ideas. I didn't tell them that this also gave slower readers an opportunity to go back and read portions they might have missed without embarrassment. In writing individual responses to their reading and then sharing it with others, they benefited from hearing other good ideas about characters and events in the book; they also learned that A students were not the only ones with admirable and powerful ideas about their reading.

Written Responses to Reading

I have deeply appreciated the double entry journals from that first experience. They have provided me a window into the minds of my students. (See examples in Figure 1.) From them, I learned that eighth graders are naturally attracted to beautiful language. One of the most frequently copied and appreciated passages from Ouida Sebestyen's book, *Words by Heart*, was " I hear you whisper, o stars of heaven, o sun, o grass of graves, o perpetual transfer of promotions. If you do not say anything, how can I say anything?" Reading students' responses to this passage, I could say nothing. I was struck dumb by the power of these words on such young readers. Appreciative responses came equally from students at all levels of reading development.

Clearly, I had underestimated my students' capacity to respond deeply to their reading. From that day to this, I have depended on my students to bring fresh,

Clearly, I had underestimated my students' capacity to respond deeply to their reading.

Journal Response to Ouida Sebestyen's *Words by Heart*

p. 18: Does it have to be stuck in you before you see what it means?	The knife was stuck through the cloth and the bread. Lena imagined it going through her father like he was dead.
pp. 35–36: Papa was coming across the yard with the sacks. He didn't seem to be struggling.	She thought he was struggling with things, but he was struggling inside his feelings.
p. 37: Something always comes along to fill the empty places.	The kittens replaced Bullet in a way. [Bullet, Lena's dog, was killed by an unknown assailant. Shortly thereafter, Lena's cat gave birth. (Ed.)]

Journal Response to T. Kroebers' *Ishi, Last of His Tribe*

p. 35: . . . foot was caught in the scalp of a woman of the people!	I thought that it was the other way around, that the Indians were the ones that scalped the white man and called it noble.
p. 100: This may be a Power Dream.	Does a Power Dream predict one's future, or does it guide them?
p. 47: Perhaps the Saldu were not taught well by their Old Ones.	What Old Ones? Whites have a mom and dad, but that's precisely where they get their teaching about life. Prejudiced parents have prejudiced children. It's really not fair, because the parents only give them one side of the story exaggerated [*sic*]. Prejudiced children who are taught from (an) early age and are unable to form their own opinion never learn why you shouldn't be prejudiced. Everybody is the same. That's the way they should be treated.

FIGURE 1.

clear, and provocative insights into the books we share and to celebrate fine writing with me. Until I provided the kind of open-ended structures that provoke students to make individual connections with the text, it would never have occurred to me that thirteen year olds could find reading aesthetically fulfilling. They might not know the phrase, but they do know the experience.

Double-entry journals can provide other valuable clues about how students read. Sometimes a first double entry journal will be a long list of words on the left side with the question "What does this mean?" on the right. At other times, as in this response to *Ishi*, a student's approach to the journal reveals one of those "walls" between reading and meaning. This student, mainstreamed from a Special Day Class and identified as a "struggling reader," selected *Ishi* to read. Curiously, he copied interesting passages on the left side, then on the right, wrote down words he didn't understand, but were not in the passages on the left.

p. 49: Ishi found Timawi in a bare oak tree where he and a wide-awake gray squirrel were answering each other in identical scolding voices.	What does Wowunupo mean?
p. 152: When he opened his eyes he saw his reflection in the still pool.	What does Moocha mean?
p. 154: Ishi lay on his back staring into the arching Sky World.	What does a pungent smell mean?

This is a clue that the students are reading word for word and not finding meaning in the context. Giving students a little reminder about what good readers do when they come to unfamiliar words and sharing other students' more detailed and personal responses moves these students out of the "reading every word" mode immediately. The relief of these readers is palpable. Once they begin to write authentic, personal responses to the text, they join our community of readers. The student mainstreamed from the special education class chose, finally, to write responses in paragraph form. He was unable to finish the book in the allotted time, but stayed with it tenaciously throughout the class reading period and eventually took it home to finish.

Graphic Response to Reading

Suzanne Langer (1979) makes the distinction between discursive and nondiscursive (formal written) modes of expression, and reminds us that most school work demands only the discursive mode. She makes a case for the powerful learning that comes from the nondiscursive, or presentational, mode of response (such as song, dance, drama, or art) to text, to ideas. The discursive mode has limitations for eliciting the truest and broadest picture of what students know and what they can do with what they are learning.

I found ample evidence for Langer's thesis as I offered my students more presentational response activities. Equal to, perhaps even exceeding, the revelatory power of writing is graphic, symbolic representation of ideas and events in a text. Students enjoy this activity more than the journals because it is so much more social and physical.

The value of graphic representations in distilling students' understanding is immeasurable. It showed up first with Eddie, a special education student who offered his group a provocative metaphor for a major concept gleaned from his reading. Creating a graphic metaphor for Kino in *The Pearl*, he suggested that the pearl itself was like an evil spider that had caught Kino in his web (see Figure 2). There was argument back and forth about whether or not Kino was the evil spider. He beat his wife, killed a man, and his baby died tragically because of his stubbornness. Was Kino evil? Was he simply trying to get justice in an unjust world? Should he have given up the pearl? After all, he had found it; it was his! Finally, the group agreed that the pearl was best represented by the spider, and Kino was a fly caught in its web. All this was part of students' discussion around the proposed metaphor. When this group presented its graphic to the class, the discussion evolved into a consideration of human greed, and whether the evil was in the pearl or in the hearts of the characters. I could not have wished for more depth or wisdom from any group of readers, and these eighth graders did it on their own, provoked by a powerful image offered by a student who had been in special education classes all his school life. It was a significant event in that young reader's life, and in my life as a teacher. It helped me trust my students, and brought home to me the power of metaphor and symbol in distilling meaning.

Oral Responses to Reading

Middle-school teachers know their students are natural actors. Even the shy ones have secret dreams of starring in front of admiring audiences. How can this natural affinity for the stage be directed in the service of learning in less formal ways than full dramatic productions? Readers Theater, the Hot Seat, and dramatic interpretations of scenes that might logically have happened to characters in the story but were not included in the story, all have the power to draw students into the text in powerful, physical ways.

The Hot Seat forces students to draw on their knowledge of setting, motivations of characters, and forces of the plot in order to respond to questions by other characters in their groups. I always start with myself as the first person in the Hot Seat to put students at ease. Once on their own, the most diverse groupings of students produce remarkable results. In one taped session on *The Pearl*, a rocker wannabe with a rice-powder-white

FIGURE 2.

face and blood-red lips, a (usually) inarticulate future soccer star, a loquacious preppie, and a shy girl who was sure she wouldn't have anything significant to contribute to the group, created a logical extension of characters' motivations through interviews and role playing:

| Juan Thomas: | Why did you shut the door in Kino's face when he took his baby to the see the doctor? |
| Doctor's Servant: | I hated turning Kino away from the doctor's door, but I work for the doctor. It's the only job I have to support my family. |

****

| Appolonia: | Why did Kino keep the pearl with him when it was dangerous? |
| Juana: | Kino had many dreams. I had dreams also, but it meant the end of our happiness. |

****

| Appolonia: | Did you blame Coyotito's death on Kino? |
| Juana: | No, I never blamed it on Kino. I blamed myself because I should have stayed in the back of the cave like Kino told me. |

> It is in the sharing of responses that students begin to pay closer attention to the possibilities for meaning in a text that they might not have considered on their own.

In their Hot Seat groups, students pull out of their memories and imaginations connections and possibilities for characters' actions that rarely surface in either formal discussions or writing. This small, structured task allows self-conscious adolescents to express their ideas in the safety of an intimate and supportive group. Sometimes I taped the results and had groups listen to each other's interviews. Other times I used the information generated by the Hot Seat as the basis for a dramatization of the scene. The results speak for themselves.

Slowly, I abandoned the assignment of a formal essay as the culminating event of our shared experiences with a core book. Instead, students developed a presentation, created a rubric, and shared their own and each other's assessments. One of my favorites was alternate scenes suggested for group dramatization at the end of *Summer of My*

German Soldier. Each group was asked to determine what they wanted their audience to learn or understand about the characters or the story from their scene. When they finished their dramatization, the audience was asked to tell what insights they had gained from the presentation. The presenting group attempted to match their own intentions with the audience response. Any discrepancy prompted discussion about the mismatch of intent and result, and became part of the evaluation.

The first time we did this, students tended to be very literal in their interpretations and what they wanted their audience to understand. With practice, however, a lesson stated as, "We want them to see that fighting and breaking windows is bad," evolved into "We wanted them to see how bad prejudice is; like when the townspeople drove the Chinese man out of town because they thought he looked Japanese." When students began to make the connections between violence and bigotry, it was a short step to move them to considerations of fear and scapegoating as tools for manipulating people's emotions into actions, and that brought us right into contemporary national and global issues. The social, collaborative effort to make sense of the reading, to bring it home, to make it relevant—this is what lures students out of apathy. It is almost irresistible to them.

Moving Forward

Now, teaching ninth graders, I still subscribe to Krashen's (1993) and Atwell's (1987) belief that students should be allowed to read anything that interests them in order to develop a habit and an enjoyment of reading. This requires a balancing act in an English curriculum with a list of required core works for students to read. I value the communal experience of reading and sharing responses to a selected book. It is in the sharing of responses that students begin to pay closer attention to the possibilities for meaning in a text that they might not have considered on their own. It is, however, a daunting task to get them to be receptive to an assigned book.

As I began to learn more about the reading process (a subject not taught to secondary credential candidates in my era), I realized that the creative activities I designed to keep my students interested were actually the ticket to encouraging reading and language development in middle-school students. I began to plan my activities much more purposefully and to look at how they promoted learning. I also garnered the courage to eliminate spelling tests, end-of-the-chapter reading questions, and grammar book worksheets. From a friend, I learned to cut down on my paperwork by reading over students' shoulders, highlighting significant passages in their written reading responses and early writing drafts. Eventually, students' primary homework assignment was to read a book of their choice for an average of thirty minutes every night. I eliminated book reports and substituted regularly scheduled small group book talks, complete with cookies. These were a resounding success.

As I continue to fret a bit about whether or not I will be able to bring my ninth-grade students to an acceptance of themselves as readers, and perhaps even an enjoyment of books, Louise Rosenblatt's (1983) words about reading reassure me:

The starting point for growth must be each individual's efforts to marshal his resources and organize a response relevant to the stimulus of the printed page. The teacher's task is to foster fruitful interactions—or more precisely, transactions—between individual readers and individual literary works. (p.26)

The key is to keep prodding students to make those interactions through carefully structured, open-ended activities in class so that these interactions become part of their internal discourse when they read on their own. If reading is a transaction with print, then our task as teachers is to help students become aware of this process of transaction and be able to use it effectively for their own purposes.

Just as my students were able to see how they could eliminate the blocks to reading they had identified, I believe most young people will respond well to reading once they understand how to remove their own reading blocks. Teachers can help in many ways. We can build a classroom library of high-interest books and allow students choices in their reading. We can provide a range of open-ended, provocative reading response activities that are not limited to writing. We can be models of what good readers do by participating in the response activities as a peer in the classroom community of readers. With good books, trust, open-ended, ongoing discussions, and a variety of engaging response strategies, the access to the reading community is no longer limited to those students who can play the game. It is available to all who will participate.

We truly never know what will make our students become avid readers. We do know some ways to lure them into the reading community. The bait we use is good books, good talk, and good practice. Once students take the bait, chances are good they will be hooked for life. Who, after all, would voluntarily leave a community that offers lifetime membership, worldwide access, and no dues? The passport to membership is a book. In years past, a surprising number of my students have joined the community of readers, not through their recreational reading, but through a core book that was required class reading. *The Outsiders, The Pearl, Summer of My German Soldier, Fallen Angels* and *Anne Frank: The Diary of a Young Girl* (the play) have been pivotal texts for different students. Although I cannot prove a direct correlation, I would like to believe that the variety of activities available to students was largely responsible for their appreciation of these books.

This year I wait anxiously to see which core works will be the turning point for some of my older, more reluctant readers. I know it is out there. The suspense and the wait for that discovery are what keep me and many of my colleagues so completely committed to our work and to our students.

I believe most young people will respond well to reading once they understand how to remove their own reading blocks. Teachers can help in many ways.

References

Atwell, N. (1987). *In the middle: Writing, reading, and learning with adolescents.* Portsmouth, NH: Heinemann.

Goodman, K. S., Smith, E. B., Meredith, R., & Goodman, Y. M. (1987). *Language and thinking in school: A whole language curriculum* (3rd ed.). New York: Richard C. Owen.

Krashen, S. (1993). *The power of reading.* Englewood, CO: Libraries Unlimited.

Langer, S. K. (1979). *Philosophy in a new key: A study in the symbolism of season, rite, and art* (3rd ed.). Cambridge, MA: Harvard University Press.

Rosenblatt, L. (1983). *Literature as exploration* (4th ed.). Urbana, IL: National Council of Teachers of English.

Adolescent Literature Cited

Frank, A. (1967). *Anne Frank: The diary of a young girl* (rev. ed.). New York: Doubleday.

Greene, B. (1984). *Summer of my German soldier.* New York: Bantam.

Hinton, S. E. (1968). *The outsiders.* New York: Dell.

Kroeber, T. (1964). *Ishi: Last of his tribe.* Boston: Houghton Mifflin.

Myers, W. (1988). *Fallen angels.* New York: Scholastic.

Sebestyen, O. (1979). *Words by heart.* New York: Little Brown.

Soto, G. (1992). Black hair. In G. Soto (Ed.), *Fire in my hands: A book of poems.* New York: Scholastic.

Lingering Questions

1. What are the best ways to accommodate and support students distracted from reading by personal crisis and stress?

2. What is the most appropriate balance between core and self-selected literature with students who do not enjoy reading and resist books assigned by the teacher from the core curriculum?

3. How can I interest teachers of other disciplines in learning reading strategies that will help change our students' perception that texts in history, science, mathematics, and so on, are not "reading"?

Note Taking/Note Making*

Note Taking/Note Making is a strategy that allows you to have a conversation with the book you are reading. It replaces the traditional end-of-the-chapter questions with your questions, the teacher's list of important words and phrases with your words and phrases, and the textbook publisher's idea of what is important in a story with your ideas of what is important. Your notes can become a form of written conversation about the book.

Here's how you do it: Divide your paper as illustrated below. As you read, mark with a self-stick note each passage that makes you stop and think or provokes a strong response from you. When you have finished reading (page, section, or chapter),

go back to your self-stick notes. Write the page and line of the passage on the left side under "Note Taking." Write as much of the passage as you need to remember what you want to say about it. After you have written all of your entries for Note Taking, go back to the passages again. Write your thoughts, reactions, questions about the copied passage on the right under Note Making. You may want to go back to the book and reread some part to refresh your memory and expand your response. Be sure to leave space between your entries under Note Taking to allow enough room for a complete response to the right of it under Note Making.

NOTE TAKING	NOTE MAKING
(example from *The Outsiders* by S. E. Hinton)	
p.20: "Nature's first green is gold . . ."	What does this mean? Why does Ponyboy say the poem to Johnny? I'll bet he would say it to Cherry if she would listen. I'm surprised there's a poem in this book.
p.110: 1.6 "Two-bit, you still got that switch?"	Two-bit should never have given the blade to Dally. I know something terrible is going to happen.

*Based on a model presented at the California Literature Project UCLA Summer Institute in 1986.

Sample Thank-You Notes in Response to Bookstore Visit

Dear Mr. and Ms. Weinberger,   10-25-94

       Thank you for opening the store up early so we could come in and take a look around last friday. Thank you for the donuts too. That was pretty nice. You have a wonderful store. The books were organized so you could find them very easily.

       I will definitely come back and get a book because I really like the selection about Vampires and really spooky books. The book that I got "Anno Dracula" I am reading already and I really really love it.

         Sincerely,
         Amber Gipson

Dear Mr and Mrs Weinberger

I appreciate how you trusted eighteen high schoolers in your store. When I first heard we where going to a book store I thought "OH Rats" But when I got there I enjoyed the atmosphere of a family run store

Thank for the great time

    your new freind,
    Scott Westerman

Oct, 25, 1994

Dear Mr and Mrs Weinburgers,
    I just wanted to thank you for letting us in your book store so early in the morning. We had a great time and thank-you for the donuts it was very nice to think of us.

I bought two books and the one that I am reading right now is very interesting. The books tittles are Near Death and Anno Dracula.

I thought that the book store was organized better then any other book store any where else. You had a lot of books to choose from and I like that in a book store. I like how you put the books in your book store.

I hope to see you again.

        Sincerly
        Stacey Bailey

Selected Readings

Atwell, N. (1987). *In the middle: Writing, reading, and learning with adolescents.* Portsmouth, NH: Heinemann.

Bird, L. B. (1989). *Becoming a whole language school: The Fair Oaks story.* Katonah, NY: Richard C. Owen.

Cordeiro, P. (1992). *Whole learning: Whole language and content in the upper elementary grades.* Katonah, NY: Richard C. Owen.

Edelsky, C. (1991). *With literacy and justice for all: Rethinking the social in language and education.* New York: Falmer.

Edelsky, C., Altwerger, B., & Flores, B. (1991). *Whole language: What's the difference?* Portsmouth, NH: Heinemann.

Gee, J. (1990). *Social linguistics and literacies: Ideology in discourses.* New York: Falmer.

Gilles, C., Bixby, M., Crowley, P., Crenshaw, S. R., Henrichs, M., Reynolds, F. E., & Pyle, C. (Eds.). (1988). *Whole language strategies for secondary students.* New York: Richard C. Owen.

Goodman, K. S. (1982). *Language & literacy: The selected writings of Kenneth S. Goodman: Vol. 1. Process, theory, research* (F. V. Gollasch, Ed.). Boston: Routledge & Kegan Paul.

Goodman, K. S. (1982). *Language & literacy: The selected writings of Kenneth S. Goodman: Vol. 2. Reading, language & the classroom teacher* (F. V. Gollasch, Ed.). Boston: Routledge & Kegan Paul.

Goodman, K. S., Bird, L. B., & Goodman, Y. (1991). *The whole language catalog.* Santa Rosa, CA: American School Publishers.

Goodman, K. S., Bird, L. B., & Goodman, Y. (1992). *The whole language catalog supplement on authentic assessment.* Santa Rosa, CA: American School Publishers.

Goodman, K. S., Goodman, Y. M., & Hood, W. J. (1989). *The whole language evaluation book.* Portsmouth, NH: Heinemann.

Goodman, K. S., Smith, E. B., Meredith, R., & Goodman, Y. M. (1987). *Language and thinking in school: A whole-language curriculum* (3rd ed.). New York: Richard C. Owen.

Goodman, Y., & Burke, C. (1980). *Reading strategies: Focus on comprehension.* New York: Holt, Rinehart and Winston.

Goodman, Y. M., Watson, D. J., & Burke, C. L. (1987). *Reading miscue inventory: Alternative procedures.* Katonah, NY: Richard C. Owen.

Heath, S. B. (1983). *Ways with words: Language, life, and work in communities and classrooms.* Cambridge: Cambridge University Press.

Peterson, R. (1992). *Life in a crowded place: Making a learning community.* Portsmouth, NH: Heinemann.

Peterson, R., & Eeds, M. (1990). *Grand conversations: Literature groups in action.* New York: Scholastic.

Pierce, K. M., & Gilles, C. J. (Eds.). (1993). *Cycles of meaning: Exploring the potential of talk in learning communities.* Portsmouth, NH: Heinemann.

Rosenblatt, L. M. (1978). *The reader, the text, the poem: The transactional theory of the literary work.* Carbondale, IL: Southern Illinois University Press.

Ruddell, R. B., Ruddell, M. R., & Singer, H. (Eds.). (1994). *Theoretical models and processes of reading* (4th ed.). Newark, DE: International Reading Association.

Smith, F. (1975). *Comprehension and learning: A conceptual framework for teachers.* New York: Richard C. Owen.

Smith, F. (1982). *Understanding reading* (3rd ed.). New York: Holt, Rinehart and Winston.

Smith, F. (1983). *Essays into literacy.* Portsmouth, NH: Heinemann.

Smith, F. (1985). *Reading without nonsense* (2nd ed.). New York: Teachers College Press.

Smith, F. (1988). *Joining the literacy club: Further essays into education.* Portsmouth, NH: Heinemann.